The
IMPEACHMENT
of
WILLIAM JEFFERSON CLINTON

The

IMPEACHMENT

of

WILLIAM JEFFERSON CLINTON

A Political Docu-Drama

by

R. EMMETT TYRRELL , Jr.

and

"ANONYMOUS"

REGNERY

Washington, DC

Library of Congress Cataloging-in-Publication Data

Tyrrell, R. Emmett.
The impeachment of William Jefferson Clinton : a political docu-drama
/ by R. Emmett Tyrrell, Jr. and Anonymous.

    p.   cm.
  ISBN 0-89526-396-3 (hardcover : alk. paper)
  1. Trials (Impeachment)—United States—Drama.   2. Presidents-
-United States—Drama.   3. Clinton, Bill, 1946-   Drama.
I. Title.
Ps3570.Y63I47 1997
812'.54—dc21   97-35882
                                                                            CIP

Published in the United States by
Regnery Publishing, Inc.
An Eagle Publishing Company
One Massachusetts Avenue NW,
Washington, DC 20001

Distributed to the trade by
National Book Network
4720-A Boston Way
Lanham, MD 20706

Design by Marja Walker

Printed on acid-free paper.
Manufactured in the United States of America

10 9 8 7 6 5 4 3 2 1

Books are available in quantity for promotional or premium use. Write to Director of Special Sales, Regnery Publishing, Inc., One Massachusetts Avenue NW, Washington, DC 20001, for information on discounts and terms or call (202) 216-0600.

To the Spirit of Warren Gamaliel Harding,
our 29th president, whose only mistake, it seems,
was being born 70 years too soon.

ACKNOWLEDGMENTS

AS THE RECENT DATE on this book's introduction indicates, its development has been swift from its fetal stage in manuscript form to full adulthood resplendent in the bookstores of America. For that matter its fetal stage was swift too, only a few months. Thus I am all the more admiring of Regnery Publishing's legendary Rapid Deployment Force, composed of my peerless Editor Richard Vigilante, Project Editor Jed Donahue, Managing Editor David Dortman, and Art Director Marja Walker. Miss Myrna Larfnik was again an invaluable resource, and let me conclude with yet another volley of thanks to my executive assistant, Lonnie Rewis, whose intelligence and grace are always unfailing.

CO-AUTHORS' NOTE

WHAT FOLLOWS IS a work of imagination, though based on actual events that have occurred in and around the White House from the day Bill Clinton took office to the present. Since most of the action and dialogue is set in the future, any resemblance between *The Impeachment of William Jefferson Clinton*, as detailed herein, and a real-time impeachment of our forty-second President is coincidental; and, of course, prescient. *It should be noted, however, that all cited documents, "reruns," and quotations dated prior to September 1, 1997 are genuine, except as otherwise noted.*

R. EMMETT TYRRELL, JR.
"ANONYMOUS"

TABLE OF CONTENTS

THE SENATE TRIAL

FOREWORD

THIS POWERFULLY PERSUASIVE volume should be required reading for every citizen of this country who cares about the integrity of our political process. Every American who is concerned with the survival of our cherished system of government, so carefully outlined by our Founding Fathers generations ago, must read this book.

Bob Tyrrell's account of the impeachment of William Jefferson Clinton was so realistic that, throughout my reading, I found myself constantly turning back to the cover, to make sure it was not the dour grey or green cover that binds every official record of proceedings in the House Judiciary Committee, including the last presidential impeachment proceedings in the House, in 1974.

Tyrrell and "Anonymous" have captured the feel of congressional proceedings in a way that few—if any—current or former Members could. They understand the purpose, process, and nuances of Congress's investigative role in a way that few citizens, in and out of Congress, do.

—CONGRESSMAN BOB BARR
SEPTEMBER 1997

INTRODUCTION

WHEN THE HISTORIAN Samuel Flagg Bemis, in 1956, finished his distinguished biography of John Quincy Adams, he headed for the golf course. When I, in 1996, finished my arguably less dignified biography of an unarguably less dignified personage, Bill Clinton, I headed for the library to read American history. *Après* an Adams from Massachusetts, one seeks recreation. *Après* the Boy President from Arkansas, one seeks a clear record of events: historic facts, everyday occurrences, norms, a cast of characters that is at least plausible. After recording all the details of Boy Clinton's life, one requires contact with reality.

Unfortunately, the first volumes I wandered into dealt with the Nixon Administration. Soon I was reading about the cover-up of Watergate, the misuse of the FBI, the public lies, the departure of presidential aides for the slammer, and the President's own departure, just a few steps ahead of a House Sergeant at Arms bearing Articles of Impeachment. Though I had sought respite from the Boy President, my mind steadily filled with images of the Arkansas Wonder shambling through the White House, winking at the truth, raking in illegal contributions and thinly veiled bribes, and calling upon the professional services of the FBI to cover his misdeeds and harass his enemies. Could I find no refuge from the chief figure of my recent scholarly researches? For five years I had ferreted out every fact available about him, and pieced them into one hundred thousand words of biography. Now Richard Nixon's historic words—"I am not a crook!"—summoned up visions of

Clinton, as well they might. There he was in the daily headlines, notifying the credulous White House press corps that "I've done nothing wrong," or "The White House was not for sale."

Slowly, steadily, I began to see a need for this book. Travelgate and Filegate were still making periodic appearances in the news, owing to the investigations of various congressional committees. Clinton's political allies and business partners were being indicted and convicted, owing to far-flung judicial proceedings by no less than two independent counsels. Then early in 1997 a riot of stories about campaign irregularities in the 1996 presidential race rampaged into the headlines. Clearly the Clinton Administration had but one genuine predecessor, the Administration of Richard Nixon, though Nixon kept things simpler. A team of his servitors broke into the Watergate offices of the Democratic Party. The President ordered a cover-up. At the time I had not been particularly disturbed. Politicians cover their blunders. But then Nixon lied repeatedly and brazenly to the American people. Worse, he imposed on the FBI and CIA to do his partisan political bidding. In a healthy democracy, law enforcement agencies, the military, and the courts must be insulated from politics. The rule of law must apply equally to all the citizenry. Without such niceties you have, well, you have the Arkansas I had written about in *Boy Clinton*.

In Arkansas I had encountered dozens of ordinary Arkansans who had been broken by Clinton's clique of cronies defying the law with impunity. The first victim I encountered was a man by the name of Freddy Whitener, who had created a small road-building company in the 1980s. As we reported in *The American Spectator*, Whitener went partners with Clinton's political supporter and business associate, James McDougal. After taking control of the finances of their real-estate development company, McDougal left Whitener holding the bag for millions of dollars of debt from McDougal's other dubious dealings. Whitener went bankrupt. Some of the debt that drove Whitener under seems to have covered contributions to Governor Clinton's 1984 campaign. When I met him, he and his wife, Dorothy, were eking out a living from a mobile home in the hills outside Bradford, Arkansas. A few hundred yards away stood his old family home, taken from him by bank regulators because of McDougal's swindle.

I have knowledge of scores of similarly broken Arkansans, including state troopers and other state employees denied their jobs, pensions, or other benefits in retaliation or simply because they were inconvenient to the Clintons. Close observers of the Clinton presidency will remember scores more who were smeared, harassed, and brutally misused when the Clintons came to Washington to practice Arkansas politics in the White House. The Clintons began early misusing the FBI to smear law-abiding workers in the Travel Office. They systematically misused government to shut down an RTC investigation into their Whitewater shenanigans and to smear honest investigators who got in their way. Continually they engaged in abuse of power, conflict of interest, obstruction of justice, and public lying of stupefying impudence. Then came the New China Lobby, the Huang-Riady axis, felons and hucksters in the White House, political corruption and misconduct so egregious that even Bob Woodward would exclaim to a national television audience, "I would give the Nixon White House credit for having a comparatively clean operation."

The blizzard of scandal was too much for most Americans to follow. Even members of the press were dizzied by charges, countercharges, convictions, pleas for human understanding, suave calumnies. Soon the whole country became inured to the Administration's deceits and arbitrary wielding of power. In American history no administration had ever committed so many violations of the law in the practice of mere partisan politics, or endangered the rule of law in so many different areas of governmental conduct. Yet public awareness was dulled. Something was needed to focus the nation's attention on the corruption that was rotting through our government. Well, few things so focus the public's attention as an old-fashioned Impeachment.

That was how it went in the case of President Andrew Johnson, and the case for impeaching him was far weaker than the case for impeaching either Nixon or Clinton. Johnson is remembered today as a sorry figure. However, before the House of Representatives began its deliberations over his conduct, he was a popular fellow. The House Committee's work erased that popularity almost overnight. Its hearings focussed the public's attention on Johnson's repeated and seemingly arbitrary flouting of the will of Congress. So it is with Clinton. In the following scenario readers will find a plentitude of causes for Clinton's impeachment. As they read the eminently plausible debates in Congress, they will come to see impeachment move from the realm of the plausible to that of the reasonable, and on to the necessary.

Along the way, "Anonymous" and I have not overlooked the absurd in our scenario, for absurdity is close to the heart of modern American politics, especially as practiced by the Clinton-Gore generation of politicians. "Anonymous" has been close to the center of politics for as long as I have known him/her. We worked easily together, anticipating the behavior of politicians, commentators, and the Clinton cabal. Between the two of us we know most of the key players in this book. Their behavior might surprise some readers. After chronicling and assessing five years of their antics, I can say for a certitude that the behavior depicted in this book is genuine Clinton-Gore *modus operandi*. So read the scenario for Bill Clinton's condign culmination. Members of Congress, taking time out from their fund-raising and hair styling, should read with special care.

Remember, Honorable Members, the observation of the poet Wordsworth: life is mostly imitation.

R. EMMETT TYRRELL, JR.
NEW YORK, N.Y., SEPTEMBER 15, 1997

THE PRELIMINARIES

The House of Representatives...
shall have the sole Power of Impeachment...

The President, the Vice President and all civil Officers of the United States, shall be removed from Office on Impeachment for, and Conviction of, Treason, Bribery, or other high Crimes and Misdemeanors.

— ARTICLE II, SECTION 4, CONSTITUTION OF THE UNITED STATES

The Senate shall have the sole Power to try all Impeachments. When sitting for that Purpose, they shall be on Oath or Affirmation. When the President of the United States is tried, the Chief Justice shall preside: And no Person shall be convicted without the concurrence of two thirds of the Members present.

— ARTICLE I, SECTION 2, CONSTITUTION OF THE UNITED STATES

QUESTION: My question to you as somebody who has enormous power to lead by example, is it good enough to say that everybody else does it?

PRESIDENT CLINTON: No, no. And I'm not trying to say that... I don't think it's good enough to say, "it is legal." I think we should be held to a higher standard ... But what I do want you to know is, when it is obvious that we have a disagreement, when I read reports or see them on television, and I think you see this in a certain way and I just honestly see it in a different way, I think it's helpful to the American people and to you and to me for me to tell how I see it. That's all ...

On the other hand, I don't believe either that we can afford to run the risk of having one party just kind of disappear from the scene because they're unwilling to do what is necessary to be competitive in raising funds in the system that exists, which is why I say to you, in the end, we should set a high standard ...

• • •

FAST-FORWARD — Senate debate on the impeachment of
William Jefferson Clinton, September 25, 1998

As I hear the various explanations and exegeses that come out of the White House — indeed, as we have all heard them, time and again, in recent years — I am reminded of nothing so much as the rationale used by the character in Marlowe's *The Jew of Malta*, who says:

Thou hast committed fornication — Yes, but that was in another country, And besides, the wench is dead.

— **SENATOR DANIEL PATRICK MOYNIHAN**

CHAPTER ONE
THE COMMITTEE OF SIX

———————————■———————————

Senator Tom Daschle
Senator John Glenn
Senator Pat Moynihan
Congressman David Bonior
Congressman Richard Gephardt
Congressman Henry Waxman

THE PRESIDENT WAS RUNNING LATE. Nothing new there, because the notion of Clinton Time had taken hold in the White House after five years, leading visitors—even distinguished visitors like the Committee of Six—to expect to wait anywhere from ten to thirty minutes before they would finally be ushered into the Oval Office.

So it was that at 2:28 PM, twenty-eight minutes after their meeting was originally scheduled, members of the committee were shown in for what they had assumed would be a closed session with the President.

Twenty-five years earlier, Richard Nixon had been alone when meeting with a similar delegation, headed by Senator Barry Goldwater. That, however, did not appear to be Bill Clinton's style in a crisis. At least not the ultimate crisis an American president could face.

"I hope you don't mind, but I've asked a few people to sit in," Clinton told members of the committee. "That is, if it doesn't pose a problem."

Typical Clinton, thought Pat Moynihan. A fait accompli, then "if it doesn't pose a problem." As if any member of the committee were about to object to Hillary Clinton's and lawyer David Kendall's presence while they were there in the room.

"Perfectly all right," said the New York senator as the committee settled in. Technically Daschle and Gephardt, as party leaders on Capitol Hill, headed the group. But forming the committee had, after all, been Moynihan's idea; and Daschle and Gephardt, for their own reasons, were only too happy to see someone else act as spokesman.

"Coffee?"

"I'm afraid, Mr. President, that this isn't a social visit, so I'll come straight to the point."

"Do that," said Hillary Clinton, in the withering tone Moynihan and other members of the committee had often heard of, but never before experienced. Moynihan, unruffled by the First Lady's tone and gelid glare, continued, fully aware that, in the well-known tradition of every White House in recent history, his every word was being taped.

WHITE HOUSE TRANSCRIPTION XB-123, Oval Office conference of 6/22/98

SENATOR MOYNIHAN: This is a painful task, Mr. President, but we've come to inform you that in all likelihood, the hearings on H.R. 104...

THE PRESIDENT: Beginning Thursday, right?

SENATOR MOYNIHAN: Thursday, yes.

MRS. CLINTON: Why can't they be postponed?

THE PRESIDENT: That's all right, Hillary. I think the answer is that they've run out of postponements. Right, Dick?

CONGRESSMAN GEPHARDT: Right, Mr. President. We just don't have the numbers...

THE PRESIDENT: Though it does seem to me that at this moment, with the President going into delicate negotiations with the new rulers of China, people in the House would hesitate...I mean, we're talking about national security and the future of the Free World... What ever happened to that hallowed principle that politics stops at the water's edge?

CONGRESSMAN GEPHARDT: We just don't have the numbers.

MRS. CLINTON: *(expletive deleted)*

SENATOR MOYNIHAN: Mr. President, do you mind if I just cut to the chase?

THE PRESIDENT: By all means.

SENATOR MOYNIHAN: What we're here to tell you is that once these hearings start, once the train leaves the station and witnesses are put under oath and begin testifying...

CONGRESSMAN WAXMAN: On television. All three networks, CNN.

THE PRESIDENT: You sure? They didn't much *(inaudible)*

SENATOR MOYNIHAN: This is different, not just another Congressional hearing... And once the impeachment process begins and continues months on end, we won't be able to...

MRS. CLINTON: I thought you said you were cutting to the chase. Cut the *(expletive deleted)* and get to the point.

THE PRESIDENT: That's all right, Hillary. I think what you're saying, Pat—correct me if I'm wrong—is that the hearings will be damaging. Damaging to the White House, to the party...

CONGRESSMAN GEPHARDT: And to two hundred Democrats running for re-election with an impeachment vote pending...

THE PRESIDENT: I see... I see where you're coming from, and don't think I'm insensitive to what you're saying, but...

DAVID KENDALL: Mr. President...

THE PRESIDENT: Let me finish this thought, Dave, because I think what you gentlemen have come here for is to ask that I *(inaudible)* into the night, but that, that's not going to happen. No, because whatever our friends in the media may suggest, the *(expletive deleted)* Post or the right-wing *(inaudible)*, I am not, not going to do a Nixon, fall on my sword...

DAVID KENDALL: Mr. President...

THE PRESIDENT: *(expletive deleted)* Dave, I said let me finish my thought... And I would further suggest, Pat, Dick, gentlemen, that I have been between a *(inaudible)* rock and a hard place before, but here I am, you see me here, and here I intend to stay.

SENATOR DASCHLE: *(inaudible)*

THE PRESIDENT: They don't call me the Comeback Kid for nothing.

CHAPTER TWO
THE CHAIRMAN

■

THE MCLAUGHLIN GROUP, 6/20/98

ELEANOR CLIFT: It's like *Alice in Wonderland*—first the lynching, then the trial.

JOHN MCLAUGHLIN: Oh, come now, Eleanor.

ELEANOR CLIFT: As if any committee chaired by Henry Hyde could be fair and impartial.

FRED BARNES: Why not? Henry Hyde is as fair...

ELEANOR CLIFT: Fair? Are we talking about the same person? The Henry Hyde who thinks women...

JOHN MCLAUGHLIN: Don't tell me you're going into the Hyde amendment again.

ELEANOR CLIFT: Why not? It's part of...

JOHN MCLAUGHLIN: Because it had nothing whatever to do with...

FRED BARNES: Well, I think he's fair.

ELEANOR CLIFT: That's because you're part of the lynch mob.

• • •

IT WAS AN ASSIGNMENT any of his Republican colleagues in the House would have relished, but Henry Hyde was past the vanity of wanting to become a media star. At age seventy-four, he had been on Capitol Hill since the Watergate era, long enough to know that making instant history—getting the star treatment—had its price.

Hyde made no secret of his thoughts about the job. In the months leading up to the impeachment hearings, he'd expressed his misgivings about being "ringmaster at a media circus" to colleagues more inclined to feed the Washington gossip mill than keep a confidence…

THE EVANS-NOVAK POLITICAL REPORT, 6/19/98, excerpt

HALF-HEARTED HENRY?

Word from Capitol Hill is that Republican leadership in the House won't be too unhappy if Henry Hyde, Chairman of the Judiciary Committee, steps down before hearings begin on the possible impeachment of President Clinton. The septuagenarian Hyde, according to one longtime GOP staffer, is thought to lack the "killer instinct" needed to take on the War Room veterans of the Clinton defense team.

HENRY HYDE READ the *Evans-Novak* item with more amusement than irritation. He had a fairly good idea where it had originated and who in the House Republican caucus was stirring up rumors that he wasn't up to the challenge of extended impeachment hearings.

Hyde knew that, contrary to Bob Novak's source, Republican leaders in both the House and the Senate thought he was exactly what pro-impeachment forces needed to fill the nation's TV screens in the months ahead: a silver-thatched, unflappable presence who, as Trent Lott put it, "looks like everybody's favorite uncle." He also knew that his biggest headache in chairing the hearings wouldn't come from the Clinton defense team in the White House, but its point-men on the Hill, committee members Barney Frank and Charles Schumer.

"I have the utmost confidence Chairman Hyde will conduct fair and impartial hearings. If you believe that, there's a piece of real estate in Florida I'd like to show you."

—REP. ROSA DELAURO (D-CT), QUOTED IN *THE BOSTON GLOBE*, 6/22/98

CHAPTER THREE
THE PRESIDENT'S ADDRESS

■

President Clinton Will Address Nation On Eve of Impeachment Hearings

—HEADLINE, *THE NEW YORK TIMES*, 6/22/98

• • •

DICK MORRIS WOULD watch Bill Clinton's pre-emptive strike against the pro-impeachment forces from his suite at the Jefferson Hotel. He would watch it alone, but with a phone at this side to take incoming calls from pollster Doug Schoen, who was monitoring not one but half-a-dozen focus groups watching the speech across the country.

After the better part of a year in political purgatory, Morris was once again *persona grata* at the Clinton White House, called in to rescue his favorite client. Was there a political risk involved in bringing the controversial spin doctor/strategist back, after his embarrassing fall from grace in the summer of 1996?

BRIEFING by White House Press Secretary
Michael McCurry, 6/18//98

QUESTION: Mike, there's a report that Dick Morris is back on board, advising the President on dealing with the impeachment hearings.

MCCURRY: Who's your source? Morris? I haven't heard anything of the sort.

Q.: Nothing?

MCCURRY: Not that I recall.

Q.: Would it make any difference if I told you I heard it from the Chief of Staff?

MCCURRY: Oh, you mean that report. Well, as a matter of fact, yes, he did—it's coming back—he did say something about an outside consultant.

Q.: Then you confirm that Dick Morris...

MCCURRY: I didn't say that. All I said was, an outside consultant. Stop trying to put words in my mouth.

MICHAEL MCCURRY PRESS BRIEFING, 6/23/98

Q.: Mike, Dick Morris was seen entering the White House grounds through the southwest gate this morning.

MCCURRY: You mean sighted like a UFO, or the Hale-Bopp comet?

Q.: No, seriously. He was seen...

MCCURRY: Any other questions? If not, this is a reminder that RSVPs on the White House press barbecue have to be in by 1700 hours today. That's 5:00 PM, for you non-military types. (Press laughter) Just let my office know...

PRESIDENT CLINTON'S ADDRESS,
TelePrompTer Copy 9:00 PM EDT, 6/24/98

MY FELLOW AMERICANS—I COME INTO YOUR HOMES TONIGHT NOT AS YOUR PRESIDENT BUT AS A CITIZEN,

HUSBAND, AND FATHER CONCERNED OVER THE FUTURE OF OUR COUNTRY AND OUR CONSTITUTION....

I KNOW FROM THE MANY THOUSANDS OF LETTERS, CARDS AND E-MAIL MESSAGES SENT TO THE WHITE HOUSE... THAT AN OVERWHELMING MAJORITY OF AMERICANS—OF ALL RACES, CREEDS, AND GENDERS—SHARE MY CONCERN.

THEY ARE ASKING THE SAME QUESTION A YOUNG GIRL ASKED WHEN I PAID A VISIT TO HER SCHOOL IN LEXINGTON, KENTUCKY, LAST WEEK—"MR. PRESIDENT," SHE SAID, "WHAT IS AMERICA COMING TO?"

(*HOLD UP LEAFLET*)

AND SHE HAD IN HER HAND THIS LEAFLET SOMEONE HAD PASSED OUT AT THE SCHOOL JUST BEFORE I ARRIVED—A HATE SHEET THAT SAID "IMPEACH BILL CLINTON"...

(*PAUSE - CLENCHED CHIN*)

AND THERE WERE SOME REFERENCES IN IT—I WON'T REPEAT THEM HERE—NOT ONLY ABOUT ME BUT ABOUT MY FAMILY, INCLUDING CHELSEA, AND...

(*PAUSE, REACT*)

EVEN OUR DAUGHTER CHELSEA—AND AS I LOOKED AT THAT YOUNG STUDENT, I HAD NO ANSWER TO HER QUESTION, "WHAT IS AMERICA COMING TO?" NO ANSWER. BUT

ON RETURNING TO WASHINGTON—HERE, IN THE LONELINESS OF THE OVAL OFFICE—THAT YOUNG GIRL'S QUESTION STAYED WITH ME.

(*PAUSE*)

"WHAT IS AMERICA COMING TO?"—AND, WHILE I CAN'T ANSWER THAT, I CAN ANSWER THE QUESTION—FOR HER AND HER PARENTS AND ALL AMERICANS OF GOOD WILL— OF HOW WE'VE ARRIVED AT WHERE WE ARE....

FROM THE VERY DAY I ENTERED THIS OFFICE ONCE HELD BY WASHINGTON AND JEFFERSON AND ABRAHAM LINCOLN—SINCE THAT DAY, WE HAVE WITNESSED AN UNPRECEDENTED AND MEAN-SPIRITED CAMPAIGN OF LIES, HALF-TRUTHS AND VILIFICATION DIRECTED AGAINST AN AMERICAN PRESIDENT DULY ELECTED BY THE AMERICAN PEOPLE....

THEY SAY THEIR TARGET IS BILL CLINTON. BUT MAKE NO MISTAKE, THIS CAMPAIGN TO BRING DOWN A PRESIDENT— THIS DESPERATE ATTEMPT TO SET ASIDE—TO OVERTHROW—THE WILL OF THE PEOPLE, ISN'T AIMED AT BILL CLINTON ALONE. IT'S AIMED AT USURPING THE CONSTITUTION ITSELF—THE VERY BEDROCK ON WHICH THE FOUNDING FATHERS BUILT THIS GREAT REPUBLIC OF OURS....

• • •

SINCE THE DAY HE LEFT the White House and took up residence at ABC, George Stephanopoulos had worn two hats: presidential insider and outside political observer. It was an incongruence that didn't seem to bother his network bosses, but on this particular night it troubled their celebrity analyst.

Stephanopoulos had watched the President's address at ABC's studios in downtown Washington with his fellow pundits, Sam Donaldson, Cokie Roberts, and George Will. He had listened to their running critique with mixed feelings. Donaldson thought the bit about the little girl was "unmitigated BS," while Roberts thought the show's *piece de resistance*—Hillary and Chelsea joining Bill on camera—was "a straight steal from Nixon's Checkers speech." Will, for his part, confined his critique to obscure Burkean quotes and an occasional groan.

Stephanopoulos's problem was that he secretly agreed with everything his colleagues said. In White House sessions before the speech, he had argued in favor of a solemn presidential appeal, no Oprah Winfrey touches. He opposed the little-girl bit—an advance man's idea, à la Bob Haldeman—and after Hillary had left the room spoke forcefully against her appearing on camera because, according to the polls, the First Lady's own legal problems were hurting the President.

But Dick Morris, as was always the case when Bill Clinton felt threatened, had carried the day. The polls said nothing of the sort, Morris insisted. The kid with the hate sheet was a "real grabber," and the Bill-and-Hillary show played to family values.

The President had agreed. "What's wrong with an Oprah Winfrey touch?" he'd asked, "It's always worked before."

• • •

TOM DASCHLE POST-SPEECH INTERVIEW, CBS Reports, 6/24/98

DAN RATHER: Down in east Texas, you know, there's an expression, "You can run buttermilk through the pipeline but that don't make it oil."

TOM DASCHLE: Pardon?

DAN RATHER: What I mean is, the President seems to be saying, they can call it impeachment, but it's really a partisan vendetta.

TOM DASCHLE: Exactly. Henry Hyde's a decent enough man, but the extremists in his party are hell-bent on payback.

DAN RATHER: For Nixon, you mean.

TOM DASCHLE: No, Gingrich. I know the right-wingers make the Nixon parallel, but it won't hold up. In fact, it's outrageous to compare Peter Rodino and Henry Hyde...

DAN RATHER: Let's make that clear—Peter Rodino, chairman of the Judiciary Committee during Watergate. You know, Senator, there's a whole generation out there...

TOM DASCHLE: —but the difference is that Rodino was out to save the Constitution and Hyde is out to scrap it.

DAN RATHER: —that can't tell a sow from a shoat.

TOM DASCHLE: Pardon?

• • •

HENRY HYDE CLICKED OFF THE SET and went back to his paperwork. He had turned down all offers to appear on the tube to respond to the President's address, knowing it would play into the hands of the White House spinmeisters who were telling Katie Couric, Ted Koppel, anybody who gave them time, that the Hyde Committee was a kangaroo court and the hearings would be a partisan charade.

Spin wasn't Henry Hyde's specialty, but he'd been around Washington long enough to know how the game was played. It didn't take a Lee Atwater to understand that public perception could make or break a congressional inquiry—that his model in chairing an impeachment hearing should be Sam Ervin, the modulated judge, not Al D'Amato, the splenetic prosecutor.

Hyde also knew that public opinion on the question of impeachment was unsettled. As he had seen twenty-four years earlier, respect for the institution of the presidency can sustain the man who holds the office long after respect for the man himself has diminished, or even disappeared.

In addition, there was the matter of what some pollsters perceive as voter-ego: having twice elected both Nixon and Clinton—by overwhelming numbers the second time around—voters (not unlike the people they elect) were understandably slow to admit they made a mistake.

Not that the American people, even while casting their ballots, didn't have misgivings about both men. Questions were raised about Nixon's character throughout his career. Clinton's very arrival on the national scene came with lurid stories about his personal life, his efforts to escape military service during the Vietnam War, and his reputation in Arkansas as "Slick Willie"—the presidential candidate who could, straight-faced, deliver the line, "I smoked, but I didn't inhale."

If anything, that reputation had grown worse in recent years. In early 1997, at the height of his popularity as President, with the economy booming and the country at peace, Bill Clinton's negative numbers—the percentage of those polled who saw him in an "unfavorable" light—still ranged in the high 40s. And that was before the Starr Report on the Whitewater cover-up and revelations on Capitol Hill portraying him as, in the words of one editorial writer, "wallowing in the sleaze of laundered campaign money" (*San Diego Union-Tribune*, 5/15/98)....

PUBLIC OPINION Fabrizio-McLaughlin survey, week of April 19–25, 1998

Do you believe President Clinton's charge that the findings of the Starr Report were "politically-inspired," and that he and

his wife Hillary Rodham Clinton "have done nothing wrong" in connection with investigations into the Whitewater case?

Believe Starr's findings were political	**34%**
Trust Starr's findings	**55%**
Don't know	**11%**

Among the charges made by the Starr Report, President Clinton is said to have "engaged in a calculated effort to use the powers of the Presidency to obstruct the Whitewater investigation." From what you have read and heard about the case, do you agree with that statement?

Yes, agree	**67%**
No, disagree	**26%**
Don't know	**9%**

Charges have been made in Congress that in raising campaign funds in 1996, the Clinton-Gore campaign broke the law. Together with the Starr Report, this has led to calls for hearings on whether President Clinton should be impeached. Would you favor or oppose such hearings?

Favor	**37%**
Oppose	**43%**
Don't know	**20%**

• • •

HYDE STUDIED THE SURVEY, then Tony Fabrizio's analysis. As the pollster saw it, Clinton's falling numbers weren't traceable to any single event or political setback, but to the sheer volume of revelations, charges, indictments that seemed part-and-parcel of Bill Clinton's incumbency; a public, in short, that had simply grown tired of reading and hearing explanations from their President about some new scandal—major or minor, political or personal.

The chairman recalled a campaign line out of the past, from another Democratic president. Jimmy Carter had staked his claim to the White House, post-Watergate, on the premise that "the American people deserve a president as good as they are."

Hyde took a final look at the mixed numbers on the question of impeachment hearings. Only 43 percent opposed. A year before it would have been 75 percent. It could be, thought the chairman, that the American people, after five years of "Slick Willie's" presidency, were coming around to Jimmy Carter's point of view.

• • •

"It would be, to say the least, premature as well as patently unfair to jump to any conclusions until all the facts are in. This is America, and the presumption, though Mr. Starr might not like it, is innocent until proved otherwise."

—CLINTON ATTORNEY ROBERT BENNETT, ON THE HIGH ROAD, REACTING TO NEWS OF THE STARR REPORT AND ACCOMPANYING INDICTMENTS.

"... lyin' witnesses, perjured testimony, a case stacked by a special persecutor who whores eight hours a day for the cancer industry..."

—CLINTON FLACK JAMES CARVILLE, REACTING TO THE SAME NEWS.

• • •

"... until all the facts are in..."

HENRY HYDE HAD a pretty good idea how long that would take, if Bob Bennett had his way. Five years, maybe ten. Sufficient time,

Hyde was sure, for Bennett's client to serve out his term, write his presidential memoirs, and be comfortably ensconced in an elder statesman's chair when the Nobel Peace Prize Committee came calling.

But that, as Hyde knew, was what seven-figure lawyers like Bob Bennett were paid for—not simply to mount a legal defense but a media offense as well. The truth of the matter wasn't that there was a shortage of facts about the high crimes, misdemeanors, and peccadilloes of the Clinton White House. If anything, the problem was information overload.

Hyde envied his predecessor, Peter Rodino. Watergate had been a simple, bungled burglary, a scandal understood from boardroom to barroom across America. It could be boiled down to a single question, "What did the President know and when did he know it?"

With the Clinton White House, however, "What did the President know and when did he know it?" was only good for starters. Which "it" was up for discussion? Whitewater? Travelgate? Filegate? Hillary's missing papers? The Riady-China connection? The suppression of the RTC investigation?

Peter Rodino's Judiciary Committee had looked down a tunnel. Henry Hyde's was headed into a maze.

• • •

WHILE HENRY HYDE was going over his opening statement and witness list for the next day's hearings, John Conyers, ranking Democrat on Judiciary, was on the phone with Donald Payne, Chairman of the Congressional Black Caucus, telling Payne about the call he'd received from the President that afternoon....

JOHN CONYERS: He asked me to pass this on to you, and that's all I'm doing-passing it on. He said... here, I took notes... he said, "Tell Don Payne and other members of the caucus to read between the lines of my speech tonight..."

DONALD PAYNE: Read between the lines? What's that supposed to...

JOHN CONYERS: Let me finish... "that I know now I made a huge mistake trying to deal with those Right-wing *(expletive deleted)*, and..."

DONALD PAYNE: He used that word..."*(expletive deleted)*"?

JOHN CONYERS: You have to understand the man. That's the way he thinks we talk. You want to hear the rest of it?

DONALD PAYNE: Just sum up.

JOHN CONYERS: Sum up? Let me put it this way: The man hasn't talked to me, one-on-one, since... when?... October '96. The campaign. So what does that tell you? He's in deep *(expletive deleted)* and looking for all the help he can get.

DONALD PAYNE: Well, I'm not, you know, happy with the man. He's two-faced, goes off in all directions. But...

JOHN CONYERS: I know what you're saying, because I come down the same way. He may be a *(expletive deleted)*...

DONALD PAYNE: —but he's our *(expletive deleted)*. Exactly.

• • •

FOR BARNEY FRANK and Charles Schumer, second- and third-ranking members of Judiciary Committee, the story was much the same. Hard-line northeast liberals, they saw Bill Clinton as a slick-talking Southerner who couldn't be trusted.

Schumer, his own political ambitions at stake, would walk a tightrope in the months to come, defending Clinton only because to do otherwise could play into the hands of his fellow New Yorker Al D'Amato in a crucial election year. Frank, whose feelings toward the President had been undisguised since the '97 budget deal with Trent Lott, saw his dilemma in simpler, more visceral terms: He disliked Clinton but hated Henry Hyde, the Republican leadership, and everything they stood for.

• • •

"If he's impeached, does that mean we can finally start the trial?"

—PAULA JONES TO HER ATTORNEY, QUOTED
ON PAGE SIX, *THE NEW YORK POST*, 6/25/98

THE
HEARINGS

COMMITTEE ON THE JUDICIARY

2138 Rayburn House Office Building
Washington, D.C. 20515

HEARINGS ON HOUSE RESOLUTION 104

MR. HYDE (ILLINOIS), CHAIRMAN

Mr. Sensenbrenner, Jr. (WI)

Mr. McCollum (FL)

Mr. Gekas (PA)

Mr. Coble (NC)

Mr. Smith (TX)

Mr. Schiff (NM)

Mr. Gallegly (CA)

Mr. Canady (FL)

Mr. Inglis (SC)

Mr. Goodlatte (VA)

Mr. Buyer (IN)

Mr. Bono (CA)

Mr. Bryant (TN)

Mr. Chabot (OH)

Mr. Barr (GA)

Mr. Jenkins (TN)

Mr. Hutchinson (AR)

Mr. Pease (IN)

Mr. Cannon (UT)

Mr. Conyers (MI), Ranking

Mr. Frank (MA)

Mr. Schumer (NY)

Mr. Berman (CA)

Mr. Boucher (VA)

Mr. Nadler (NY)

Mr. Scott (VA)

Mr. Watt (NC)

Mr. Lofgren (CA)

Ms. Jackson-Lee (TX)

Ms. Waters (CA)

Mr. Meehan (MA)

Mr. Delahunt (MA)

Mr. Wexler (FL)

Mr. Rothman (NJ)

Thomas E. Mooney, Sr.
Chief of Staff/General Counsel

Perry Applebaum Minority (Democratic) Counsel

CHAPTER FOUR

THE FIRST DAY

■

Impeachment Process Begins Today; Rep. Hyde Pledges "Fair, Open" Panel

— BANNER HEADLINE, *NEW YORK TIMES*, 6/25/98

Poll Says Majority Sees Impeachment As "Partisan Politics"

— FRONT PAGE, *USA TODAY*, SAME DAY

Hyde S&L Case Back in Court

— FRONT PAGE, *CHICAGO SUN-TIMES*, SAME DAY

THE *SUN-TIMES* STORY was by Basil Talbott, who had covered the settlement of the Clyde Savings-and-Loan case a year before. Henry Hyde, one of a dozen officers and directors of the failed S & L, had been cleared of wrongdoing by federal regulators, but now the settlement was being challenged by a Chicago stockholder. Asked about the timing of the suit—on the same day the impeachment hearings were to begin—the plaintiff's lawyer said it was "pure coincidence."

OPENING STATEMENT of Chairman Henry Hyde, Judiciary
Committee hearings on H. Res. 104, 6/25/98

MR. HYDE (CHAIRMAN): Let me make clear my view, as chairman, of
what these hearings are about. "Impeachment" is an often-misun-
derstood word, but a reading of Article I, Section 2 of the
Constitution defines our responsibility as members of the House...
Finally, it's important to know that we are not here as a court to try
the President. We are here to gather and assess facts and determine
whether sufficient cause exists for the Senate to try him for conduct
violating his oath of office...

This is not an easy task, and I, for one, would urge that my colleagues on both sides of the aisle recognize that we too have taken
an oath... and neither the Constitution nor the people of the
United States will be served if, in the course of these hearings, we
descend to partisan bickering...

• • •

THERE WAS AN UNEASY STIR in the chamber when Hyde brought up
the matter of partisan bickering. The room quieted immediately,
however, when he went on to frame the issue to be resolved by the
Congress in these proceedings. The issue was abuse of power as
outlined in the impeachment clause of the Constitution. Proof of a
statutory crime was not necessary, and even if there were such
proof it might not be relevant. The Constitution spoke of a "high
crime," and at least since Watergate most scholars agreed that the
Founding Fathers considered it a "high crime" for a president to
fail to observe the moral standards expected of him. Impeachment
then and now had to do with standards of political morality.
Language found in the second article of the impeachment of
Richard Nixon suggested the scope of the task facing the committee now. Nixon, the Rodino Committee had charged, had violated
"his constitutional oath faithfully to execute the office of the
President of the United States and, to the best of his ability, pre-

serve, protect, and defend the Constitution of the United States...." And he had disregarded "his constitutional duty to take care that the laws be faithfully executed...."

• • •

OPENING STATEMENT of John Conyers (D-MI), Ranking Democrat, Judiciary Committee hearings on H. Res. 104, 6/25/98

JOHN CONYERS: I'm gratified to know that our colleague from Illinois (Mr. Hyde) is aware of the harm done to the Constitution and the American people by narrow, mean-spirited partisanship. But that only begs the question of what we're doing here—rehashing old, discredited accusations aimed at a President who has been unfairly targeted, since the day he took office, by those who want to turn back the clock...

OPENING STATEMENT of Charles Schumer (D-NY), Judiciary Committee hearings on H. Res. 104, 6/25/98

CHARLES SCHUMER: ... Have we forgotten the growing gap between rich and poor? The ongoing crisis of our inner cities? The tragedy of homelessness? A justice system in critical disrepair? A rising incidence of spousal- and child-abuse in the American home? An unequal tax burden, with middle-class Americans carrying the load for corporate chiselers? Aren't these the issues we were sent here to deal with? Not wallow, as some seem to prefer, in the bilious back-water of charges made and refuted, time-and-again...

OPENING STATEMENT of Bill McCollum (R-FL), Judiciary Committee hearings on H. Res. 104, 6/25/98

BILL MCCOLLUM: I applaud the Chairman's call for an end to partisan bickering as we enter these hearings, but it's obvious by now that as far as this White House is concerned, personal, partisan attacks are the order of the day...

Given the experience of the past five years—beginning with the false accusations and innuendo leveled at the President's critics in the Travelgate and Filegate scandals—it comes as no surprise that...

At this point, Bill McCollum was interrupted by Barney Frank and the following colloquy took place:

BARNEY FRANK: Point of order, Mr. Chairman. It was my understanding that opening statements were confined to the general subject matter of these hearings, and not...

BILL MCCOLLUM: May I be allowed to finish? I believe we were allotted up to ten minutes and Mr. Frank will have ample opportunity...

BARNEY FRANK: I have the right to make a point of order. All I ask is that you stick to the agreed format.

HENRY HYDE (GAVELING): ... You'll have your chance, Mr. Frank. The format, as you call it, was only suggested, not...

BARNEY FRANK: My understanding was...

HENRY HYDE (GAVELING): —required... You've made your point, Mr. Frank. Let's move on.

BILL MCCOLLUM: As I was saying... The Chairman's call for an end to partisan bickering...

• • •

THOUGH ONLY IN HIS second term, Georgia Republican Bob Barr had already shown himself to be a congressman ahead of the curve on the question of impeachment. As early as March, 1997, Barr had asked Henry Hyde to begin an inquiry into whether Bill Clinton should be removed from office. Coming as it did at the peak of Clinton's post-election popularity, the request seemed an exercise in partisan futility. But Barr pursued the issue in a way that impressed the chairman. Now, with Clinton's Whitewater and campaign fund-raising problems having reached critical mass, Hyde was more receptive to suggestions from the thirty-eight-year-old former prosecutor with the Tom Dewey-like mustache.

At a closed session of the committee, Barr argued that past congressional inquiries into the operations of the Clinton White House—the D'Amato inquiry, the Clinger inquiry, the Leach inquiry—had floundered because the committees involved used a "scattershot" approach in summoning witnesses. He submitted an agenda that broke the hearings down into categories—"scandal by scandal" as Barr put it—beginning with...

FROM SAFIRE'S POLITICAL DICTIONARY, Third Edition (1998)

GATE. Derived from Watergate, the all-purpose term used to describe a complex network of political, financial, and criminal transactions that formed the basis of impeachment proceedings against President Richard M. Nixon. Since 1973, an obligatory suffix applied to scandals involving White House operations. See also...

■ ■ ■

TRAVELGATE. Catchword attached to one of the earlier scandals involving the Clinton White House. When seven longtime employees of the non-political White House Travel Office, including its director, Billy Dale, were summarily fired in May, 1993, the ostensible reason given was financial irregularities in the handling of funds used to make travel arrangements for reporters covering the President's foreign and domestic trips. But as later admitted by David Watkins, then in charge of White House administration, the charges were only a cover for Hillary Clinton's real purpose—to turn the lucrative travel business over to personal friends.

Once exposed, the plan collapsed. Five of the fired employees were reinstated, the President apologized for what he variously called "a mistake" and an "inappropriate action." Dale, brought to trial for alleged embezzlement, was exonerated by a District of Columbia jury.

■ ■ ■

FILEGATE. Catchword attached to a Travelgate scandal spin-off. While investigating the Travelgate affair, the House Government Reform and Oversight Committee gained access to documents revealing that two mid-level White House operatives, Craig Livingstone and Anthony Marceca, had in their possession not only the raw FBI file on Billy Dale, but 900 other confidential files on members of previous administrations, including former Secretary of State James A. Baker III. Though President Clinton termed this unprecedented access to FBI files "a bureaucratic snafu," prima facie evidence that Livingstone and Marceca had violated the Privacy Act led to full-scale investigation by Independent Counsel Kenneth Starr.

CHAPTER FIVE
STEPHANOPOULOS

———————————■———————————

RE-RUN —

"I'd say, 'Gee, I just don't remember what happened back then,' and they won't be able to indict me for perjury and that, maybe that's the principal thing that I've learned in four years ... I just intend to rely on that failure of memory."

— **CLINTON WHITE HOUSE COUNSEL CHARLES RUFF in 1977, telling Bob Woodward how he'd answer future congressional inquiries about his conduct as special prosecutor in the Watergate case.**

GEORGE STEPHANOPOULOS entered the hearing room in much the same way he entered the press room when he was White House communications director, the first year of the Clinton presidency: sporting a prime-cut Armani suit, unruly (albeit blown-dry) hair, and an attitude that informed his reply to every question with the unspoken words, "How dare you?"

The chamber was packed. Over four hundred news correspondents from around the world had been given credentials, all but twenty-five consigned to watching on television in adjoining rooms. Lawyers and lobbyists made up a large part of the audience, with a smattering of familiar Hollywood faces available to news directors for TV cutaways. And from neighboring Orange County, the President's favorite televangelist, the Reverend Robert Schuller.

A gaggle of female staffers from various congressional offices had shown up early to watch the witness dubbed "Gorgeous George" by columnist Liz Smith take first turn before the Hyde Committee...

TESTIMONY OF GEORGE STEPHANOPOULOS,* 6/25/98

HENRY HYDE: Mr. Stephanopoulos, let me read from a report of the Committee on Government Reform and Oversight. I quote: "Travelgate is a story about the failure of the Clinton White House to live up to the ethical standards expected of the highest office in the land. The wrongdoing of this administration lies not only in the firings of the seven Travel Office employees. They severed at the pleasure of the President. If the President chose to fire them to reward political cronies, that was his prerogative. And he must reap the consequences. Rather, the wrongdoing occurred after the firings. It resulted from a desire to hide the truth about who actually fired them and why." Unquote. You were White House communications director at that time, is that correct?

GEORGE STEPHANOPOULOS: At the time of the Travel Office turnover, yes.

HENRY HYDE: Turnover? You mean the firings?

GEORGE STEPHANOPOULOS: I was communications director at that time.

HENRY HYDE: In charge of what's generally called damage control, correct?

---

* Stephanopoulos was the first of 138 witnesses who either testified in open session or were deposed by the Hyde Committee in its sixteen-week Impeachment Inquiry. Highlights of the testimony of pivotal witnesses, along with key documents, are included herein, but for those desiring a complete transcript of proceedings, see Document 12074-98: House Judiciary Committee Inquest re the Impeachment of President William Jefferson Clinton, available either from the Government Printing Office as printed text, or via the Internet at http:// www.clint.imp

GEORGE STEPHANOPOULOS: If by that you mean, responsible for putting together the White House statement on the matter, yes.

HENRY HYDE: And in that capacity, did you call a meeting at your office on Friday, May 21, 1993, a meeting that included White House Counsel Bernard Nussbaum, Deputy Counsels William Kennedy and Vincent Foster, and John Collingwood of the Federal Bureau of Investigation?

GEORGE STEPHANOPOULOS: I've answered that question many times, Mr. Hyde, under oath, in depositions...

HENRY HYDE: Well, if you don't mind answering it one more time.

GEORGE STEPHANOPOULOS: Yes, a meeting was held in my office, I believe that day, to update the counsel's office on the FBI's findings.

HENRY HYDE: Findings. You're referring to...

GEORGE STEPHANOPOULOS: What the bureau had learned in its preliminary investigation of the Travel Office.

HENRY HYDE: That was it? To update Mr. Nussbaum and his staff? No other purpose?

GEORGE STEPHANOPOULOS: Well, yes, to coordinate anything said by the bureau about the investigation with our own statements.

HENRY HYDE: "Coordinate"—in other words, spin control.

GEORGE STEPHANOPOULOS: That's your characterization, not mine.

HENRY HYDE: On the contrary, it's the characterization made by your deputy at the time, Dee Dee Myers, to describe the function of your office.

GEORGE STEPHANOPOULOS: It's still not my characterization. Ms. Myers had what you'd call a flair for colorful quotes...

HENRY HYDE: But you didn't find it unusual, odd, that members of the White House staff were, as you say, coordinating statements with the FBI in an ongoing investigation?

GEORGE STEPHANOPOULOS: Odd? No. It was—the investigation, after all, was inside the White House itself. There was reason to believe, at least at that time, that funds had been mis—mismanaged.

HENRY HYDE: But as the investigation proved, they weren't.

GEORGE STEPHANOPOULOS: No, but with due respect, Mr. Hyde, we're going over something five years in the past, a matter that's been gone over again and again, and as the President said at the time, there were mistakes made, some inappropriate steps taken.

HENRY HYDE: That's why we're here, Mr. Stephanopoulos, to determine the extent of those improprieties. Mr. Collingwood's presence at your meeting that day—was he there by invitation, or order?

GEORGE STEPHANOPOULOS: Invitation, of course. We weren't in the habit of issuing orders to the FBI, if that's what you mean.

HENRY HYDE: Still, you didn't bother to go through proper channels, the Department of Justice, to invite Mr. Collingwood, did you? You went directly to the FBI.

GEORGE STEPHANOPOULOS: Yes, but again, Mr. Hyde, as we said at the time, we were new to the White House, just settling in. There were mistakes we later corrected—a learning process, the kind that goes on in every new administration.

JOHN CONYERS: Excuse me, Mr. Stephanopoulos, but an inquiry to the chair... Is it your intention, going back five years, to call this Collingwood as a witness? Otherwise, I see no purpose in badgering this witness...

HENRY HYDE: My purpose, Mr. Conyers, is to ascertain why and how the FBI was used by the Clinton White House in an investigation of charges that proved unfounded, that unfairly smeared seven innocent people. And how a White House aide with this witness's background can plead ignorance of a fundamental rule of law and procedure, one that's applied to every administration until this one—that the White House must go through the Justice Department when it wants to contact the FBI.

JOHN CONYERS: Oh? It seems to me that, back during the Nixon years...

HENRY HYDE: No sir, no sir. Never during the Nixon administration, not even during Watergate, did we ever see the official spokesman for the Federal Bureau of Investigation just summoned to the White House... That was Mr. Collingwood's job, wasn't it, Mr. Stephanopoulos?

GEORGE STEPHANOPOULOS: I believe so.

HENRY HYDE: Weren't you aware at the time that the Federal Bureau of Investigation operates, strictly operates, under the Department of Justice, at arms-length from the White House? Or has, under past administrations.

GEORGE STEPHANOPOULOS: I don't understand the question. Was I aware...?

HENRY HYDE: Let me put it this way, Mr. Stephanopoulos—you're a Rhodes scholar, with a degree in political science, summa cum laude, isn't that right?

GEORGE STEPHANOPOULOS: Yes.

HENRY HYDE: And you've had considerable experience in Washington, up here on the Hill in fact, before you joined the Clinton staff.

GEORGE STEPHANOPOULOS: Yes.

JOHN CONYERS: If the chair...

HENRY HYDE: Permit me to finish, Mr. Conyers, then you can question—then how, Mr. Stephanopoulos, please tell me and the other members of this committee how you could plead ignorance, could possibly be unaware of the impropriety of the FBI's being called in by the White House to work out a damage control program.

GEORGE STEPHANOPOULOS: It was not a damage control program, Mr. Hyde. And let me add, any implication that the purpose of the meeting was, in your word, to "smear" members of the Travel Office is a smear in itself. Our only purpose, everyone there, was an open exchange of information on the status of the case.

HENRY HYDE: You're sure of that.

GEORGE STEPHANOPOULOS: *(inaudible)*

HENRY HYDE: Well, allow me, Mr. Stephanopoulos, to read two press releases issued by Mr. Collingwood, the first prior to your meeting on May 20, 1993, the second after, on May 21. I quote from the first: "At the request of the White House, the FBI has had preliminary contact with... the auditors brought in to audit the White House Travel Office. We anticipate receiving the final report of the auditors soon and will analyze their findings to determine the next steps in the investigation..." Is the witness familiar with that statement?

GEORGE STEPHANOPOULOS: Familiar? After five years *(inaudible)*

HENRY HYDE: And here, the second statement, issued the following day, May 21, 1993, I quote: "At the request of the White House, the FBI has had preliminary contact with the auditors brought in to audit the White House Travel Office."... So far the two statements are identical. But then, I quote, "That contact produced sufficient information for the FBI to determine that additional criminal investigation is warranted. We anticipate receiving the final report of the auditors soon, and will analyze their findings to determine the next steps in the investigation..." Unquote. Now sir, those two statements...

BARNEY FRANK: Will the Chair yield for a question?

HENRY HYDE: Not at this moment, Mr. Frank, I'd like to make my point. Those two FBI statements, one issued before your meeting with Mr. Collingwood, one issued afterward, are identical save for one difference—the addition of the line that includes the word "criminal." Says, in other words, that there was reason to believe the seven Travel Office employees fired were guilty of having committed a crime, a charge that proved baseless. Wouldn't you agree, Mr. Stephanopoulos, that that constitutes a smear?

GEORGE STEPHANOPOULOS: May I see...

BARNEY FRANK: Will the Chair yield? Because I see where this is headed, and I think it's important at this early stage to set the parameters...

HENRY HYDE: No, Mr. Frank, the chair will not yield until we've finished questioning...

(At this point, Chairman Hyde, his hand over the microphone, turned to hold a private discussion with Committee General Counsel Thomas Mooney, Sr.)

HENRY HYDE: You mention, Mr. Frank, parameters. If it's a point of order you have in mind...

BARNEY FRANK: A point of order, yes... The scope of these hearings, Mr. Chairman, as I understand H.R.104, is to determine whether grounds exist to impeach a president, under Article Two, Section Four of the Constitution. This is uncharted territory, virtually uncharted, since the only precedent we have is the Johnson impeachment, 130 years ago. Now Andrew Johnson, as we know, was never elected President, had served only two years...

HENRY HYDE: Spare us the history lesson, Mr. Frank, and make your point. We have a witness waiting.

BARNEY FRANK: My point is that the questions you've asked the witness are irrelevant to the mandate of this committee. Whatever occurred five years ago—the alleged, and I emphasize alleged, crimes, misdemeanors, whatever the chair is trying to lay at the feet of the President...

HENRY HYDE: Abuse of power, Mr. Frank. Wrongful misuse of the FBI to deprive seven innocent people of their rights.

BARNEY FRANK: I repeat, this entire matter has been hashed, re-hashed, and was known at the time of the 1996 election. It was all out there—the rumors, leaks, trumped-up charges—and the ultimate authority in a democratic society, the people, heard the so-called evidence and rejected it.

BOB BARR: Mr. Chairman...

HENRY HYDE: One moment, Mr. Barr. Is it—let me try to understand this, Mr. Frank—are you contending that some kind of statute of limitations exists for presidential crimes?

BARNEY FRANK: No, because no crimes have been committed. Only alleged. And since everything you've gone over with this witness was known years ago...

BOB BARR: But everything wasn't known. By withholding documents, stonewalling...

HENRY HYDE: One at a time, Mr. Barr. Your point is noted, Mr. Frank, a question best taken up in executive session, without imposing on our witnesses' time.

JOHN CONYERS: Let the record show that I join my colleague from Massachusetts in raising the question, legitimate question, of the mandate of this committee under Article Two, Section four, and of the right Congress has, any Congress, to set aside the judgment rendered by the people in a free election.

CHARLES SCHUMER: Seconded. Unless we reverted to the status of a banana republic...

HENRY HYDE (GAVELING): The ruling of the chair is that Mr. Frank's point will be taken up in executive session. We will proceed questioning the witness, in order.

• • •

LUNCH BREAK AT THE WHITE HOUSE, and the President, having long since abandoned the herbivorous diet imposed by his doctors, was dispatching a guacamole special rushed in from his favorite California Pizza Kitchen, on Connecticut Avenue. With equal relish, he had taken in Barney Frank's deft insertion of the mandate issue, a central point in his defense against impeachment:

Does Congress have the right to override the decision made by the American people in a free, fair election? Was that what the framers of the Constitution intended when they wrote the impeachment clause?

In the days to come, friendly columnists and commentators would speculate on the origin of this defense, tracing it to a five-page memorandum variously credited to Dick Morris, pollster Doug Schoen, and constitutional scholar Laurence Tribe. It would take a series of phone calls from the White House press office, speaking on background, to set the record straight: The constitutional scholar who had written the memorandum was the President himself. Had even his friends forgotten that in real life, before he got into the blood sport, Professor Bill Clinton had dazzled impressionable young students of law at the University of Arkansas?

● ● ●

TESTIMONY OF GEORGE STEPHANOPOULOS, (continued)

JOHN CONYERS: Back to the matter of the Travel Office books, Mr. Stephanopoulos. Isn't it true that what triggered that investigation was an audit by an independent accounting firm?

GEORGE STEPHANOPOULOS: Yes. Peat-Marwick conducted an audit that raised questions, serious questions, about how funds were being handled. There were—there apparently were some irregularities.

JOHN CONYERS: And it was at that point that the FBI was called in.

GEORGE STEPHANOPOULOS: I believe so. Understand, Mr. Conyers, my responsibility was in the communications area. All I know, I knew, at the time, was what was told me. But it was my impression that Peat-Marwick conducted an audit and uncovered irregularities, yes.

JOHN CONYERS: So the reason for the investigation, the motive for it, was based on hard evidence, not political considerations, as your previous questioner implied.

GEORGE STEPHANOPOULOS: As far as I knew, yes, that was the case.

• • •

JAMES SENSENBRENNER, JR. (R-WI): You say Peat-Marwick was brought in to conduct an audit. What was the occasion for that—was it routine? Were audits conducted across-the-board, in every White House office? Say, the White House Mess, the kitchen operation?

GEORGE STEPHANOPOULOS: I don't know.

JAMES SENSENBRENNER: But you're positive that the only White House operation the FBI and Peat-Marwick worked on was the Travel Office.

GEORGE STEPHANOPOULOS: Is that a question or a statement?

JAMES SENSENBRENNER: Take it either way, just answer yes or no.

GEORGE STEPHANOPOULOS: If the Congressman...

JAMES SENSENBRENNER: Yes or no, wasn't the Travel Office the only area of White House operations the FBI and Peat-Marwick were called in on?

GEORGE STEPHANOPOULOS: To the best of my recollection—no, I really can't say.

JAMES SENSENBRENNER: All right, let me put it another way: It was the only White House operation you, the communications director, were called in on, to meet with the FBI. Is that correct?

GEORGE STEPHANOPOULOS: Yes, to the best...

JAMES SENSENBRENNER: No further questions, Mr. Chairman.

• • •

HOWARD BERMAN (D-CA): Mr. Stephanopoulos, just to put things back on track—we're here, presumably, to look into questions raised about possible Presidential misconduct... Let me ask, did President Clinton know about your meeting with Mr. Collingwood, your contact with the FBI?

GEORGE STEPHANOPOULOS: Not to my knowledge.

HOWARD BERMAN: He was almost totally absorbed at the time—correct me if I'm wrong—those were the first months of the new administration, and his time was occupied organizing, getting a handle on the more serious problems, foreign and domestic, facing the country. Is that a fair assessment?

GEORGE STEPHANOPOULOS: Almost totally absorbed. There was, I believe, Haiti for one, and the worsening situation in Bosnia, all taking up his time... But let me make it clear, when the Travel Office problem came down, when it was shown that we, his staff, had made mistakes in handling it, President Clinton nevertheless stood up and took full responsibility.

HOWARD BERMAN: Even though...

GEORGE STEPHANOPOULOS: Even though, as you've said, he was totally absorbed in more serious problems.

• • •

BOB BARR: You make it sound, Mr. Stephanopoulos, as if the FBI was brought in as a result of the Peat-Marwick findings. But isn't it a fact that the bureau was brought in first, then an audit drummed up to justify the investigation?

GEORGE STEPHANOPOULOS: I'm not following, Mr. Barr. Is what you're saying...

BOB BARR: First, the fact is, a political decision was made to fire the Travel Office Seven and turn the operation over to Hillary Clinton's cronies...

CHARLES SCHUMER: That's out of line. Is the chair going to allow...

(At this point in the proceedings, shouts were heard from the audience, and uniformed police escorted a protester out of the chamber.)

HENRY HYDE (GAVELING): Any further disturbance and—I don't want to clear the room, but these hearings will not be conducted as a media circus.

CHARLES SCHUMER: If the Chair means what he says, then remind Mr. Barr that his reference to "cronies"...

HENRY HYDE: Mr. Barr...

BOB BARR: *(inaudible)*—but if our colleague from New York finds "Hillary Clinton's cronies" offensive, strike it and put in its place, "Clinton campaign contributors." Mr. Stephanopoulos, are you still with us?

GEORGE STEPHANOPOULOS: Unfortunately, yes. *(Audience laughter)*

BOB BARR: Just prior to the interruption, I was inquiring how Peat-Marwick was brought in to justify the FBI's involvement. Could you enlighten me on that point?

GEORGE STEPHANOPOULOS: They were brought in, to the best of my knowledge, to determine whether there were irregularities in the Travel Office books.

BOB BARR: I believe the term "independent accounting firm" was used. Was that the way you described Peat-Marwick?

GEORGE STEPHANOPOULOS: I don't recall using that phrase, but yes, it was an independent accounting firm.

BOB BARR: Do you—did you at that time—know a Mr. Larry Herman, a member of that firm?

GEORGE STEPHANOPOULOS: Yes. Only slightly, but I knew him.

BOB BARR: Was Mr. Herman the person contacted by the White House staff in retaining Peat-Marwick?

GEORGE STEPHANOPOULOS: I didn't make the contact.

BOB BARR: But Larry Herman was the Peat-Marwick auditor contacted, is that not right?

GEORGE STEPHANOPOULOS: I believe so.

BOB BARR: Mr. Stephanopoulos, would you please tell us where Mr. Herman was working at the time? I mean, the specific job that he, as a member of Peat-Marwick, was assigned to?

GEORGE STEPHANOPOULOS: *(inaudible)*

BOB BARR: Then let me refresh your recollection. At the time Mr. Herman was contacted to bring Peat-Marwick in to conduct an audit of the Travel Office, he was attached to a government management study known as the National Performance Review. Does that ring any bells?

GEORGE STEPHANOPOULOS: I can't say...

BOB BARR: Mr. Stephanopoulos, you were communications director at the time. Surely you can tell us who headed the White House National Performance Review.

BARNEY FRANK: If the chair...

BOB BARR: That's quite all right, Mr. Frank. If the witness is reluctant to answer, I'll answer for him. At the time Larry Herman's accounting firm, Peat-Marwick, was called in to conduct its so-called non-political audit of the Travel Office, his boss—the man in charge of the National Performance Review—was none other than Vice President Al Gore.

• • •

GRETA VAN SUSTEREN and Roger Cossack were keeping score and handing out grades. The impeachment hearings having been packaged by CNN for what the network hoped would be a long, lucrative run ("The President on Trial"), its two courtroom experts were

From the 1996 Report of the House Committee on Government Reform and Oversight (Henceforth the Clinger Committee Report) on Travelgate

As Admitted Into the Record of the House Judiciary Committee hearings on H. Res. 104:

WHITE HOUSE OFFICIALS COVERED-UP THE REAL REASONS FOR THE FIRING OF THE WHITE HOUSE TRAVEL OFFICE EMPLOYEES. THE FIRINGS WERE NOT BASED ON THE PEAT MARWICK REVIEW, BUT RATHER WERE DECIDED BEFORE PEAT MARWICK EXAMINERS EVER SET FOOT IN THE WHITE HOUSE

> At the very latest, the decision to fire the Travel Office employees was made by May 12, 1993, a full day before the FBI was called to the White House and 2 days before the Peat Marwick review team came to the White House. On May 12, Harry Thomason told David Watkins that he had talked with Mrs. Clinton and she was "ready to fire them all that day." The decision to fire was made first; the White House rationale was sought later.

THE WHITE HOUSE MISREPRESENTED THE PEAT MARWICK REVIEW. IT WAS NEITHER AN AUDIT NOR INDEPENDENT AND WAS DIRECTED BY A WHITE HOUSE WHICH DID NOT WANT AN AUDIT TO BE CONDUCTED

> The Peat Marwick employee who was called in to conduct a supposed "audit" already had volunteered his services to the Vice President's National Performance Review in a May 10, 1993, meeting with Jennifer O'Connor. The Peat Marwick work, as explained in its own engagement letter and subsequent draft and formal reports was a review conducted in keeping with and limited by the White House's needs.
>
> The findings of the Peat Marwick review have been seriously misrepresented by the White House. His notes state: [auditors] "strongly disagree[d] with [the] review conclusion" of the Management Review.

given the job of appraising each day's witnesses and their question-ers in the manner they had perfected in the O.J. Simpson trial…

CNN COMMENTARY following the testimony
of George Stephanopoulos.

GRETA VAN SUSTEREN: On balance, I'd say though the witness did well, it wasn't a particularly good day for the defense.

ROGER COSSACK: You mean the President. I agree, Stephanopolous kept his poise and didn't rattle, but Henry Hyde and his fellow Republicans made some telling points. But Greta, I think it's important that folks understand the procedure involved here. What we're watching is the equivalent of a grand jury taking testimony. If the testimony is thought sufficient, the grand jury will hand up an indictment—which in this case is called impeachment.

GRETA VAN SUSTEREN: And then the trial takes place in the Senate, where it requires a two-thirds vote to convict.

ROGER COSSACK: Just to make that clear.

GRETA VAN SUSTEREN: Right. But back to today's hearings, it looked to me as if the prosecution—the Republicans—have a game plan in mind as they cross-examine the witness, and the name of the game is volleyball: Hyde serves, they volley, and Barr comes in for the spike.

ROGER COSSACK: Interesting you should put it that way, Greta, because I saw it as something of a game, too. Except the game I saw was soccer, with John Conyers as the goalie, Barney Frank as the striker…

CHAPTER SIX
ULTRA VIRES

∎

Gore Denies Role in Travelgate Audit

— HEADLINE, *THE WASHINGTON TIMES*, 6/30/98

• • •

AL GORE WAS feeling sorry for himself. Dick Morris, in one of his sly backdoor moves, had called to reassure him that his poll numbers (62 percent favorable, 18 percent unfavorable) were holding up, but Gore wasn't so sure. He had worked six years to bond with Bill Clinton, to shape the two-peas-in-a-pod image recommended by his own P-R advisors, but now...

Not that it was unusual for a vice president to be squeezed between his own ambition and loyalty to a failing White House. But how many of his predecessors had to share a pod with a President facing impeachment, not to mention a law suit for sexual harassment?

• • •

VICE PRESIDENT GORE'S NEWS CONFERENCE,
Los Angeles airport, 6/29/98

QUESTION: Any response to yesterday's testimony that Larry Herman...

AL GORE: As I've said, I am not going to comment on day-to-day testimony being given the Judiciary Committee. When I have something to say...

Q: But this involves a member of your staff, Larry Herman. George Stephanopoulos says...

AL GORE: First of all, George Stephanopoulos didn't say it, a Republican on the committee did. Second, Larry Herman was simply an accountant, and to my understanding, all he did was help conduct an audit. That's what accountants are for.

Q: According to the committee, he was also a member of the spin squad—Stephanopoulos, Kennedy, Watkins, Dee Dee Myers—who briefed the press about the reason the FBI was brought in.

AL GORE: Let's—let's set the record straight, keep in mind that you're talking about a person only attached to my office to conduct a performance review. Not a member, technically, a member of my staff, only an outside consultant brought in for a limited purpose. Whatever he, Larry Herman, did beyond that was purely, strictly ultra vires. That's all I have to say about the matter.

CHAPTER SEVEN
"MISTAKES WERE MADE"

TESTIMONY OF WILLIAM KENNEDY III, former Associate
White House Counsel, 7/8/98

HENRY HYDE: Mr. Kennedy, do I understand that it's your wish to assert your privilege as a witness under House Rule 3F2?

WILLIAM KENNEDY III: Yes, Mr. Hyde, it is.

HENRY HYDE: The committee will stand in recess for five minutes.

(Recess)

HENRY HYDE: This is unusual, but not unprecedented in other committee hearings. Accordingly, after consultation with the House Parliamentarian as to whether the rule applies to impeachment hearings, we will accede to your wish.

SONNY BONO (R-CA): Let the record show, Mr. Chairman, that I object to invoking this rule in hearings as important as these, and point out that if every witness claims this privilege, the public's right to be fully informed...

HOWARD BERMAN: The rule is pretty clear, Mr. Bono, and the witness has a right to invoke it.

SONNY BONO: Privilege, not a right.

HENRY HYDE: The gentleman from California makes a good point...

SONNY BONO: Which gentleman from California? *(Audience laughter)*

HENRY HYDE: Both gentlemen, actually, but we'll allow the privilege in this case, and if it comes up again, take another look at it. Therefore, pursuant to the rule, I now instruct that all lenses on television and other cameras be covered, and that all microphones be turned off.

(Cameras and broadcast microphones remained off for the duration of Mr. Kennedy's testimony.)

THOMAS MOONEY (COMMITTEE GENERAL COUNSEL): Mr. Kennedy, let me outline a scenario, a sequence of events, based on what we know about the May, 1993, firings at the Travel Office: Early on, in the first few weeks of the administration, one of President Clinton's cousins—an alleged cousin, Catherine Cornelius—you know Ms. Cornelius...

WILLIAM KENNEDY: Yes.

THOMAS MOONEY: ...who handled transportation during the 1992 campaign, wrote a memorandum outlining a plan to replace the Travel Office staff with Clinton appointees. You're familiar with the Cornelius memorandum, aren't you, Mr. Kennedy?

WILLIAM KENNEDY: I know of a memorandum Catherine Cornelius wrote covering Travel Office operations and how to make them more efficient, if that's the one you mean. But it fell into the category of White House personnel, outside my area.

THOMAS MOONEY: Understood. The chain of command on personnel matters was, correct me if I'm wrong, Chief-of-Staff Thomas McLarty, and David Watkins, head of personnel. That's the official chain, but unofficially, isn't it true that Mrs. Clinton played a pivotal role in restructuring White House operations?

WILLIAM KENNEDY: She was an interested party, yes. But pivotal, I can't say.

THOMAS MOONEY: Well, pivotal in your case, certainly. You, Deputy Counsel Vincent Foster, and Counsel Bernard Nussbaum—isn't it fair to say that if it hadn't been for the First Lady you wouldn't have been hired at the White House?

WILLIAM KENNEDY: You might see it that way, Mr. Mooney, but I like to think that I had some other things going for me.

THOMAS MOONEY: But you and Vince Foster, like Webster Hubbell over at the Justice Department, were all Hillary Clinton's operating partners at the Rose law firm in Little Rock before you came to Washington. Isn't that right?

WILLIAM KENNEDY: We were associates, yes.

THOMAS MOONEY: And your boss at the White House, Bernard Nussbaum, he owed his job as White House counsel to Mrs. Clinton, didn't he? Even though he wasn't a member of the Arkansas Mafia.

BARNEY FRANK: I object, Mr. Chairman.

JOHN CONYERS: That was uncalled for, Mr. Mooney. I think the Chair has an obligation to...

HENRY HYDE: You were speaking colloquially, I know, Mr. Mooney, but there might be some to take offense at your choice of words.

THOMAS MOONEY: Withdrawn, Mr. Chairman. All I meant to say was that Mr. Nussbaum's ties to the First Lady came through her having worked for him as a staff member during the Nixon impeachment hearings.

BARNEY FRANK: Withdrawn is fine as far as it goes, but I think an apology is due as well. Ethnic slurs of that kind...

SONNY BONO: Apology to who, Arkansas or the Mafia? (*Audience laughter*)

HENRY HYDE (GAVELING): The committee will be in order. Counsel will proceed with questioning the witness...

THOMAS MOONEY: Back to Catherine Cornelius's plan, Mr. Kennedy, what she essentially proposed was a switch from the air-charter company used by the Travel Office—UltrAir, I believe—to another firm, TRM, a company that included as partners one David Martens—do you know Mr. Martens?

WILLIAM KENNEDY: Not well, but I know him.

THOMAS MOONEY: And Harry Thomason, a close friend of Mrs. Clinton. You know Mr. Thomason, of course.

WILLIAM KENNEDY: Yes.

THOMAS MOONEY: And under Catherine Cornelius's plan, not only would Mrs. Clinton's friends, Thomason and Martens, get the White House air charter contract, but the previously non-political Travel Office staff would be replaced by people from the Clinton campaign, is that correct?

WILLIAM KENNEDY: As I've said, Mr. Mooney, that was David Watkins' department, not mine.

THOMAS MOONEY: Is that so... Then tell us, Mr. Kennedy, since it wasn't your department, how you, Vincent Foster and the White House counsel's office happened to get involved in the Travel Office firings. You're not denying your involvement, are you?

WILLIAM KENNEDY: No, sir, I'm simply pointing out that my involvement, as you call it, didn't come up until questions were raised about mismanagement, the handling of money in the Travel Office.

THOMAS MOONEY: Raised by whom? Ms. Cornelius? Mr. Thomason? Or perhaps you're referring to the Peat-Marwick audit.

WILLIAM KENNEDY: I believe—to the best of my recollection, the Peat-Marwick audit. We're going back, you know, five years.

THOMAS MOONEY: But Peat-Marwick didn't come into the picture until, according to the White House's own report, May 14. Yet according to the same report, you and Mr. Foster attended a meeting with David Watkins, Catherine Cornelius and Harry Thomason two days before, on May 12. Do you recall the nature of that meeting?

WILLIAM KENNEDY: The nature of the meeting?

THOMAS MOONEY: Yes, the nature of the meeting. Wasn't it to discuss the Travel Office takeover and how to expedite the transfer of the air charter contract from UltrAir to TRM?

WILLIAM KENNEDY: My recollection—I'm not sure about the dates—is that yes, I sat in on a meeting with the parties you named and Travel Office matters were discussed.

THOMAS MOONEY: "Sat in on a meeting"—You make it sound as if you were just a passive observer, an incidental figure at the meeting. Isn't it true, Mr. Kennedy, that immediately following that conference between you, Watkins, Foster, and Cornelius—isn't it true that you placed a call to Unit Chief James Bourke of the Criminal Investigative Division of the FBI, demanding that the bureau send agents to the White House to investigate the Travel Office for alleged criminal irregularities?

WILLIAM KENNEDY: *(inaudible)*

THOMAS MOONEY: No, that's not what I asked. I asked whether it was true that in a second conversation with Bourke the following morning, May 13, you told him you wanted an affirmative answer within fifteen minutes, or you'd turn the matter over to the IRS?

WILLIAM KENNEDY: Mr. Mooney, I've been over this matter many times before...

THOMAS MOONEY: You're an experienced lawyer, Mr. Kennedy, and you know that it's irrelevant how many times you've been asked a question in other forums. I'll ask you again...

CHARLES SCHUMER: Stop badgering the witness, Counsel. Mr. Chairman, I object to the tone used with this witness. Mr. Kennedy is not on trial.

BOB BARR: Yet.

CHARLES SCHUMER: Mr. Chairman...

HENRY HYDE (GAVELING): We're going to strike that last remark, Mr. Barr, and ask members of the committee on both sides to restrain their personal comments. I realize we're dealing with matters that touch a nerve, but we can't let, aren't going to let things get out of hand... Counsel?

THOMAS MOONEY: Thank you, Mr. Chairman. If we may proceed, Mr. Kennedy—we were getting into your conversation with James Bourke of the FBI. You don't deny that you called Mr. Bourke, do you?

WILLIAM KENNEDY: No, but I dispute, vigorously dispute, the characterization you gave it. I did not threaten the FBI in any way. The gist of our conversation was, I told him we had some concern with the handling of funds in the Travel Office, and asked if the Bureau could give us a hand checking it out.

THOMAS MOONEY: You understand, Mr. Kennedy, that there are witnesses and testimony that say otherwise.

WILLIAM KENNEDY: What I understand, sir, is that I'm being asked questions about a conversation that took place over five years ago. I repeat, whatever I told Mr. Bourke, it was not intended as a threat, however he may have heard it.

THOMAS MOONEY: Let me quote, Mr. Kennedy, from the White House Review, the review headed by then-Chief of Staff McLarty and then-OMB Director Leon Panetta. And this, keep in mind, is from your own White House colleagues, who said, quote: "such comments" as you made to the FBI on May 13 and thereafter, "should not have been made" because, continuing to quote: "Comments like these risk the perception that the FBI is being improperly pressured." Unquote. Do you have any...

WILLIAM KENNEDY: No, sir. I stand by what I said...

THOMAS MOONEY: Mr. Chairman?

HENRY HYDE: Thank you, Counsel. Mr. Kennedy, let's pin this down: Whatever your tone or intention, did you or did you not tell James

Bourke that if the FBI didn't agree to investigate the Travel Office, you'd turn the matter over to the IRS? Yes? No?

WILLIAM KENNEDY: Not in that way. What I recall saying was, we had a potentially criminal problem, and if the FBI didn't feel it could handle it, the IRS might be the proper agency.

HENRY HYDE: But as it turned out, there was no criminal problem, was there?

WILLIAM KENNEDY: I—no, as it turned out, no…

HENRY HYDE: One more point, just to clarify matters—whose money are we talking about, Mr. Kennedy? There was some confusion about that at the time. I recall President Clinton saying the sole purpose of the Travel Office shake-up was to save taxpayers' money. But we aren't in fact talking about taxpayers' money, are we?

WILLIAM KENNEDY: You mean—I don't understand the question, Mr. Hyde.

HENRY HYDE: The money in the Travel Office, the funds you thought had been so mismanaged that the FBI or IRS ought to be brought in. Those funds weren't government funds, taxpayer money, were they, Mr. Kennedy? In fact, they were funds furnished by the various news organizations that use the air charters that accompany the President when he travels. Isn't that true?

WILLIAM KENNEDY: My understanding, sir, yes, that's the case.

HENRY HYDE: Well, that being the case, wouldn't it have been reasonable for you, a seasoned attorney, to have inquired if any of the news organizations paying the freight, so to speak, had lodged any complaint about the handling of the funds?

WILLIAM KENNEDY: Reasonable?

HENRY HYDE: Yes, reasonable to find out if…

JOHN CONYERS: Mr. Chairman, exactly where is this headed? The witness has told us what he knows, now you're asking him to tell us about things he doesn't know. Are we—it appears to me we're off on a fishing expedition.

HENRY HYDE: What I'm fishing for, Mr. Conyers, if you'll allow me to proceed, is the who and why behind the witness's effort to bully—and that's what it appears to be—bully the FBI into an investigation the bureau was reluctant to make. Well, if the shake-up in the Travel Office wasn't done for the benefit of the taxpayer, and it wasn't done for the benefit of the press, because they weren't complaining, who benefited? Ms. Cornelius wanted to run the Travel Office, so she would have benefited. But I find it hard to believe that a low-to-mid-level campaign worker like Catherine Cornelius could have gone as far with her plan as she did without high-level help. Harry Thomason would have benefited. A major supporter of the Clintons. So who benefits from helping Harry Thomason?

(At this point, General Counsel Mooney engaged the Chairman in side conference, after which Mr. Hyde resumed questioning.)

HENRY HYDE: Mr. Kennedy, the General Accounting Office report on the Travel Office, you're familiar with that, are you not?

WILLIAM KENNEDY: Yes, sir, though not...

HENRY HYDE: Yes?

WILLIAM KENNEDY: ...not in detail, and it's been some time since I looked at it.

HENRY HYDE: Well, to refresh your recollection, the report refers to, specifically, your conference with FBI Agent Howard Apple, head of the bureau's Crimes Unit. A conference held at the White House May 13, 1993, in which you told Agent Apple that the Travel Office matter was, I quote the report, "directed at the highest levels of the White House." Unquote. Do you recall that conversation?

WILLIAM KENNEDY: As I've said before, Mr. Hyde, I don't recall making any such statement.

HENRY HYDE: Then, Mr. Kennedy, it's a case of your word against Agent Apple's. Can you think of any reason or motive that would lead him to lie about something like this? He is, after all...

WILLIAM KENNEDY: I'm not accusing anyone of lying, Mr. Hyde. All I'm saying is, I don't recall making that statement.

HENRY HYDE: In other words, Agent Apple either misheard or misinterpreted what you said...

WILLIAM KENNEDY: Yes, sir.

HENRY HYDE: —in the same way Agent Bourke did earlier. You seem to have, Mr. Kennedy, a singular problem making yourself clear to FBI agents, wouldn't you agree?

WILLIAM KENNEDY: *(inaudible)*

• • •

JOHN CONYERS: Mr. Kennedy, we've heard a lot of talk, reference to putting things into perspective, so I want to lead off by asking you to tell us, if you will, the job status of White House Travel Office employees.

WILLIAM KENNEDY: Job status? By that, do you mean...?

JOHN CONYERS: Are they civil service employees? How are they hired?

WILLIAM KENNEDY: Oh, yes. Right. They serve—they're hired and serve at the pleasure of the President.

JOHN CONYERS: At the pleasure of the President. No job tenure, in other words, so that contrary to what's been said here previously, Mr. Dale and the so-called Travel Office Seven, were not, by any stretch, non-political employees. They could be hired and fired at any time, at the pleasure...

WILLIAM KENNEDY: Yes, sir, at any time.

JOHN CONYERS: So this business of some sort of outrage having been committed by their dismissal was, is, completely off base. A distortion, a mountain made of a molehill.

WILLIAM KENNEDY: That's correct, sir, at least in my opinion.

JOHN CONYERS: And in mine, Mr. Kennedy. I have no further questions for this witness, but I think it's appropriate to point out that nothing we've heard from Mr. Kennedy, or any other witness to date, has told us anything we didn't already know—that mistakes were made by some of the president's subordinates, that others may have overstepped their authority, or even broken the law. But nothing, I repeat, nothing we've heard connects President Clinton in any way with any wrongful action, much less "high crime" that would justify these hearings.

HENRY HYDE: May I ask—are you saying, Mr. Conyers, arguing that in order to justify an impeachment, it's necessary to prove that a president personally committed or took part in the commission of a crime? Because that's not the test, as you well know.

JOHN CONYERS: My statement speaks for itself.

HENRY HYDE: *(to Mr. Mooney)* Do you have the report, the Rodino report, available?... Thank you—Mr. Conyers, you were a member of the Rodino Committee, the last committee of this kind to consider the impeachment of a president, so I'm sure you're familiar with that part of the report that goes into this very question. In fact, Chairman Rodino specifically outlined the criteria for impeachment in his opening statement to his committee. Do you recall it?

JOHN CONYERS: I'm well aware of the report.

HENRY HYDE: Well, for the benefit of those members of the committee who aren't—and in view of your statement a few moments ago—let me point out that the Rodino Committee held, correctly, I believe, that impeachment goes to the broader question of political morality—whether there's been a breach of the ethical standards set for a president or those working for him, his subordinates. And in that regard, I think the evidence we've heard to date is significant. Highly significant.

JOHN CONYERS: We obviously disagree.

HENRY HYDE: Yes, well, it won't be the first time.

JAMES SENSENBRENNER, JR.: Let me get this straight, Mr. Kennedy. You say, and I agree it's the case, that the President could have fired employees of the Travel Office at any time, without cause. They served at his pleasure.

WILLIAM KENNEDY: Yes, sir.

JAMES SENSENBRENNER: Well, why didn't he, then?

WILLIAM KENNEDY: Why didn't he what?

JAMES SENSENBRENNER: Just fire them. Let them go. Why was it necessary to bring in the FBI, Peat-Marwick, the IRS, to make false accusations that impugned the reputations of innocent people, if all the President had to do was fire them?

WILLIAM KENNEDY: I can't answer that, Congressman. All I was doing was—

JAMES SENSENBRENNER: Following orders, is that what you want to say? The Little Rock defense. *(Audience laughter)*

BARNEY FRANK: Pardon, I didn't get all of that last comment. What defense?

JAMES SENSENBRENNER: Little Rock defense, Mr. Frank, Little Rock defense.

BARNEY FRANK: Is that supposed to be witty? Comparing...

JAMES SENSENBRENNER: Not witty, Mr. Frank, just accurate.

Mr. Kennedy, I was not quite clear on one of your answers to Mr. Hyde before. Mr. Hyde asked if you told Agent Apple that the Travel Office matter was directed at the "highest levels of the

"CONSTITUTIONAL GROUNDS FOR PRESIDENTIAL IMPEACHMENT,"

February 1974 Report of the House Judiciary Committee
THE RODINO COMMITTEE

As Admitted Into the Record of the
House Judiciary Committee Hearings on H. Res. 104:

... Impeachment, as Justice Joseph Story wrote in his *Commentaries on the Constitution* in 1883, applies to offenses of "a political character":

> ... growing out of personal misconduct or gross neglect, or usurpation, or habitual disregard of the public interests, in the discharge of the duties of political office. These are so various in their character, and so indefinable in their actual involutions, that it is almost impossible to provide systematically for them by positive law. They must be examined upon very broad and comprehensive principles of public policy and duty....

The post-convention statements and writings of Alexander Hamilton, James Wilson, and James Madison—each a participant in the Constitutional Convention—show that they regarded impeachment as an appropriate device to deal with offenses against constitutional government by those who hold civil office, and not a device limited to criminal offenses....

Impeachment and the criminal law serve fundamentally different purposes. Impeachment is the first step in a remedial process—removal from office and possible disqualification from holding future office. The purpose of impeachment is not personal punishment; its function is primarily to maintain constitutional government....

The criminal law sets a general standard of conduct that all must follow. It does not address itself to the abuses of presidential power. In an impeachment proceeding a President is called to account for abusing powers that only a President possesses....

White House." Now, did you say that you did not recall saying that or that you did not say it?

WILLIAM KENNEDY: I do not recall saying it.

JAMES SENSENBRENNER: OK. OK. So what do you say now?

WILLIAM KENNEDY: Congressman?

JAMES SENSENBRENNER: Was it directed at the highest levels of the White House? You say you don't recall saying it was. But was it directed at the highest levels of the White House?

WILLIAM KENNEDY: Congressman, I'll remind you that at the time I was at a pretty high level in the White House myself. So was Vince Foster. So it all depends on what you mean by "highest levels" and what was directed. Those questions are so subjective and complicated at this point that, frankly, Mr. Congressman, your assessment of that is as good as mine.

HENRY HYDE: Let's move it along. Does the gentleman from Wisconsin have any further questions?

JAMES SENSENBRENNER: No questions, Mr. Chairman, but I would like to follow up on what was said earlier about the political status of the White House Travel Office. For the record, Mr. Dale, director of that office, had been on the job there for over thirty years before being dismissed—told to pack up his things and be gone by the end of the day. And the same is true of Gary Wright, the deputy director. Thirty-two years' loyal service at the pleasure of both Democrat and Republican presidents—I'd say that's as non-political as you'll find in this country, anywhere outside the witness' home state of Arkansas…

• • •

BILL MCCOLLUM: Mr. Kennedy, among your contacts with the FBI, do you recall meeting with Special Agent Thomas Carl, on or about May 14, 1993?

WILLIAM KENNEDY: I recall a conversation with an Agent Carl, though I'm not certain about the date.

BILL MCCOLLUM: Let's not play word games, Mr. Kennedy. A conversation is something you have when you run into someone in the hallway. I'm talking about a formal meeting—in fact, two meetings—with Thomas Carl. One on the fourteenth, the second on or about the fifteenth, in your office.

WILLIAM KENNEDY: We talked. I'd call that a conversation.

BILL MCCOLLUM: You talked about bringing in the Internal Revenue Service to audit UltrAir, isn't that right? Putting pressure on the IRS to dig up something on the Travel Office.

WILLIAM KENNEDY: No, sir. Under no circumstances did I talk to Agent Carl or anyone else about putting pressure on the Travel Office.

BILL MCCOLLUM: But you did talk about pressure, didn't you? About the pressure you were getting from high-level White House sources to, quote, "do something" about the Travel Office.

WILLIAM KENNEDY: No, sir. I don't recall that as part of our conversation. What I do recall is telling Agent Carl about reports that the Travel Office had some serious bookkeeping problems, and the people I worked under, Mack McLarty and Vince Foster, were very concerned about them.

BILL MCCOLLUM: Anybody else? Isn't it true that the First Lady was pressuring McLarty and Foster to fire the Travel Office staff and replace them with her friends?

WILLIAM KENNEDY: If you're asking whether the First Lady was concerned about the situation in the Travel Office, my answer is yes. But only because she heard reports about fiscal mismanagement.

BILL MCCOLLUM: Are you familiar—I'm sure you're familiar with David Watkins' memorandum on that subject. The so-called "soul cleansing" memorandum he sent to Mack McLarty?

WILLIAM KENNEDY: I'm familiar with it, but frankly David Watkins

Document IV

DRAFT

DRAFT   DRAFT

PRIVILEGED AND CONFIDENTIAL

MEMORANDUM FOR

FROM: DAVID WATKINS

SUBJECT: Response to Internal White House Travel Office Management Review

In an effort to respond to the Internal Travel Office Review, I have prepared this memorandum, which details my response to the various conclusions of that Report. This is a soul cleansing, carefully detailing the surrounding circumstances and the pressures that demanded that action be taken immediately. It is my first attempt to be sure the record is straight, something I have not done in previous conversations with investigators — where I have been as protective and vague as possible. I know you will carefully consider the issues and concerns expressed herein.

DRAFT

business to a single charter company, and told her that the functions of that office could be easily replaced and reallocated.

Once this made it onto the First Lady's agenda, Vince Foster became involved, and he and Harry Thomason regularly informed me of her attention to the Travel Office situation — as well as her insistence that the situation be resolved immediately by replacing the Travel Office staff.

Foster regularly informed me that the First Lady was concerned and desired action — the action desired was the firing of the Travel Office staff. On Friday, while I was in Memphis, Foster told me that it was important that I speak directly with the First Lady that day. I called her that evening and she conveyed to me in clear terms that her desire for swift and clear action to resolve the situation. She mentioned that Thomason had explained how the Travel Office could be run after removing the current staff — that plan included bringing in World Wide Travel and Penny Sample to handle the basic travel functions, the actual actions taken post dismissal (?) and in light of that she thought immediate action was in order.

On Monday morning, you came to my office and met with ~~myself~~ *me* and Patsy Thomasson. At that meeting you explained that this was on the First Lady's "radar screen." The message you conveyed to me was clear: immediate action must be taken. I explained to you that I had decided to terminate the Travel Office employees, and you expressed relief that we were finally going to take action (to resolve the situation in conformity with the First Lady's wishes). We both knew that there would be hell to pay if, after our failure in the Secret Service situation earlier, we failed to take swift and decisive action in conformity with the First Lady's wishes. You then approved the decision to terminate the Travel Office staff, and I indicated I would send you a memorandum outlining the decision and plan, which I did.

This memo, known as the David Watkins "soul cleansing" memo, was later referred to by Rep. William Clinger as the "smoking gun" connecting Hillary Clinton with the Travelgate episode. In it, Watkins says he fired White House Travel Office employees under pressure from Hillary, and misled investigators about her role in the events.

From the 1996 Clinger Committee Report on Travelgate

As Admitted Into the Record of the House Judiciary Committee hearings on H. Res. 104:

HARRY THOMASON WHO HAD A FINANCIAL STAKE IN THE TRAVEL BUSINESS, INSTIGATED THE FIRING OF THE TRAVEL OFFICE EMPLOY-EES. MR. THOMASON HAD PERSONAL AND FINANCIAL STAKES IN ENSURING THAT THE FORMER TRAVEL OFFICE EMPLOYEES WERE FIRED WHICH MADE IT CLEARLY INAPPROPRIATE FOR HIM TO HAVE ANY INVOLVEMENT IN THIS MATTER

> Harry Thomason was the first person to pass along rumors about the Travel Office employees to Mrs. Clinton and President Clinton. (While Mrs. Clinton has suggested that Vincent Foster may have told her first about the rumors, Foster's own notes indicate that he did not know about the rumors until May 12, 1993, when Watkins and Harry Thomason first approached him. Mrs. Clinton only raised this issue with Foster the following day.) Neither Mrs. Clinton nor anyone in Mrs. Clinton's office could identify any alternative source of the rumors....
>
> The suggestion by President and Mrs. Clinton that there were "rumors everywhere" and Harry Thomason's sworn testimony about "a buzz in the air" of wrongdoing in the Travel Office are not consistent with the more than 70 depositions conducted by the committee and dozens of informal interviews. Virtually no one—except those in direct contact with Harry Thomason—heard rumors. Both the General Accounting Office review and the DOJ Office of Professional Responsibility ("OPR") review concluded that Harry Thomason passed on the rumors to Mrs. Clinton....

HARRY THOMASON ABUSED HIS OFFICIAL STATUS AND WHITE HOUSE ACCESS AT A TIME WHEN HE HAD A FINANCIAL STAKE IN THE TRAVEL BUSINESS. HARRY THOMASON'S ACTIVITIES... MAKE HIM A SPECIAL GOVERNMENT EMPLOYEE TO WHICH THE CONFLICT OF INTEREST LAWS APPLY

> Darnell Martens, Harry Thomason's partner in his air charter consulting company, TRM, wrote a January 29, 1993

memo to Thomason outlining how they should pursue "Washington opportunities" in the early days of the Clinton administration. These opportunities included seeking White House travel business as well as a quarter-of-a-million dollar GSA contract to survey all non-military Government aircraft.

Documents provided to this committee and only subsequently provided to the Justice Department, clearly establish that TRM was seeking both Travel Office business and the GSA contract.

Darnell Martens, with the assistance of his partner Harry Thomason, contacted Billy Dale in February 1993 seeking the Travel Office business. Martens' post-May 19, 1993, explanations that he was seeking the business on behalf of others, contradicts his own documents of March 5, 1993, in which he advocates that "the Administration... disband the... system in favor of the functions being outsourced to TRM/Air Advantage."

has told so many different stories since he left the White House that it's hard to give credibility to anything he says.

BILL MCCOLLUM: I'm not talking about something he said after he left the White House. The memorandum to McLarty was written while he was still on the payroll.

WILLIAM KENNEDY: That may be, Mr. McCollum, but what I said about Watkins' credibility stands. Everyone knows by now that...

BILL MCCOLLUM: But if everyone knows it, why did the White House do everything it could to keep his memorandum from the public? Were they afraid...

WILLIAM KENNEDY: Mr. McCollum...

BILL MCCOLLUM: —the American people would find out what role, key role, Hillary Clinton played in the Travelgate firings?

JOHN CONYERS: Since the Congressman knows all the answers, why does he even bother questioning the witness? Mr. Chairman, once again I object...

BILL MCCOLLUM: To get at the truth, Mr. Conyers. Mr. Chairman, I find it interesting, ironic, that the gentleman from Michigan, the only member of the present Judiciary Committee who also served as a member of the committee that voted to impeach Richard Nixon—I find it interesting that he's suddenly so solicitous of White House witnesses.

JOHN CONYERS: I asked a simple question, Mr. McCollum. Since you seem to know all the...

BILL MCCOLLUM: As a matter of fact, on reviewing the transcript of the Nixon hearings, I found that far from being concerned about witness rights, Mr. Conyers...

(Opposite page) In her written responses to questions presented by Rep. William Clinger investigating the firing of the White House Travel Office, Hillary Clinton denied being behind the firings and said she "had no role in the decision to terminate the employees." Her statement contradicted earlier testimony, most notably that of David Watkins.

LAW OFFICES

WILLIAMS & CONNOLLY

725 TWELFTH STREET, N.W.

WASHINGTON, D. C. 20005

(202) 434-5000

FAX (202) 434-5029

EDWARD BENNETT WILLIAMS (1920-1988)
PAUL R. CONNOLLY (1922-1978)

DAVID E. KENDALL

(202) 434-5145

March 21, 1996

BY HAND DELIVERY

The Honorable William F. Clinger, Jr.
Chairman, Committee on Government Reform
    and Oversight
House of Representatives
2157 Rayburn House Office Building
Washington, D.C. 20515-6143

Dear Mr. Chairman:

    I enclose the responses of Mrs. Clinton to the
questions transmitted to her by you last month.

              Sincerely,

              David E. Kendall

"1. Mrs. Clinton does not know the origin of the decision
     to remove the White House Travel Office employees
     She believes that the decision to terminate the
     employees would have been made by Mr. Watkins with the
     approval of Mr. McLarty.

2.   Mrs. Clinton was aware that Mr. Watkins was
     undertaking a review of the situation in the Travel
     Office, but she had no role in the decision to
     terminate the employees.

3.   Mrs. Clinton did not direct that any action be taken
     by anyone with regard to the Travel Office, other than
     expressing an interest in receiving information about
     the review.

4.   Mrs. Clinton does not recall this conversation with
     the same level of detail as Mr. Watkins. She recalls
     that on Friday, May 14, she had a very short telephone
     call with Mr. Watkins. Mr. Watkins stated that Mr.
     Foster had mentioned that Mrs. Clinton was interested
     in knowing what was going on with the Travel Office.
     Mrs. Clinton knew that Mr. Watkins was out of town.
     Mr. Watkins conveyed to her that even though he was
     not in Washington, his office was taking appropriate
     action.

5.   Mrs. Clinton has a general recollection of having
     conversations with Mr. Foster and Mr. McLarty about
     the Travel Office situation prior to the termination
     of the Travel Office employees. She has no specific
     recollection of any particular conversation with Mr.
     Thomason on this issue at that time.

     Mrs. Clinton believes that she spoke with Mr. Foster
     about the Travel Office before her telephone call with
     Mr. Watkins. She also believes that she had a very
     brief conversation with Mr. McLarty sometime before
     she spoke with Mr. Watkins. In that conversation, she
     told Mr. McLarty that she had heard about problems in
     the Travel Office and wanted Mr. McLarty to be aware
     of it.

     Mrs. Clinton does not recall seeing the May 17
     memorandum from Mr. Watkins to Mr. McLarty until after
     the Travel Office employees were terminated."

HENRY HYDE (GAVELING): Let's back off a few minutes, gentlemen, cool down… Mr. Kennedy, I know it's been a long day, but with everyone's indulgence, I'm going to call a fifteen-minute recess, after which the gentleman from Florida can resume questioning…

CHAPTER EIGHT
THE BEST OF MY RECOLLECTION

■

NINA TOTENBERG COMMENTARY, National Public Radio, 7/9/98

NINA TOTENBERG: ... As for the chairman's repeated promise to keep the hearings from veering into the swamp of partisan politics, no one is really surprised he hasn't matched deeds to words, allowing his Republican colleagues to repeatedly cross the line between questioning and baiting the witness... What's more, according to committee sources, the situation is likely to get worse. The big debate among Republican members, we're told, is whether to subpoena the First Lady. The more virulent Clinton-haters in Hyde's party are eager to, in the words of one, "haul her in." But cooler heads, including it's said the chairman himself, are afraid that, considering Hillary Clinton's already embattled status in the courts, a mauling by the committee might create a sympathetic backlash in her favor.

TESTIMONY OF WILLIAM KENNEDY III (continued)

BILL MCCOLLUM: Only a few more questions, Mr. Chairman... Mr. Kennedy, so that I understand you correctly, is it your testimony that in all your urgent phone calls and meetings with the FBI in May, 1993, you neither felt nor heard of what David Watkins referred to as, quote, "irresistible pressure" from Hillary Clinton to...

WILLIAM KENNEDY: No, sir, I didn't.

From the 1996 Clinger Committee Report on Travelgate

As Admitted Into the Record of the House Judiciary Committee hearings on H. Res. 104:

BILL KENNEDY ABUSED THE FBI BY REPEATEDLY INVOKING THE "HIGHEST LEVELS" OF THE WHITE HOUSE IN MEETINGS WITH THE FBI

Bill Kennedy sought to and in fact did abuse and compromise the FBI by invoking the "highest levels" of the White House in order to involve FBI headquarters officials rather than a field agent as would have been the normal procedure. Mr. Kennedy provided inaccurate and incomplete testimony to this committee and numerous other investigative bodies regarding his statements to the FBI.

White House officials hoped to fire the employees on May 13 and drafted talking points on May 13, 1993, discussing the Travel Office firings and claiming an FBI investigation was underway. The FBI, however, could not move that quickly and did not believe it had sufficient predication to launch a criminal fraud audit....

FBI headquarters never should have been contacted directly on this matter. Such allegations normally would have been handled by a field agent or even the local police.

BILL MCCOLLUM: ...I'm not finished... to, quote, "get our people in, and get those people out of the Travel Office"?

WILLIAM KENNEDY: No, I didn't.

BILL MCCOLLUM: Mr. Kennedy, let me remind you that you're under oath. According to the GAO report on the Travel Office firings, you specifically told the FBI...

HENRY HYDE (GAVELING): The gentleman's time has expired.

WILLIAM KENNEDY: I'm well aware that I'm under oath, Congressman, and I repeat that to the best of my knowledge and recollection...

• • •

MAXINE WATERS: If you don't mind, Mr. Chairman, my questions to the witness will be directed at what I assumed these hearings were all about—whether the President is guilty of crimes and misdemeanors. Not the First Lady, not the Chief of Staff, not this witness, but President Bill Clinton. Am I correct in that assumption?

HENRY HYDE: Correct, Ms. Waters. You may proceed.

MAXINE WATERS: Thank you, Mr. Chairman... Mr. Kennedy, whether or not you talked to the FBI, the IRS, the CIA, whatever, and whether or not you or any other member of the White House staff did anything, or tried to do anything illegal—I'm not saying that you did, just setting up a hypothetical—whatever took place at the Travel Office, my question is, did President Clinton know any of this was going on?

WILLIAM KENNEDY: Congressman—Congresswoman—Waters, I have no knowledge, absolutely none, that the President was involved in any of this.

MAXINE WATERS: By any of this, you mean... ?

WILLIAM KENNEDY: The Travel Office turnover, investigation, anything of that nature. In all of it, I don't recall hearing his name mentioned. It was, at least it was looked at, as a low-level staff decision the President shouldn't have to concern himself with.

MAXINE WATERS: Did you ever have a meeting or a conversation with the President about any of these matters?

WILLIAM KENNEDY: Frankly, I didn't, wasn't at the level the President would...

MAXINE WATERS: Whatever level, did you ever meet with or talk to the President about anything having to do with the Travel Office?

WILLIAM KENNEDY: To the best of my recollection, no.

MAXINE WATERS: Did you ever hear, however remotely, of anyone else meeting or talking to the President about the Travel Office?

WILLIAM KENNEDY: To the best of my recollection, no.

MAXINE WATERS: Did you ever receive instructions or feel, in Mr. McCollum's word, "pressure" from President Clinton on this matter? I mean, about talking to the FBI, IRS, or anyone else?

WILLIAM KENNEDY: To the best of my recollection, no.

MAXINE WATERS: In short, to your knowledge and recollection, the President was neither directly nor in any other way involved in the Travel Office matter?

WILLIAM KENNEDY: To my knowledge, not involved, though I did hear that, like Mrs. Clinton, once he heard of possible mismanagement in the Travel Office, he became concerned.

MAXINE WATERS: But not involved.

WILLIAM KENNEDY: Not involved, no.

MAXINE WATERS: You're an attorney, aren't you, Mr. Kennedy?

WILLIAM KENNEDY: The last I heard. *(Audience laughter)*

MAXINE WATERS: An attorney, familiar with the Constitution. Now I'm going to ask you the question, the sixty-four-dollar question, that this committee is, or should be, concerned with: In your time at the White House, in anything you did as the President's associate counsel, in anything you ever heard about the President's conduct of office, was President Clinton in any way, shape or form, involved in anything remotely resembling a high crime or misdemeanor violating the oath he took to defend and protect the Constitution?

HOWARD COBLE (R-NC): Mr. Chairman, with due regard to the witness's status as a lawyer, I've got to object to this question on grounds that it's not relevant...

MAXINE WATERS: Not relevant? It's the only thing relevant...

HOWARD COBLE: Please, Ms. Waters, let me finish my objection—not relevant to his purpose here as a witness. He hasn't been called as a constitutional expert, and for that matter there isn't an expert who can answer that question. It's solely for the members of this committee to determine. Anything the witness has to say on the subject...

MAXINE WATERS: He's as qualified as any member to answer...

HENRY HYDE (GAVELING): I'm going to let the witness respond, Mr. Coble, though I agree that the question, bottom line, is for the committee to decide.

MAXINE WATERS: Thank you, Mr. Chairman. Mr. Kennedy?

WILLIAM KENNEDY: The question... ?

MAXINE WATERS: Do you think President Clinton should be impeached?

WILLIAM KENNEDY: No, absolutely not.

SONNY BONO: Are you sure of that, or is it only to the best of your recollection? *(Audience laughter)*

• • •

HOWARD COBLE: Going back, Mr. Kennedy, to the question raised earlier about UltrAir and the Internal Revenue Service, is it your testimony that you never talked to anyone at the IRS?

WILLIAM KENNEDY: Yes, sir, though as I said I might have asked someone whether it was appropriate to contact the IRS.

HOWARD COBLE: Contact them about what? Harassing?... as you know, we have testimony, depositions, to the effect that the idea behind the Travel Office firings, in addition to the jobs, was to replace UltrAir with an air carrier run by Mrs. Clinton's friends. So my question is whether you talked to anyone about getting the IRS to harass UltrAir?

WILLIAM KENNEDY: No, sir, I at no time asked anyone to harass anybody.

HOWARD COBLE: Because that would be illegal, wouldn't it? An abuse of power, to pressure or influence any law enforcement agency, the FBI or IRS, to investigate somebody without cause, purely for political ends. Is that right, Mr. Kennedy?

WILLIAM KENNEDY: Yes.

HOWARD COBLE: I'm glad we agree, because we have evidence, hard evidence, that not long after you met with members of the FBI hierarchy in Washington, an FBI agent called the regional office of the IRS, suggesting it would be, as you like to say, appropriate to investigate UltrAir. And on May 21, 1993—does that date mean anything to you, Mr. Kennedy?

WILLIAM KENNEDY: No, sir, not particularly.

HOWARD COBLE: Well, it does to the folks at UltrAir, because on that day, that morning, a horde of IRS inspectors suddenly showed up at their offices in Smyrna, Tennessee, to inspect their books. Highly unusual, wouldn't you say?

WILLIAM KENNEDY: *(inaudible)*

HOWARD COBLE: Speak up, Mr. Kennedy, we can't hear you.

WILLIAM KENNEDY: I said, I wouldn't know if it was unusual or not.

HOWARD COBLE: A coincidence, then? An associate counsel at the White House talks to the FBI, then the FBI talks to the IRS...

WILLIAM KENNEDY: No, sir! That scenario...

HOWARD COBLE: It's not a scenario, Mr. Kennedy. It's in the GAO report. The IRS came down on a law-abiding business without any reason other than its being in the way...

BARNEY FRANK: That's not what the GAO said.

HOWARD COBLE: If you mean it didn't specifically say, "The IRS was pressured by the White House to harass this small, independent company," you're right, Mr. Frank. But for anyone reading this report without blinders, it's spelled out in fairly clear terms. Mr. Kennedy...

WILLIAM KENNEDY: Mr. Coble, let me say... let me say that who and why the IRS chooses to inspect is beyond me. All I can say is, I didn't pressure or attempt to pressure the FBI, IRS or anyone else to investigate UltrAir, and as both a former member of the White House staff and a citizen, I deeply resent any insinuation that I did.

HOWARD COBLE: That's a fine speech, Mr. Kennedy, but the evidence says otherwise. No further questions, Mr. Chairman.

• • •

NBC NIGHTLY NEWS, 7/13/98

TOM BROKAW: Former White House aide William Kennedy finished another grueling session before the Hyde Impeachment Committee this afternoon with a vigorous defense of both the President and Mrs. Clinton that unfortunately—because of a ruling by the Chair—wasn't seen by anyone outside the hearing room. Reports from Andrea Mitchell on Capitol Hill and Lisa Myers, with the First Lady in California.

BARNEY FRANK (ON TAPE, OUTSIDE THE COMMITTEE ROOM): Don't believe the hype, these aren't congressional hearings—they're Star Chamber hearings. And that's spelled with one "r."

ANDREA MITCHELL (OUTSIDE THE CAPITOL): Angered at what they term the high-handed tactics of Chairman Henry Hyde, Barney Frank and other Democrats on the House Impeachment Committee met behind closed doors late today to consider what action to take if Hyde orders a ban on future television coverage.

Though Republican staff members argued the ban was imposed at William Kennedy's request, not the chairman's, Frank sees the news blackout as part of a larger Republican scheme, adding that any attempt by Hyde to invoke the rule with future witnesses may result in court action on behalf of the people's right-to-know... Andrea Mitchell, NBC News, the Capitol.

LISA MYERS: (OUTSIDE THE CENTURY PLAZA, LOS ANGELES): This is Lisa Myers. Hillary Clinton came to Los Angeles today to honor a long-standing commitment to speak at a fund-raiser held for Barbara Boxer's Senate campaign. But from the moment Mrs. Clinton's plane touched down, it was clear her appearance here would be overshadowed by the larger drama unfolding three thousand miles away.

HILLARY CLINTON (ON TAPE, LOS ANGELES AIRPORT): I've come to California to speak on behalf of my good friend Barbara Boxer...

REPORTER: Mrs. Clinton, have you been following Bill Kennedy's testimony to the Hyde Committee?

HILLARY CLINTON: ...a wonderful senator we need to keep on the job in Washington, not only for California's sake, but the good of the country. Thank you very much, that's all I have to say.

LISA MYERS: Mrs. Clinton was also greeted in downtown Los Angeles by protesters carrying placards that read, "TIPPER FOR FIRST LADY, 1998." In her remarks to a closed audience of some 2000 party loyalists, Mrs. Clinton staunchly defended the administration's record, according to Senator Boxer, but made no mention of either her husband's impeachment hearings or her own legal problems.

TOM BROKAW: Lisa, did you get any vibrations of what sort of toll all this is taking on the First Lady?

LISA MYERS: Good question, Tom. The word we get is that Hillary Clinton's main concern right now is the effect these hearings are having on her daughter Chelsea, who came down from Stanford to spend the day with her mother. But to the outside world, as one of the First Lady's close friends put it, "Hillary is all chin high, stiff upper lip."

TOM BROKAW: Lisa Myers, from Los Angeles, reporting on Hillary Clinton's day... Meanwhile, overseas, news of the impeachment hearings continues as the top story. In London, Prime Minister Tony Blair, in a ringing endorsement of the man he likes to call "Cousin Bill," told the House of Commons that the President's impeachment would represent, in Blair's words, "a terrible setback, if not a catastrophe, for NATO and the democratic idea in Europe and throughout the world... "

• • •

WILLIAM KENNEDY MIGHT be called back to testify on other issues, Henry Hyde informed his Republican colleagues, but David Watkins would not be summoned as a Travelgate witness. Neither would Mack McLarty, Catherine Cornelius, Jeff Eller, Patsy Thomasson, or a dozen other Clinton staffers implicated, one way or another, in the Travel Office firings. Instead, their testimony before the Clinger Committee in 1996 would be included in the record.

Hillary Clinton? No plans to call the First Lady, said the chairman. "Not at this time." Slowly, patiently, Hyde spelled out the less-is-more strategy that he and Bob Barr had worked out for the hearings—though his listeners weren't always receptive. He had no trouble convincing Republicans on his committee, but there were others who subscribed to what the chairman viewed as the kitchen-sink strategy that had only worked to Bill Clinton's advantage in past Congressional hearings.

It was like the O.J. Simpson case, Hyde would explain in terms even non-lawyers could appreciate: When the prosecution has more evidence than a jury can digest, the shrewd prosecutor win-nows out the redundant witness, the extraneous exhibit. Keep it simple, keep it clear. Especially when dealing with a defendant like Bill Clinton, a master of extrication, the Houdini of political escapes...

RERUN — Excerpt, President Clinton's town-hall appearance, *CBS This Morning*, 5/26/93

PRESIDENT CLINTON: We found out that there were seven people working in the Travel Office, primarily to book travel for the press, and that the press were complaining that the cost was too high. So, there were all these recommendations made to change it, but noth-ing was done until an accounting firm came in and reviewed the operations and found serious management questions in terms of unaccounted funds and things like that. So then the person in charge of that made the decision to replace them... That is literally all I know about it.

CONTINUED RE-RUN — Excerpt, White House news conference on the Travel Office firings, held two days later, 5/29/93.

PRESIDENT CLINTON: Let's not obscure what happened.

• • •

THE WASHINGTON TIMES **FRONT PAGE,** 7/17/98

Former Travel Director Tells of Clinton White House 'Mugging'

BY PAUL BEDARD

Former Travel Office Director Billy Dale, in sometimes emotional testimony, told the House Judiciary Committee today that he and six other members of that office "saw our careers ruined and rights trampled" as a result of being fired by the Clinton White House five years ago in "a politically-arranged mugging."

Mr. Dale, who was later cleared by a District of Columbia jury of charges he had illegally appropriated Travel Office funds, testified as the final witness in the Travelgate phase of the committee's impeachment hearings, now entering their third week.

Sources say that Chairman Henry Hyde, Republican of Illinois, has arranged the Committee schedule to go next into what he calls "adjunct" outgrowths of the Travel Office firings, including charges that the Clinton staff gained improper access to over 900 FBI "raw" files and engaged in a cover-up operation in the hours following the suicide of White House Deputy Counsel Vincent Foster in July, 1993....

CHAPTER NINE
THE FILES AND THE FIFTH

■

TESTIMONY OF CRAIG LIVINGSTONE and Anthony Marceca,
7/22/98

HENRY HYDE: Let the record show that the witnesses, Craig
Livingstone and Anthony Marceca, have both been interrogated by
the committee on camera, and under advice of counsel refused to
answer questions relating to their conduct as members of the
President's staff. It is the opinion of the chair that the refusal of
White House employees to forthrightly answer questions about their
duties is per se evidence to be considered by this committee. It is also
something the American people are entitled to see and know.

JOHN CONYERS: Let the record also show that a committee minority
objects to wasting time and taxpayer money in a charade of questioning witnesses who have nothing to say unless granted immunity—an option the chair has refused to take.

HENRY HYDE: I think the gentleman from Michigan knows, but
apparently chooses to forget, that what we've turned down is blan-
ket immunity, and you and your colleagues joined in that decision.

BARNEY FRANK: When? At what point did I ever...

RANDY TURK (ATTORNEY FOR CRAIG LIVINGSTONE): If the chair please...

HENRY HYDE: Yes, Mr. Turk?

RANDY TURK: Since the subject has come up again, I re-submit my
offer on behalf of my client to waive his Fifth Amendment rights in

return for a guarantee of total immunity. He stands ready to cooperate, to answer all questions, but not at the unreasonable risk of possible prosecution.

HENRY HYDE: We've covered this ground before, Counsel, but the sticking point remains. There's no guarantee if it's found the witness is lying. Mr. Conyers, Mr. Frank, does that...?

JOHN CONYERS: It distorts my position, but...

BILL MCCOLLUM: Distorts which position? Talk about charades—Mr. Chairman, it's obvious what our Democrat colleagues are up to. Anything to obfuscate, befog the issues... Mr. Frank, I'm looking at the transcript of our last executive session, and I'll be glad to read into the record exactly what you said at that time on the subject of immunity.

HENRY HYDE (GAVELING): If the members will—Mr. Mooney, let's just move on with the witnesses or we'll be here all day and half the night.

THOMAS MOONEY, SR.: Yes, sir. We'll begin, Mr. Livingstone, by asking the nature of your job, your job description, and the dates of your joining and leaving the White House staff.

CRAIG LIVINGSTONE: Under advice of counsel, I respectfully decline to answer on grounds it may tend to incriminate me.

THOMAS MOONEY: In what way, Mr. Livingstone? It's no crime to work on the White House staff.

CRAIG LIVINGSTONE: That's a question, right?

THOMAS MOONEY: A question, yes.

(At this point the witness engaged in a side conference with his attorney.) *

THOMAS MOONEY: Mr. Livingstone?

---

* Livingstone, it was obvious, was confused and had to be reminded by his lawyer of the rule governing use of the Fifth Amendment before Congressional committees. A witness cannot be selective in responding to questions. He must either invoke the Fifth for all questions, answer all questions, or risk being cited for contempt.

CRAIG LIVINGSTONE: Mr. Mooney, under advice of counsel, I respectfully decline to answer on grounds it may tend to incriminate me.

THOMAS MOONEY: Very well, I'll then ask you—what we're interested in is the nature of your employment at the White House as director of personnel security and the role you played in gathering some 900 sensitive, confidential FBI files on American citizens—"raw" files, as they're called—beginning with Billy Ray Dale's. Who initiated the request for those files, Mr. Livingstone? Mr. Dale's file in particular.

CRAIG LIVINGSTONE: Under advice of counsel, I respectfully decline to answer on grounds it may tend to incriminate me.

THOMAS MOONEY: Well, you do know Anthony Marceca, don't you? The individual on your staff who gathered the files?

CRAIG LIVINGSTONE: Under advice of counsel, I respectfully decline...

THOMAS MOONEY: The question is simple enough, Mr. Livingstone. Do you know Anthony Marceca?

(The witness again conferred with his attorney.)

CRAIG LIVINGSTONE: Under advice of counsel, I respectfully decline to answer that question because my answer might tend to incriminate me.

THOMAS MOONEY: Mr. Livingstone, we have information, depositions, that tell us you were the White House supervisor who hired Mr. Marceca. You do recall hiring him, don't you? Let me rephrase the question. Look to your left. Do you know that individual, the person seated next to you at the witness table?

BARNEY FRANK: Mr. Chairman...

CRAIG LIVINGSTONE: Under advice of counsel...

BARNEY FRANK: If the witness will—hold it, Mr. Livingstone, just— Mr. Chairman, if I didn't know better, I'd swear we've been caught in a time warp, a throwback to the 1950s, when humiliating a witness for asserting his constitutional rights was commonplace. There's a word for this kind of thing...

HENRY HYDE: Is this a point of order Mr. Frank? If not, I'll remind you that anything you have to say about the...

BARNEY FRANK: —the word is McCarthyism. And it strikes me, as I'm sure it does millions of viewers watching this, it strikes me as the ultimate hypocrisy that a chairman supposedly concerned about abuse of power should tolerate this sort of travesty.

CHARLES SCHUMER: Let me add my voice...

BOB BARR: Mr. Chairman, that's not a point of order.

HENRY HYDE: A moment, Mr. Schumer, Mr. Barr—a few moments, on a point of personal privilege, to respond to our colleague from Massachusetts, since I've been called many things over the years, but "hypocrite" has never been one of them. As I said earlier, it's fundamental to me that the people of the United States have a right to expect the highest standards from their President and members of his White House staff. President Clinton himself has said that repeatedly, from the day he took office.

The highest standard. That doesn't mean that a public-spirited citizen who takes a job on the President's staff relinquishes any of his or her rights. But a refusal to tell a legally-constituted body—a court, grand jury, this or any congressional committee—about public business taking place in the White House—a refusal based on the possibility of self-incrimination—raises serious questions, critical questions.

BARNEY FRANK: Mr. Chairman, if I may...

HENRY HYDE: Two more points—the first relating to what my colleagues on the other side have variously called a "charade" and a "travesty." I take it that means putting a Fifth Amendment witness in the dock and requiring that he assert his claim point-by-point. Some may argue that this is a waste of time, but the assertion of the Fifth Amendment in this case points out, in dramatic form, that the highest standard hasn't been met, something the public has a right to know.

Mr. Frank calls this a "travesty," but in fact—he may be too young to remember—this is the very technique, modus operandi, used by his colleague from Massachusetts, John F. Kennedy, and Committee Counsel Robert F. Kennedy, when they set out to prove, to shed light on the corrupt leadership of the Teamsters Union in the 1950s. Question-after-question, to witnesses taking the Fifth, and if you're under the impression Tom Mooney here is "humiliating" this witness, I invite you to go back into the record of the Senate Labor Racketeering Committee in the mid-Fifties, and find out how it's really done. Finally...

BARNEY FRANK: If the Chair will permit...

HENRY HYDE: I'm winding up, Mr. Frank, then you'll have your chance to respond. Finally, as to the charge of "McCarthyism," I think we understand that term, as it's been used over the years, to mean the reckless, irresponsible use of government power and resources to intimidate and harass, to smear personal reputations by use of rumor and innuendo on the order of that found in the FBI's so-called "raw" files. Which is why, traditionally, those files have always been considered highly confidential, off-limits except under extraordinary circumstances.

Yet what do we find here? We have testimony, depositions, enough to fill a room, that—how many?—first a few, then a hundred, then four hundred, then nine hundred of these "raw" files, including those on past administration officials like Secretary of State Jim Baker—nine hundred were in the hands of these two witnesses, White House employees who come before this Committee and refuse to answer legitimate questions about their activities as members of the White House staff.

That's disturbing, Mr. Frank, and I would think, I wonder where our friends at the American Civil Liberties Union, who had a great deal to say about President Nixon's transgressions twenty-five years ago, I wonder why we haven't heard from them on this issue.

(At this point in the proceedings there was audience applause.)

HENRY HYDE (GAVELING): Members of the audience will refrain—now, Mr. Frank?

BARNEY FRANK: Only one point, Mr. Chairman. We disagree, profoundly disagree, on most points—including your view, I might say, of what took place in this country in the 1950s—but my use of the word "hypocrisy" was unfortunate. I ask that it be amended to read "inconsistency"…

HENRY HYDE: I thank my colleague from Massachusetts—though I presume, Mr. Frank, that "travesty" still stands. *(Audience laughter)*

BARNEY FRANK: "Travesty" stands.

• • •

LIVINGSTONE AND MARCECA would be at the witness table the better part of a morning, long enough to raise questions that would be addressed the next day by a witness who, far from refusing to answer, seemed to relish the live-grenade combat of committee testimony.

CHAPTER TEN

FROM: BERNARD W. NUSSBAUM

■

TESTIMONY OF BERNARD NUSSBAUM, 7/29//98

HENRY HYDE: Mr. Nussbaum, before we begin questioning, do you have a statement you'd like to introduce into the record?

BERNARD NUSSBAUM: No. Let me make it clear, Mr. Hyde, that I resent, bitterly resent, being called down here to testify on matters that are already of record, under oath, in prior testimony that could have served the purpose of this committee.

HENRY HYDE: Then you do have a statement.

BERNARD NUSSBAUM: No, I simply want to make my position clear.

HENRY HYDE: Mr. Mooney?

THOMAS MOONEY: Thank you, Mr. Chairman. Mr. Nussbaum, what we're specifically interested in is your role in, and knowledge of, the gathering of 900 FBI files in...

BERNARD NUSSBAUM: Look up my testimony before the Clinger Committee. I've told everything I know about it. It happened, it was a mistake, and as soon as the mistake was discovered, it was corrected.

THOMAS MOONEY: It wasn't quite that simple, Mr. Nussbaum, since it took Congressman Clinger's committee...

BERNARD NUSSBAUM: I'm not here to cavil with you, Counselor. You asked a question, I gave you my answer.

THOMAS MOONEY: Then let me try this out, Mr. Nussbaum, since the record shows that the mistake, as you call it, carried your signature: On December 20, 1993, a White House memo requesting Billy Dale's FBI file was sent to the agency...

BERNARD NUSSBAUM: You don't have to read me the record, I already know it.

HENRY HYDE: Mr. Nussbaum, this will go a lot easier all around if you let counsel do his job.

THOMAS MOONEY: Thank you, Mr. Chairman. Let me repeat, Mr. Nussbaum: on the twentieth of December, 1993, the White House sent a memo to the FBI asking for Billy Dale's "raw" file—seven months after Mr. Dale had been summarily fired. My question is why, and whether, that request had anything to do with an ongoing White House campaign to discredit Mr. Dale and the Travel Office Seven. Can you, given your position at the time as counsel to the President, shed any light on this?

BERNARD NUSSBAUM: As I told the Clinger Committee...

THOMAS MOONEY: Tell us, if you will.

BERNARD NUSSBAUM: My responsibilities at the time were such that one memo, more or less...

THOMAS MOONEY: Let me refresh your memory. This particular memorandum was addressed to: "FBI, LIAISON, FROM: BERNARD W. NUSSBAUM" and specifically said that the file was needed because Mr. Dale was being considered for a White House Access pass. Does that strike you—given the fact that Mr. Dale was seven months gone at the time—strike you as odd?

BERNARD NUSSBAUM: It doesn't strike me any way, odd or ordinary. Who was or wasn't on the access list was David Watkins' department, not mine.

THOMAS MOONEY: But your name was on the request—Bernard W. Nussbaum—not Watkins. What you're telling us is that under

COPY

THE WHITE HOUSE

WASHINGTON

DEC 20 1993
_____
(Date)

TO: FBI, LIAISON

FROM: BERNARD W. NUSSBAUM

SUBJECT: FBI Investigations

Subject's Name DALE, BILLY RAY _____

Date of Birth 04-05-37 _____   Place of Birth Grundy, VA _____

Present Address _____

We request: _XX___   Copy of Previous Report

               _____   Name Check

               _____   Expanded Name Check

               _____   Full Field Investigation : Level I___ Level II___

               _____   Limited Update

               _____   Other

The person named above is being considered for:

               _____   White House Staff Position

               _____   Presidential Appointment

               _XX___   ACCESS (S) _____

                                   NON-RESPONSIVE MATERIAL REDACTED
Attachments:

               _____   SF 86

               _____   SF 87, Fingerprint Card

               _____   SF 86, Supplement

                                                   CGE 043641

White House memo from Bernard Nussbaum requesting Billy Dale's FBI "raw" file—
months *after* Dale had been fired as Travel Office Director.

ordinary circumstances, an access request would go through Watkins. So what we're talking about is something out of the ordinary. Isn't that a reasonable conclusion?

BERNARD NUSSBAUM: If you've jumped to it based on my name being on the request, no, it's not reasonable at all. It was a form memo, a print signature.

THOMAS MOONEY: But your signature—not Watkins' or McLarty's or that of George Stephanopoulos.

BERNARD NUSSBAUM: Mine, yes, but that doesn't say or prove a thing, Counselor, and if you knew anything at all about how the White House works, you'd understand that…

• • •

BILL MCCOLLUM: Let me see if I understand you correctly, Mr. Nussbaum: You say the fact that the request for Billy Dale's file carried your name on it really didn't matter, because the signature was printed, a form signature. Is that correct?

BERNARD NUSSBAUM: Correct.

BILL MCCOLLUM: You didn't even know the request was being made, is that what you're saying? The way they do things around the White House—this White House, at least—is, the counsel to the President signs his name, they print it up by the dozens, hundreds, thousands, on a form, and anybody and everybody can use it.

BERNARD NUSSBAUM: No, sir, not anybody and everybody. Only those in the counsel's office.

BILL MCCOLLUM: Fine, now we're getting somewhere. Winnowing the list of possibilities of who ordered up the Billy Dale file. The only way the form could have gone over to the FBI, then, was through someone working directly for you.

BERNARD NUSSBAUM: Or someone delegated by me, yes.

BILL MCCOLLUM: And the same would hold true, I suppose, for the other eight-hundred ninety-nine?

BERNARD NUSSBAUM: Pardon?

BILL MCCOLLUM: The other eight-hundred ninety-nine requests for FBI "raw" files that went out over your signature—your printed signature. There were nine-hundred or so files in Craig Livingstone's...

BERNARD NUSSBAUM: Wait just a minute, Congressman. I didn't say, and I am in no way responsible for, forms that went out...

BILL MCCOLLUM: But you just said everybody couldn't use the forms, only those working directly for—or delegated by—you. Doesn't that make you responsible?

BERNARD NUSSBAUM: That's absurd.

BILL MCCOLLUM: Why is it absurd, Mr. Nussbaum? You're a lawyer, and from what we know, a good one—counsel to a President, before that a staff member for an impeachment committee... Tell me, what would you have said to a member of President Nixon's staff, if he'd come before the Rodino Committee, and told them, "I don't know how those files wound up at the White House, it wasn't my signature, it was a form letter"?

CHARLES SCHUMER: Mr. Chairman, I object to this line...

BILL MCCOLLUM: Withdraw the question, Mr. Chairman. Not that it's not relevant, but I think my point's been made.

HOWARD BERMAN: Mr. Nussbaum, did the President have any advance knowledge of the firing of the seven employees in the Travel Office?

BERNARD NUSSBAUM: He was told there was a problem, but he wasn't—it wasn't at a level that required his attention. Personnel changes were taking place throughout the White House, so it was no—except for word there was fiscal mismanagement—no big deal.

1996 Clinger Committee Report on Travelgate

As Admitted Into the Record of the House Judiciary Committee hearings on H. Res. 104:

On May 17, 1993, McLarty met with Watkins and told him the Travel Office was on Mrs. Clinton's radar screen. Watkins, responding to pressure from McLarty, Foster and Mrs. Clinton, decided to fire the employees because he thought there "would be hell to pay" if he did not accede to the First Family's wishes. McLarty approved the decision and the May 17 memo on the firing was "cc'd" to "Hillary Rodham Clinton" and faxed to President Clinton in California....

President Clinton denied knowing anything about the Travel Office firings even though he had been briefed on the matter two days before the firings. This was known to at least Bruce Lindsey and Jeff Eller. Such statements by the President had to have sent a chilling message to all those individuals who were aware of President Clinton's prior knowledge of the firings, in effect creating a conspiracy of silence. The fact that President Clinton was briefed prior to the firings was not disclosed publicly until this investigation.

HOWARD BERMAN: Was the President aware Billy Dale's file, or any other file, had been ordered from the FBI?

BERNARD NUSSBAUM: To the best of my knowledge, the first he heard about that was when the story broke in the papers.

HOWARD BERMAN: Then what happened?

BERNARD NUSSBAUM: He asked for a briefing and I, along with other members of the staff, gathered the facts and laid them out.

HOWARD BERMAN: You briefed him. Do you recall, can you tell us, what his reaction was?

BERNARD NUSSBAUM: What you'd expect. He was angered, furious that at a critical time, in the first weeks of his presidency, he'd been let down by sloppy, inept staff work.

HOWARD BERMAN: A breakdown in the system.

BERNARD NUSSBAUM: A mid-level bureaucratic foul-up. Exactly.

• • •

HOWARD COBLE: Mr. Chairman, before questioning Mr. Nussbaum, I'd like to raise in public session the point I made at our last closed session, regarding the curious role played by FBI Director Louis Freeh in the Filegate affair—beginning with Mr. Freeh's pen-pal correspondence with Craig Livingstone during the period that Livingstone and his assistant Anthony Marceca were collecting hundreds of FBI "raw" files at the White House.

The record shows that Director Freeh and Craig Livingstone were on "Dear Craig" and "Louie" terms, reflected in no fewer than five letters in which the director thanked Livingstone for various favors Livingstone had given the director's family, including private White House tours and special help given the director's son. What makes this relationship especially troubling is the fact that Mr. Freeh was brought to the FBI to restore discipline and arms-length integrity to an agency that many feared had become

From the 1996 Clinger Committee Report on Filegate

As Admitted Into the Record of the House Judiciary Committee hearings on H. Res. 104:

On May 30, 1996, the White House produced 1,000 documents to the committee in order to avoid a vote by the House of Representatives on the contempt citation against [White House Counsel Jack] Quinn. That production included Dale's FBI background file and the memorandum from Bernard Nussbaum, then Counsel to the President, to the FBI liaison requesting the file. That was the first time the committee learned of the White House improperly requesting, maintaining, and withholding the FBI background file of Billy Ray Dale.

Investigators for the committee were reviewing the White House documents when they came upon memoranda of an extremely personal nature about Dale and his family. Affixed to these documents was a December 20, 1993 memorandum from Nussbaum to the FBI requesting a copy of a 'previously requested report' for the background file of Billy Dale. Mr. Dale was dismissed from the White House 7 months before the request, and had no need for White House access.

too politicized. Instead, what we've witnessed in recent years is an alarming tendency by the FBI Director and his top aides—notably his former counsel, Howard Shapiro—to ingratiate themselves with the Clinton White House.

Some recent history: it was two years ago, almost to the day, that the Government Reform and Oversight Committee uncovered the notorious White House memorandum—approved by the witness here—asking the FBI to forward the Dale file to the White House...

• • •

BERNARD NUSSBAUM: Notorious memorandum? Am I here to answer questions or take insults?

HOWARD COBLE: Be patient, Mr. Nussbaum. I'll get around to questions.

BERNARD NUSSBAUM: Let's start with that, that notorious memorandum, as you call it. Though it doesn't seem to have registered...

HENRY HYDE: The witness will be in order. Mr. Coble, I assume you're keeping track of the time.

HOWARD COBLE: I am, Mr. Chairman, but allow me a moment for a point of personal privilege: Mr. Nussbaum, you may not like what I have to say, or for that matter the way these hearings are being run, but let me remind you, this is 1998, not 1974. This time around, you're the witness, not the interrogator, and the imperious style that marked your career as a Watergate prosecutor and White House counsel doesn't go over too well, at least not with this Congressman.

HENRY HYDE: You have three minutes remaining, Mr. Coble.

HOWARD COBLE: Thank you, Mr. Chairman. The point I want to make is that when Reform and Oversight discovered that the White House had called up Billy Dale's "raw" file—an ugly attempt to dig up dirt, to smear a man already victimized—the director of the FBI, Louis Freeh, dismissed this call-up as, quote, "a routine procedure" in response to "a type of request routinely made." And it wasn't until nine days later, June 14, 1996—after the prevailing publicity winds had shifted and it was clear the request had not been "routine" in prior administrations—that Mr. Freeh, shocked, shocked, that such a thing could have happened on his watch, stated that his friend Craig Livingstone's actions constituted "egregious violations of privacy" and the FBI had been, quote, "victimized" by the White House...

JOHN CONYERS: Point of order, Mr. Chairman. I wasn't aware we'd been convened to review the record of the director of the FBI. Or is he also up for impeachment?

HOWARD COBLE: Abuse of police power is one of the elements of impeachment, Mr. Conyers, and the fact that the Clinton White House not only attempted to corrupt the Federal Bureau of Investigation but may have succeeded because of a compliant director is very much part of this committee's agenda.

HENRY HYDE: Your time is...

HOWARD COBLE: One question, Mr. Nussbaum. In the mounds of paperwork, thousands of documents subpoenaed from the Clinton White House, we find memcons, memorandums of conversations, and other notes from various participants, including all members of your staff, the chief of staff, heads of other White House offices. But none made by you. I find that odd.

BERNARD NUSSBAUM: There's nothing odd about it. I didn't take notes.

HOWARD COBLE: Not a one? You're sure of that?

BERNARD NUSSBAUM: Yes. If there's anything I went to the White House knowing, it's that people who take notes at meetings are asking for trouble.

HOWARD COBLE: Asking for trouble?

BERNARD NUSSBAUM: Stupid.

CHAPTER ELEVEN
HER COSMIC COLOR

———————————■———————————

HILLARY CLINTON WAS WEARING PINK. Not the same dress, but the same shade of pink she had worn at her fabled news conference back in 1994, the all-star performance in which she'd established (to everyone's satisfaction but the Right-wing crazies) her innocence of any wrong-doing in the Whitewater affair, her quick-profit ventures—all those malicious charges levelled by the professional Clinton-haters.

Pink, her lucky color. Her cosmic color. That, at least, was what a pop psychologist of New Age predilection had advised during her trip to Los Angeles. Wear pink, she'd said, the chroma of innocence. It will make you feel better, and release cosmic vibrations sure to disarm your enemies.

Well, she'd been half-right: it did make the First Lady feel better. As for her enemies…

All in pink (Versace), seated in the conference room of her attorney's plush law offices, Hillary watched with mixed emotions—both admiration and anger—as her old Watergate mentor Bernie Nussbaum testified before the Hyde Committee: admiration for Nussbaum, her kind of lawyer, who never apologized, seldom explained, and thought the best defense in any given situation was, in his words, "a good swift kick in the *(expletive deleted)*"; anger at his churlish inquisitors, whom she'd taken to calling "Hyde's hyenas."

That the First Lady had to travel three blocks to confer with her lawyers was the result, she felt, of Nussbaum's forced departure from his job as counsel. If Bernie had been on the job, the Supreme Court decision that the attorney-client privilege didn't apply inside the White House would have gone otherwise. As matters stood, the only way she could talk to her lawyers in absolute safety was to go to their offices.

"Hyde's hyenas": predators hungry for blood. What was it Kissinger had said? *Even paranoids have enemies.* The First Lady recalled quoting that line to Vince Foster back in 1993, shortly after the Travel Office story had broken. *Let up*, Foster had advised. *Just because someone worked in the Bush White House doesn't mean he's an enemy. Don't be so damn paranoid.*

Reliable, trusting Vince. He'd laughed when she quoted Kissinger, but if he were alive now, he might have second thoughts about the First Lady's feeling they were Washington outsiders surrounded by enemies. Enemies on Capitol Hill, like Henry Hyde and his bloodthirsty friends; enemies in the media, like the toxic *Washington Times*, the excretal *American Spectator*, the abominable Rush Limbaugh. And unseen enemies as well, enemies who came at you with smiles, embraces. But when your back is turned...

Just who did Al Gore think he'd fool, putting that girl in Los Angeles up to waving that ridiculous placard: TIPPER FOR FIRST LADY, 1998 ? Hillary knew, was sure in her own mind, that it had come from the Gore people. Who else? Certainly not the Right-wingers, who hated the Gores as much as they despised the Clintons. And who did Gore think he'd fool, inserting that line into his recent speech to the Detroit Economic Club, the line that read, "It's time Americans, like the eagle in flight, shed the molting plumage of the past..."

Molting plumage of the past? After all she and Bill had done for the Gores? It appeared what Harry Truman had said about Washington was right: You want loyalty in Washington? Get a dog.

CHAPTER TWELVE

ADVERSE OR DEROGATORY INFORMATION

———————————————■———————————————

TESTIMONY OF BERNARD NUSSBAUM (continued)

BOB INGLIS (R-SC): As we know, Mr. Nussbaum, Washington is a town of mysteries, and the biggest mystery to come along in recent years is the identity of the person—the "Deep Throat"—who hired Craig Livingstone. Can you shed light on that subject, tell us what you know about it?

BERNARD NUSSBAUM: As I've told a dozen committees, grand juries and investigators, I have no idea who hired Mr. Livingstone. None whatsoever.

BOB INGLIS: But he did work in your department. According to the White House table of organization, Mr. Livingstone's job as head of the office of personnel security fell under the jurisdiction of the counsel's office.

BERNARD NUSSBAUM: Technically that's correct—on paper—but the way things actually worked we had very little to do with Livingstone's operation.

BOB INGLIS: What you're saying is, he operated on his own, without supervision.

BERNARD NUSSBAUM: Don't put words in my mouth, Congressman.

BOB INGLIS: I'm not putting words in your mouth, Mr. Nussbaum. You said Livingstone was under your jurisdiction, but you had little to do with his operation. Then whose office in the White House did? Could it have been the First Lady's?

BERNARD NUSSBAUM: That's a ridiculous insinuation, and you know it.

BOB INGLIS: But Livingstone did know the First Lady—no, withdraw that for the moment. Let's get back to whether he was supervised or operated on his own, ordering up 900 files from the FBI—sensitive information, rumors, uncorroborated charges about former Cabinet members and private citizens. You claim you didn't authorize that, even though your name was on every order. Is that right?

BERNARD NUSSBAUM: If you're asking whether I knew anything about the files...

BOB INGLIS: Or authorized their being sent to the White House.

BERNARD NUSSBAUM: No, I didn't.

BOB INGLIS: So he ordered them up—he and his friend Tony Marceca—ordered them up on their own. Would that be fair to say?

BERNARD NUSSBAUM: *(inaudible)*

BOB INGLIS: Pardon?

BERNARD NUSSBAUM: Yes.

BOB INGLIS: Then he was operating on his own, without supervision, as I said... Mr. Nussbaum, a little background for those not familiar with the procedure followed during prior administrations regarding FBI "raw" files: Isn't it true—we have testimony and depositions from several of your predecessors in the White House counsel's office, including Boyden Gray from the Bush years—isn't it true that all White House requests for FBI files were closely supervised by the counsel?

BERNARD NUSSBAUM: Are you asking whether I've talked to Boyden Gray on the subject?

BOB INGLIS: No, what I'm asking is why those standards, those strict standards for dealing with sensitive information about individuals, were thrown out the window when the Clinton team moved into the White House... Let me put it another way: are you familiar, Mr. Nussbaum, with the SG-86 questionnaire filled out by new White House employees, then sent to the FBI to form the basis of an employee's "raw" file?

BERNARD NUSSBAUM: Yes, I am.

BOB INGLIS: A questionnaire designed, in the words of another of your predecessors as White House counsel, A.B. Culvahouse, to— quote—"affirmatively encourage the furnishing of adverse or derogatory information" about the employee. Do you find any fault with that definition?

BERNARD NUSSBAUM: Fault, no. What are you getting at, Mr...

BOB INGLIS: Inglis. What I'm getting at, Mr. Nussbaum, is that if these reports fell into the wrong hands, they could be used for any number of purposes. Intimidation, blackmail...

BERNARD NUSSBAUM: Blackmail?

BOB INGLIS: No one's accusing you, Mr. Nussbaum. I'm just pointing out why all White House operations, prior to the Clintons', regarded these files as sensitive, subject to close—the closest— supervision. Now, in those prior administrations—Republican, Democrat alike—the director of personnel security was a professional, a career person. Not a political appointee. Isn't that right?

BERNARD NUSSBAUM: What's right, Congressman, is that you've insinuated, as much as said, that as White House Counsel I either engaged in or authorized the use of files for blackmail, and that is a damned lie, outrageous conduct coming from a member of Congress, and I ask for, demand, an apology before I submit to any further questions.

(At this point in the proceedings, the witness stood, as if to leave the Committee room, and after what appeared to be a heated side conversa-

tion between Mr. Hyde and Mr. Conyers, the chairman recessed the hearings until the next day.)

• • •

RUSH LIMBAUGH SHOW, 7/31/98

RUSH LIMBAUGH: —Not in time for this year's Academy Award ceremony, but Bernie Nussbaum's performance yesterday deserves some kind of Oscar... (thump)... Maybe the Oscar Mayer baloney award for the Best Impersonation of an Outraged Innocent by a Clinton Mouthpiece (thump)... How, Bombastic Bernie wanted to know, how could anyone possibly imagine the Clinton White House would ever, ever try to intimidate or blackmail anyone with those 900 confidential files that Hillary's choirboys, Craig Livingstone and his sidekick Tony Marceca ordered up from the FBI... ?

How, indeed... The FBI calls these files "raw," folks, because that's what they are—rumors, gossip, unsubstantiated charges—the sort of thing a responsible White House wouldn't want in the grubby hands of political hit men and barroom bouncers whose sole recommendation was, they'd paid their dues as dirty tricksters in the Clinton-Gore campaign of 1992 (thump)...

• • •

RERUN — Excerpt, *The Washington Post* (FOCUS) 9/8/96

On February 10, 1994, Tony Marceca, who was supposed to help keep persons with questionable backgrounds out of the White House, got a sharply worded call from an FBI agent about his own past.

"You took money for warrants, and double-billed the county for travel," Agent Cecilia Wood told him, evidently referring to his days as a constable in Pennsylvania. "You lied about it then—you're lying about it now."

When Marceca denied it, Wood accused him again. "You are lying now," she said.

"I think I need to get an attorney to deal with with this," Marceca said, recording the exchange on a Post-It note in his appointment dairy.

Marceca left the White House the next day, but not soon enough to spare President Clinton the embarrassment of still another controversy over a White House function that was supposed to be as routine as counting heads. In six months in the once-obscure White House office of Security, Marceca collected more than 700 confidential FBI background reports on White House pass-holders from Republican administrations.

Discovery of Marceca's collection of files on Republicans in early June inevitably called to mind the notorious "enemies list" devised by the Nixon White House 25 years ago. Suspicions were reinforced by reports that Marceca's friend and boss, Craig Livingstone, had been loose-mouthed about private information in FBI background reports, and that both Livingstone and Marceca had once tried to use derogatory information in a political campaign.

Marceca's wrongful acquisitions were only the most blatant example of how poorly the security office functioned. While he busily assembled files on former pass-holders in whom the White House should have had no interest, more than 100 active White House employees were allowed to work for months—some for more than a year—without obtaining proper clearances or background checks.

The two men met in early 1984 as campaign workers for Senator Gary Hart (D-Colo.), then a presidential candidate. Neither... impressed Dennis Casey, a Pennsylvania political consultant who said he met them on the 1984 Hart campaign. He said Livingstone strongly advocated using derogatory information about Mondale backers—including rumors about "sexual peccadilloes"—to force them into the Hart camp. "I just got a very bad taste in my mouth," Casey said. "He felt it was my duty to go to these people and try to coerce them into supporting Senator Hart."

• • •

RERUN (3)

"I did not know him. I did not have anything to do with his being hired, and I *do* not remember *even meeting him until some time in the last year."* *(Emphasis supplied)*

—HILLARY CLINTON ON THE SUBJECT OF CRAIG LIVINGSTONE, JULY 10, 1996

"Hi, Craig."

—HILLARY CLINTON, PASSING CRAIG LIVINGSTONE IN THE WEST WING, AS RECALLED BY A WHITE HOUSE STAFFER, CIRCA SUMMER, 1994.

CHAPTER THIRTEEN
IN FOSTER'S OFFICE

■

NUSSBAUM WAS BACK at the witness table the following morning, still surly but ostensibly placated by Chairman Hyde's public assurance that his colleague Bob Inglis didn't mean to imply any criminal wrongdoing on the witness's part. A check of the transcript made that obvious, but Hyde knew from experience that, given the Washington media, what is actually said or done in a political controversy is less important than the way it's played...

Conyers Charges "Gutter Tactics" in GOP Questions to Witness

—HEADLINE, *THE NEW YORK TIMES*, 7/31/98

"Smear" Queries Trouble Legal Experts
PART ONE OF A TWO-PART SERIES

—HEADLINE, *THE WASHINGTON POST*, 8/4/98

IT WAS A DIVERSION, of course, but as Hyde told young Bob Inglis, arguing about the media's spin on yesterday's news only keeps the spin going today and tomorrow. The evidence against Livingstone and Marceca was overwhelming, and the chain of culpability ran through Nussbaum to Hillary Clinton, on into the Oval Office. In many ways, thought Hyde, the Filegate episode offered the strongest argument in favor of impeachment: a White House operation of the kind Richard Nixon was accused of in 1974. (Nixon aide Charles Colson, as Pat Buchanan pointed out in a newspaper column, was sent to the penitentiary for unauthorized use of only one FBI file.)

• • •

"Seven-hundred, nine-hundred, ten thousand files— what difference does it make? There was a mistake made by over-zealous staff members, it was corrected, apologies were made. And to this day it's never been shown, no matter how many files were involved, that even one of them was misused."

—WHITE HOUSE AIDE PAUL BEGALA IN FULL CRY, CROSSFIRE, 8/5/98

"The point is, they're out there, who knows where? How many Xerox copies were made? They were left around his office, on desks, cabinets, open to every passing eye. Marceca even took files home. Why? That's what's chilling, the potential for blackmail, intimidation, and the President, even if he didn't initiate it, condoned it."

—BOYDEN GRAY RESPONDING, SAME PROGRAM.

• • •

TESTIMONY OF BERNARD NUSSBAUM (continued)

BOB INGLIS: Mr. Nussbaum, you were interviewed by FBI Agent Dennis Sculimbrene, in March 1993, regarding the employment of Craig Livingstone by the White House.

197

WFFO: 161 F-HQ-10455??
KDS/mje   1

EMPLOYMENT
Executive Office of the President
Office of the Counsel
Old Executive Office Building
Washington,D.C.

          The following investigation was conducted by SA M.
Dennis Sculimbrene regarding DAVID CRAIG LIVINGSTONE on 3/1-
3/93.

          LORI STALLINGS, Supervisory Personnel Assistant, The
White House Office, Personnel Office, advised that the appointee
is listed on the rolls with the EOP in the Office of the Counsel,
but is not officially employed at the White House Office as a
Security Assistant to the Counsel to the President at this
current time(March 4, 1993). He began work on a volunteer basis
about 5 weeks ago, on a temporary/part time basis. She said that
these are unofficial records, and official records would not be
available for an indefinite period.

          BERNARD NUSSBAUM, Counsel to the President, advised
that he has known the appointee for the period of time that he
has been employed in the new administration. He had come highly
recommended to him by HILLARY CLINTON, who has known his mother
for a longer period of time. He was confident that the appointee
lives a circumspect life and was not aware of any illegal drug or
alcohol problems. He said that the appointee will work at the
White House on security matters. He said that in the short period
of time that the appointee has worked for him he has been
completely satisfied with his performance, conduct and
productivity. He recommended the appointee for continued access
in his current capacity.

          WILLIAM HOLDER KENNEDY, Associate Counsel to the
President, advised that he has known the appointee since he
arrived himself, to take over the office responsibilities that he
currently handles. He did not hire the appointee, and was aware
that the appointee may not stay in his current position. He was
aware that the appointee was attempting to head the Military
Office. KENNEDY said that if the appointee stays in his current
position, he would recommend his access to the complex, based on
the understanding that he makes such recommendation on the short
period of time that he has known the appointee.

Exhibit in testimony given at an August 1, 1996, hearing of the Committee on
Government Reform and Oversight. In his interview with Nussbaum, FBI agent
Dennis Sculimbrene says Nussbaum claimed that Craig Livingstone "had come
highly recommended to him by Hillary Clinton...." The First Lady had earlier denied
ever recommending Livingstone.

BERNARD NUSSBAUM: That again.

BOB INGLIS: Yes, that again. Do you recall telling Agent Sculimbrene at that time that Livingstone had, quote, "come highly recommended by Hillary Clinton?" That's what Sculimbrene wrote in his notes taken imediately after the interview.

BERNARD NUSSBAUM: No, I don't recall it, because I didn't say it to Sculimbrene or anyone else at any time.

BOB INGLIS: You're sure of that—the notes, understand, were written three years before Livingstone, so to speak, made a name for himself. Why would Sculimbrene invent such a statement?

BERNARD NUSSBAUM: I'm not a mind-reader, Congressman. You'll have to ask him.

BOB INGLIS: We have. He swears his notes are accurate... *

• • •

BOB BARR: One area we haven't touched on, Mr. Nussbaum—an outgrowth of the Travel Office as well as Whitewater problems—concerns the clean-up operation in Vince Foster's office the night of his suicide. We have a witness—a Secret Service agent—who says under oath that he saw Craig Livingstone carrying boxes of papers, documents out of Foster's office that night. You were in charge of that operation, were you not?

---

* Agent Sculimbrene had been questioned by two investigators dispatched to his house by FBI General Counsel Howard Shapiro following the Clinger Committee's revelation of his interview with Nussbaum. He would leave the Bureau, under pressure, after 27 years at the White House, serving under four Presidents. Two Secret Service agents who made statements counter to the official White House line on Livingstone would also suffer career-ending consequences. When the White House claimed that Reagan-Bush personnel files had come into Livingstone's hands "because the Secret Service had supplied out-of-date lists," Agents John Libonati and Jeffrey Undercoffer told Congressional committees that sort of error hadn't and couldn't occur. Following their testimony, the Treasury Department's Inspector General, authorized by Secretary Robert Rubin, opened an investigation of the two agents for "possible perjury." The investigation went nowhere but, as with Billy Dale and Sculimbrene, the Clinton White House had sent a message: Libonati and Undercoffer are no longer with the Secret Service.

BERNARD NUSSBAUM: As Counsel, yes. Since Foster was my deputy, the documents he was working on, he had in his office, were my concern, my responsibility.

BOB BARR: Your responsibility. So you're the right person to ask about depositions we have from witnesses who say that many of those documents were carried to the residential section of the White House—Whitewater documents, billings from the Rose law firm, as well as Travel Office papers. Could you tell us...

BERNARD NUSSBAUM: Whatever documents left the Foster office were, let me assure you, confidential, relating to White House business, and properly removed.

BOB BARR: Not if it's shown there were Whitewater papers and Rose law firm billings, but—let me ask, Mr. Nussbaum, a question that may go to the heart of this, of what our problem may be: When you were, when you served as White House counsel, did you see yourself as working for the office of the President or for Bill Clinton personally?

BERNARD NUSSBAUM: What's the question?

BOB BARR: When you were White House counsel, did you see yourself as representing the office of the President, or Bill Clinton personally?

BERNARD NUSSBAUM: Both.

BOB BARR: Both?

BERNARD NUSSBAUM: Yes, because I'm a practicing lawyer, Congressman, not a law-review theorist, and in my view, the office of the President and the President are one and the same.

BOB BARR: But you're aware that most of your predecessors, White House counsels in past administrations, viewed it otherwise. They saw themselves as representing the institution, not the individual.

BERNARD NUSSBAUM: That's a nice legal point, fine in theory but not in practice. The office and the man are one and the same.

From the 1996 Clinger Committee Report on Travelgate

As Admitted Into the Record of the House Judiciary Committee hearings on H. Res. 104:

THE WHITE HOUSE'S OBSTRUCTION OF THE REVIEW OF VINCE FOSTER'S DOCUMENTS WAS DUE IN PART TO CONCERNS ABOUT TRAVELGATE DOCUMENTS IN FOSTER'S CUSTODY

> White House Counsel Bernard Nussbaum conducted a sham review of the documents in Foster's office following Foster's death. Mr. Nussbaum did not adequately or accurately describe to law enforcement officials relevant documents in Foster's office, including the Vince Foster Travel Office file....
>
> Mr. Nussbaum withheld information ... from GAO, Public Integrity and FBI investigators for almost a year following Foster's death....
>
> Following Vincent Foster's death, high-ranking White House officials quietly killed efforts by TRM to obtain the GSA contract, concealed all documents pertaining to these efforts from the ongoing General Accounting Office investigation, and long-delayed their production of documents to the Justice Department's Public Integrity unit investigating possible criminal conflicts of interest by Harry Thomason....

MRS. CLINTON INSTRUCTED WHITE HOUSE STAFF ON THE HANDLING OF FOSTER DOCUMENTS AND THE FOSTER NOTE FOUND ON JULY 26, 1993, AND SENIOR WHITE HOUSE STAFF COVERED UP THIS INFORMATION AND KEPT IT FROM INVESTIGATORS

> Mrs. Clinton personally was involved in the discussions regarding the White House's handling of documents in Vince Foster's office following his death....
>
> Mrs. Clinton directed that Mack McLarty and others not inform the President about the discovery of the Foster "suicide" note on July 26, 1993. This note essentially defended Foster's and the White House's actions in the Travel Office firings and Mrs. Clinton suggested that executive privilege research be done regarding the note.
>
> The White House's delay in turning over the Foster note was due to senior staffers' deference to Mrs. Clinton's wishes.

BOB BARR: Well, you're not alone in that view, Mr. Nussbaum, though you should know that the last President who thought that way...

BERNARD NUSSBAUM: One and the same.

BOB BARR: ...was Richard Nixon.*

● ● ●

DEPOSITION OF PHILIP HEYMANN, former Deputy Attorney General, on the reason for his resignation from the Justice Department, 8/3/98

PHILIP HEYMANN: I was very concerned about maintaining the integrity of Foster's office as a possible crime scene. I told Mr. Nussbaum that we needed career prosecutors and investigators to take control of the matter immediately. He agreed. Not only was this a good idea from the standpoint of the department's being better equipped than the National Park Service to investigate the Foster death, but we both felt—and this was even more important—that from an appearance standpoint the public would have more confidence in an investigation conducted by career department professionals than in one run by the White House. By the conclusion of our conversation I had a firm commitment that two of my deputies would have unrestricted access to the Foster office, beginning the next morning.

Q: So you sent two department attorneys over?

PHILIP HEYMANN: Yes.

Q: And what happened?

PHILIP HEYMANN: Mr. Nussbaum blocked both from access to Mr.

---

* In Barr's book on the Clinton impeachment (*High Crimes*, Regnery), he wrote that while Nussbaum was portrayed by the press as the Committee's toughest witness, "it was actually his testimony, particularly his answer to my last question, that opened the way for approval of our first Article, covering abuse-of-power."

Foster's files. They were instructed to be seated and do nothing while Mr. Nussbaum reviewed the files and decided what they could and could not see.

Q: Was that arrangement consistent with your understanding of the previous day?

PHILIP HEYMANN: Absolutely not.

From the 1996 Clinger Committee Report on Travelgate

As Admitted Into the Record of the House Judiciary Committee hearings on H. Res. 104:

[A]n enormous and elaborate cover-up operation, housed in the White House Counsel's Office, sought to prevent numerous investigations from discovering not only the roles of who fired the workers and why, but also their efforts to persecute the victims. In the process, the administration may have severely damaged the credibility and prestige of the White House: it obstructed and frustrated all investigations; it turned the Office of the White House Counsel into a political damage-control operation; it made frivolous claims of executive privilege; it abused its powers to smear innocent citizens; and most important, it failed to level with the American people.

As a result, it is the committee's view that the White House stands in contempt of its own constitutional responsibilities to faithfully uphold and execute the Constitution and laws of the Nation. Never before has a President and his staff done so much to cover up improper actions and hinder the public's right to learn the truth....

The much-heralded White House Management Review (hereinafter "WHMR") proved to be nothing more than a whitewash overseen by then-Chief of Staff and childhood friend of Bill Clinton, Mack McLarty, the very person who had authorized the Travel Office firings. In the course of the committee investigation, evidence of a vast cover-up of President Clinton's knowledge and dealings with his close friend Harry Thomason as well as his staff's deliberate minimization of Hillary Clinton's role emerged and still continues to unfold....

Despite President Clinton's misleading press accounts that he knew little about the firings, we learned Bill Clinton actually was briefed on the firings two days before they occurred....

And then-Assistant to President Clinton for Management and Administration, David Watkins reluctantly became the designated fall guy for the firings in order to protect the higher-ups who had directed his actions.

We learned of the long-hidden notebook kept by Vincent Foster that had been in the office of White House Counsel Bernard Nussbaum following Mr. Foster's death. The notebook chronicled Mr. Foster's anguish over Hillary Clinton's role in the firings, Harry Thomason's potential criminal liability, and whether the White House scandal containment strategy could be maintained to stop at the level of David Watkins.

We learned that Mrs. Clinton directed President Clinton's Chief of Staff, Mack McLarty not to tell President Clinton about the torn up "suicide" note found in Vincent Foster's briefcase on July 26th, 6 days after his death. Mrs. Clinton instructed the President's senior aides to wait until a "coherent position" was developed before informing the President....

The note was essentially an outline of a defense of the Travel Office firings. When it took more than a day to turn the note over to the proper law enforcement authorities, both the Attorney General and Deputy Attorney General were so concerned that the Deputy Attorney General immediately initiated an FBI investigation into the delay in turning over the note....

CHAPTER FOURTEEN
"WE HAVE TO TALK FUTURE"

———————————◼———————————

THE PRESIDENT, returning from Boston, where he addressed a fundraiser (the Portuguese-American Friendship Committee) on Joe Kennedy's behalf, put down the newspaper and turned to his guest aboard Air Force One. Is there any chance, he wanted to know, that we could put together a ceremony celebrating the fiftieth anniversary of the Berlin Airlift?

STROBE TALBOTT: You mean, talk to Kohl...?

THE PRESIDENT: It's Dick Morris's idea—the President overseas, standing tall, invoking Harry Truman...

STROBE TALBOTT: I don't think... no, definitely not.

THE PRESIDENT: ...while these midgets on the Hill are up to their ears in *(expletive deleted)*, talking impeachment.

STROBE TALBOTT: Reviving memories—the Cold War, you know. I don't think the Germans or the Russians would, uh, go for it.

THE PRESIDENT: Well, it's—the basic idea is still a winner. Foreign trips—like Morris says, you really can't lose. Try to come up with— if the airlift idea won't work, see what else is out there...

● ● ●

FROM THE DAY HENRY HYDE and the Republican leadership decided to take up H. Res. 104, there was never a doubt, either on Capitol Hill or at the White House, that the bill would move through the Judiciary Committee and pass the House. The Republican leadership would never have allowed the hearings to begin had the outcome been in doubt. The decision to proceed with the hearings was in effect the decision to impeach—unless the hearings backfired badly. But there were no signs of backfire yet.

The facts, Clinton's critics believed, were already in, the case overwhelming. They quoted, with relish, British historian Paul Johnson's assessment (*The American Spectator*, May, 1998) that the Clinton administration was "the most venal in American history, alongside which the tinny corruption of the Harding years pales by comparison."

Once that harsh assessment of his presidency moved beyond the realm of conservative critics and into the American heartland, Clinton had little chance of avoiding impeachment by a Republican House. Only onetime *Crossfire* host Michael Kinsley, writing in cyberspace from an aerie in Washington state, thought otherwise, arguing in Microsoft's *Slate* of "the distinct possibility that a dozen Republican members, repelled by the tawdry machinations of their leadership, will think twice and either abstain or vote 'no'."

Closer to the ground, observers viewed impeachment as only a matter of time, of how long Hyde chose to run the hearings. Once past the committee, H. Res. 104 would be put on a fast track for an early House vote, the bill would be passed along straight party lines and sent across the Capitol, to the Senate.

It was there, in the Senate, that the decisive battle would take place—ten days to two weeks, at the most, of heated rhetoric and behind-the-scenes maneuver.

Assuming Trent Lott was able to keep his Republican troops in line, pro-impeachment forces would need thirteen additional Democratic votes to reach the super majority required to remove Bill Clinton from office. Two-thirds, sixty-seven votes.

Hyde's problem was with the Young Turks in his party who didn't seem to understand this simple arithmetic. In the end, the chairman's point of view would prevail, but it took all his powers of persuasion to convince his hot-eyed colleagues that whatever the merits of Paula Jones's case and the untold story behind Vince Foster's suicide, to include them in the Articles of Impeachment might alienate fence-straddling Democrats.

Orrin Hatch, Hyde's counterpart on the Senate side, agreed. As chairman of the Judiciary Committee, Hatch would serve as lead prosecutor in the Senate trial. Like Hyde, he believed that, given the Big Spin capability of the White House—and its friends in the media—the case against Clinton would be only as strong as its weakest link.

NBC NEWS, 8/6/98

BRIAN WILLIAMS: The House Judiciary Committee leadership today took a key step in the Republican-led effort to remove President Clinton from office in circulating an article of impeachment for alleged "abuse of power" in the so-called Travelgate and Filegate affairs of five years ago. While Chairman Henry Hyde plans not to bring any of the several expected articles to a vote until all the articles are ready, the draft of the first article gives a clear indication of Hyde's strategy. His office told NBC that the committee now plans to move into the second phase of its hearings, covering White House fund-raising efforts in the 1996 presidential campaign.

BRIEFING by White House press secretary Michael McCurry, 8/7/98

Q: What was the President's reaction to the report that Republicans on the Hyde Committee have already informally approved a first article of impeachment?

MCCURRY: He was disappointed, Helen, but not surprised. This—we might as well clear the air now because these hearings are going to be dragged out, squeezed for every headline—we're not going to respond to this on a day-to-day, hour-by-hour basis. The President will have something to say when the hearings are over. A lot to say, in fact.

Q: Has he talked to Harold Ickes lately?

MCCURRY: No, why should he? All the President wants his people—staff and former staff—to do if they're called to testify, is tell the truth and nothing but the truth...

• • •

WHITE HOUSE TRANSCRIPTION XB-672, telephone conversation, the President and Harold Ickes, Jr., 8/6/98

THE PRESIDENT: Just between—I wouldn't want this to go any farther, Harold, but I'm drowning in this *(expletive deleted)*, up to my ears in...

HAROLD ICKES, JR.: Yeah, I can imagine, with those *(expletive deleted)* on the Hill.

THE PRESIDENT: Not the Hill, that's not the problem. I could, we could handle that if I just had the right people around, someone like you, who could get his head out of his *(expletive deleted)* long enough to...

HAROLD ICKES, JR.: Well...

THE PRESIDENT: You don't have to say it, Harold, I'll say it for you. I made a mistake, big-time, probably the worst *(expletive deleted)* mistake since I've been here, letting you leave.

HAROLD ICKES, JR.: Not leave. I mean, it wasn't as if I...

THE PRESIDENT: No, no, of course not. You'd never have left if I hadn't...

HAROLD ICKES, JR.: No, I—look, don't misunderstand, but I'd just as soon not rehash all that, you know? It's history, and...

THE PRESIDENT: Yeah, well… I know where you're coming from, old buddy.

HAROLD ICKES, JR.: —it seems to me, no disrespect, but we've had this same conversation before I was scheduled to testify last summer.

THE PRESIDENT: Last summer? Jesus, to tell you the truth, I'd…

HAROLD ICKES, JR.: So why, why don't we just leave it, you know what I'm saying? Because if you're calling about my Hyde testimony…

THE PRESIDENT: Hyde testimony? You're testifying there? I had no…

HAROLD ICKES, JR.: That's my point, I'm not. They had me scheduled, along with Fowler and McLarty, but at the last minute decided they didn't need my testimony, they already had it.

THE PRESIDENT: So you're not testifying. Okay, but you see what I mean, Harold? Nobody let me know, which just proves what I've been saying. It's gone to *(expletive deleted)* around here since you left, and as soon as we put all this behind us, I think…

HAROLD ICKES, JR.: Yeah, well…

THE PRESIDENT: —we have to talk future.

CHAPTER FIFTEEN
THE CHINA SYNDROME

■

Hyde Moves to Speed Clinton Hearings
Labor Day Deadline is Set for House Impeachment Vote

—HEADLINE, *THE WASHINGTON TIMES*, 8/10/98

• • •

IT WAS ONE OF THE FEW things Republicans and Democrats on the Judiciary Committee could agree on: Voted up or voted down, the impeachment issue had to be resolved before election day. Whether pro- or anti-Clinton, the folks back home were tired of reading and hearing about scandals, investigations, charges and counter-charges. Bill Clinton's second term had become, as Charles Krauthammer described it, "a second national nightmare," and whatever the outcome—whether he survived impeachment and served out his term or left the White House in disgrace—Clinton's legacy, like Nixon's in the seventies, would be one of deep public cynicism about politics and government.

Less than a year had gone by since not one, but two separate Congressional committees had turned the subject of campaign funding inside-out, summoning White House staffers, party officials, access hustlers, contributing fatcats, contributing Buddists, contributors-with-no-visible-means-of-support—testimony that followed a money trail running from Little Rock to the Lincoln Bedroom, from the Democratic National Committee's

Washington headquarters through the Commerce Department to Beijing...

• • •

RERUN — Excerpt, Michael Kelly in *The New Republic*, 7/14/97

What matters is not whether the Chinese government sought to subvert the American electoral process. It's whether the American government sought to subvert the American electoral process. Did the White House direct a fund-raising operation intended, on a vast, knowing and systematic basis, to subvert the law? Was this operation, in its greed, so aggressively unconcerned with legality and even the appearance of ethical conduct that it signaled to the Chinese—and to others with dirty money and needful of favors—a willingness to do back-door business?...

• • •

THESE WERE THE QUESTIONS that Fred Thompson's Senate Governmental Affairs Committee had hired a small army of lawyers and investigators to answer in the summer of 1997. A few months later, Dan Burton's Government Reform and Oversight Committee had followed suit, covering much the same ground with the same cast of characters: John Huang, Charles Yah Lin Trie, Xi Ping Wang, Yue Chue, Maria Hsia, Johnny Chung, Nora and Gene Lum, Wang Jun, James Riady, Roger Tamraz, Yogesh Gandhi, Mr. Wu...

So it was that Henry Hyde, after polling the Republican members of his committee decided to forgo yet another round of extended hearings on campaign funding. As he told Larry King, the decision served two purposes: It would speed up the process while highlighting the fact that the aim of an impeachment inquest wasn't so much to gather evidence as to weigh facts already on hand.

LARRY KING LIVE, CNN, 8/11/98

LARRY KING: Henry Hyde, chairman of the House Judiciary Committee, and I'm pleased you could be with us tonight, Mr. Chairman.

HENRY HYDE: Glad to be here, Larry.

LARRY KING: I had, you know, White House spokesman Lanny Davis on a few evenings ago, right after you cancelled hearings into campaign funding. He said...

HENRY HYDE: That's not quite the way it happened, Larry. We haven't cancelled anything. We've just cut the amount of time we'll spend gathering evidence that's already...

LARRY KING: Just repeating what he said.

HENRY HYDE: Which is why I'm here—to correct any misconception his appearance may have made about the direction we're headed. The question of how much testimony we needed on this phase of the hearings has always been open, and I think Lanny Davis and the people he works for know that.

LARRY KING: By people he works for, you mean...

HENRY HYDE: President Clinton and his legal team—Charles Ruff, David Kendall, Robert Bennett...

LARRY KING: Let's back up a minute. The White House says—what Lanny Davis told us, sitting in the same chair you're sitting in—was that you cancelled hearings into campaign funding because you knew a case could be made that the Clinton-Gore campaign didn't do anything that past Republican administrations haven't done... Reagan in the eighties... Bush in 1992...

HENRY HYDE: That's White House spin, far from true. But even...

LARRY KING: Just repeating what he said.

HENRY HYDE: —if you buy that argument, keep in mind, this is the same President who arrived in Washington, January 1993—paraded in over Memorial Bridge—promising he'd give the American people the most ethical White House in history. Not "I don't do anything worse than my predecessors," but "the most ethical."

LARRY KING: Sounds like Ross Perot.

HENRY HYDE: It's what Bill Clinton said, Larry. It's on film. Look it up.

LARRY KING: No need. I'll take your word for it.

• • •

MICHAEL KELLY HAD WRITTEN of what he called "the China syndrome"—the corruption of the American electoral process by a foreign government, with the winking connivance of a White House "aggressively unconcerned with legality."

That alone, borne out as it was by a flood of evidence in the Thompson-Burton hearings, would be enough to support impeachment. More than enough, thought the Chairman, reflecting on how far the country had come since his younger days, when "White House scandal" meant an Eisenhower aide's leaving office in disgrace for accepting a vicuna coat for his wife.

• • •

TESTIMONY OF SAMUEL (SANDY) BERGER, 8/1/98

HENRY HYDE: Good morning. Before we get underway, I have a brief statement to make about the second phase of these hearings, in which we intend to hear testimony regarding alleged illegalities that occurred in fund-raising activities in and around the Clinton White House during the period 1993-96.

First, the committee yesterday decided by majority vote to incorporate into its final report all findings made by the House and Senate committees that looked into these matters last year. Second, for the guidance of the news media, following this phase we intend to go into a third and final phase, covering allegations of possible obstruction of justice regarding investigations into Whitewater and related matters... Counsel?

THOMAS MOONEY, SR.: Thank you, Mr. Chairman... Mr. Berger, we have your testimony before the Burton and Thompson committees last year, when you were assistant to the President for national security affairs. During the time frame we're looking at—1992 through 1996—you were, I believe, deputy assistant, is that correct?

SANDY BERGER: Yes, under Tony Lake.

THOMAS MOONEY: So you're familiar then with the area of fund-raising we're most interested in—the efforts of foreign governments and nationals to gain access to the President and other members of his administration for the purpose of shaping, or at least influencing U.S. foreign policy.

SANDY BERGER: Yes, though I don't know that there's anything I can add to my previous testimony on the subject.

THOMAS MOONEY: You have no opening statement, then.

SANDY BERGER: None, other than to repeat what I've said before: At no time, to my knowledge as a member of the White House staff concerned with national security, have the interests or security of the United States ever been compromised or jeopardized by the President as a result of campaign contributions or the promise of campaign contributions.

THOMAS MOONEY: To your knowledge—would you expand on that a bit, Mr. Berger. A few questions...

SANDY BERGER: Yes, sir.

THOMAS MOONEY: You're familiar—we're all familiar by now—with the varied activities of John Huang, who it's fair to say emerged as a central figure, if not the central figure, in last year's hearings.

SANDY BERGER: I know Mr. Huang—knew him—but only on a casual basis. I didn't, frankly, pay that much attention to him.

THOMAS MOONEY: Do I understand you to say that you weren't aware of John Huang's employment by the Lippo Group, his ties to Indonesia, and his special interest in China?

SANDY BERGER: If I was, Mr. Mooney, it would have been only a peripheral awareness. Mr. Huang was simply one person seen around the White House from time to time, and my responsibilities were such that—just say, they precluded giving special consideration to any one individual. Other than the President, of course.

THOMAS MOONEY: What about Eric Hotung?

SANDY BERGER: You already have my answer to that, Mr. Mooney, in the testimony I gave last summer. Mr. Hotung was a Hong Kong businessman who offered a special insight into the situation in that area.

THOMAS MOONEY: And he wanted to pass that special insight, as you call it, on to the President or someone who had direct access to the President. Is that why you met with him?

SANDY BERGER: He wanted to meet with someone and present his views, yes.

THOMAS MOONEY: You describe Mr. Hotung, I believe, as a Hong Kong businessman. Wouldn't Hong Kong billionaire be more accurate?

SANDY BERGER: He was—at least I was told—a very successful businessman, yes.

THOMAS MOONEY: Who, according to the record, contributed $100,000 to the Democratic National Committee, is that correct?

SANDY BERGER: Again, I went over that last year, Mr. Mooney, and my answer now is the same as it was then. At the time I met with Mr. Hotung, I was unaware—and for that matter disinterested—in any political contribution he may have made to the Democratic National Committee, or anyone else.

THOMAS MOONEY: You were unaware...

SANDY BERGER: Only after I met with him, and only through reading about it in the papers, did I become aware of it.

THOMAS MOONEY: Who then suggested that you meet with Mr. Hotung? I assume you didn't, don't have time to meet with every successful foreign entrepreneur with special insights.

SANDY BERGER: Who suggested...?

THOMAS MOONEY: Was he referred through the State Department? The CIA? Some other foreign policy agency?

SANDY BERGER: I believe—as I've said before, to the best of my recollection—the reference came through Doug Sosnik.

THOMAS MOONEY: Douglas Sosnik—the White House political affairs staff, correct? Did Sosnik specialize, was he an expert on foreign affairs in Mr. Hotung's part of the world? What I'm trying to determine, Mr. Berger, is why you, a senior member of the President's foreign policy apparatus, would take the recommendation of a domestic political aide regarding who to listen to about foreign policy matters. Can you enlighten the committee on that point?

SANDY BERGER: All I can do, Mr. Mooney, is repeat that my meeting with Mr. Hotung had nothing to do with any contribution to the DNC, nothing whatsoever.

HENRY HYDE: Excuse me, Counsel... Mr. Berger, I think what Counsel is asking is the reason you did meet with Mr. Hotung, not the reason you didn't. If, as you say, it wasn't because he happened to be a big contributor, then what was it? Since the request came from the White House political office, didn't that raise some question in your mind? An inkling, perhaps...

SANDY BERGER: No sir. Doug Sosnik was a member of the White House staff for whom I had, have the utmost respect, and to my mind his request was both reasonable and appropriate.

HENRY HYDE: You're evading the question, Mr. Berger. Whatever your respect for Mr. Sosnik, what we're trying to get at here is the modus operandi of the Clinton White House regarding domestic politics, on one hand, mixing it with foreign policy on the other. You've been around Washington for some time, sir, you know how things operate around here as well or better than anyone in this room.

SANDY BERGER: I take that—I assume that's meant as a compliment, Congressman. (*Audience laughter*)

HENRY HYDE: Indeed it is, Mr. Berger. The country's fortunate to have someone with your experience looking after our foreign policy interests at the White House—which is why we're puzzled about your meeting with Mr. Hotung. Let's be frank...

SANDY BERGER: By all means, Mr. Chairman.

HENRY HYDE: When a call comes in from the White House political office—not State, not CIA, but the political office—to set up a meeting with a wealthy businessman, an experienced Washington hand doesn't have to think too long to figure out what's going on. I have a memorandum here—thank you, Counsel—a memorandum, September 20, 1995, just prior to your meeting with Mr. Hotung. It's from Democratic National Committee Co-Chairman Don Fowler to Doug Sosnik—are you familiar with it?

SANDY BERGER: I can't say...

HENRY HYDE: It has to do with your meeting—Fowler to the White House, and here's what he said: After describing Mr. Hotung's special interest in U.S.-China relations, Fowler writes, "Mr. Hotung has several policy options that he would like to suggest for consideration by administration officials." Unquote. And following this memorandum, Sosnik called you, and you met with Mr. Hotung. And after his meeting with you, he also had a private session with the top White House intelligence expert on Asia, Robert Suettinger. You're aware of that, aren't you?

SANDY BERGER: Somewhat.

HENRY HYDE: Somewhat?

SANDY BERGER: By that I mean, since my meeting with Mr. Hotung took place some three years ago, any recollection I have is vague. The meeting wasn't unusual, and the idea that he might have met with Bob Suettinger afterward...

HENRY HYDE: Not unusual? We said we'd be frank, Mr. Berger, one old Washington hand to another, so let me ask a question that doesn't call on your memory, only your experience: Do you think Eric Hotung would have been granted an audience with the number-two man at NSC, yourself, and the number-one intelligence expert on Asia, Mr. Suettinger, if he hadn't contributed $100,000 to the Democratic National Committee?

JOHN CONYERS: I see we're back to asking hypotheticals.

HENRY HYDE: If you will, Mr. Conyers, let's give Mr. Berger a chance to answer, because the question goes to the heart of the problem raised during last year's hearings and to what the American people want to know—need to know: Does money buy access to American foreign policy, to the decision-makers who shape that policy in the Clinton White House? Mr. Berger?

SANDY BERGER: Your question, Mr. Chairman, if I understand it correctly, is whether I would have met with Mr. Hotung had he not been a campaign contributor...

HENRY HYDE: Correct.

SANDY BERGER: —and my answer remains, that at the time I met with Mr. Hotung I had no idea he was a contributor.

HENRY HYDE: That's not what I asked, Mr. Berger. The fact that you didn't know he was a contributor is irrelevant. What's relevant here is that someone at the top level—Don Fowler at the DNC, Sosnik at the White House—did in fact know, and proceeded to set up the meeting as a matter of routine. So whether you knew or were simply being used, the result was the same. The contribution was made, the meeting took place, quid pro quo.

SANDY BERGER: That's not—I don't see myself, Mr. Chairman, as being used, at any time.

HENRY HYDE: Well, somebody was, Mr. Berger. We're not just talking about White House coffee sessions—$50,000 to rub shoulders and shake hands with the President, which is bad enough—but one-on-one meetings between a Hong Kong billionaire with an axe to grind and President Clinton's top foreign policy advisers. When access is bought and sold at that level—when it comes at $100,000 a meeting, somebody or something is being used... No further questions... Mr. Conyers?

JOHN CONYERS: May I take a look at that memorandum?

HENRY HYDE: Certainly.

JOHN CONYERS: Just to find out if it's the smoking gun it's made out to be.

HENRY HYDE: No one claimed it was a smoking gun, only that it reflects the way this White House mixes politics into foreign...

JOHN CONYERS: A pop gun then. It makes a noise, but on examination, you find out that's all there is—noise. I see here, Don Fowler asks the White House to give Mr. Hutong—Hotung—a hearing, to listen to any ideas the man might have in any area of the world where, God knows, we need all the ideas we can get. So what?

BOB BARR: So what?

JOHN CONYERS: My time, Congressman—I repeat, so what? Does anyone who's been around Washington—anyone with the experience our colleague talks about—seriously doubt that when George Bush was President, Haley Barbour was sending this kind of request over from the Republican National Committee?

HENRY HYDE: I doubt it, seriously. Haley Barbour wasn't at the

Republican National Committee when George Bush was President.

BARNEY FRANK: Lee Atwater.

JOHN CONYERS: Right, Lee Atwater then.

BOB BARR: If you have a letter to that effect, Atwater to Bush, Mr. Conyers, let's see it. Otherwise...

HENRY HYDE (GAVELING): In order, Mr. Barr, you'll have your chance. Mr. Conyers, the witness...

JOHN CONYERS: I have just one question, and it's to the point—Mr. Berger, tell us, if you will, in the time you spent with Mr. Hotung— did the man ask, even hint, that he wanted something in return for any contribution he might have made?

SANDY BERGER: No, sir. I don't recall everything that was said, it was several years ago—but on that point I can answer unequivocally, no. Nothing like that ever came up...

• • •

BILL MCCOLLUM: Mr. Berger, would you tell the committee what you know about the President's Foreign Intelligence Advisory Board? You're familiar with the board, I'm sure.

SANDY BERGER: Yes, though I can't claim to be an expert on how it operates. It's, as I understand, an independent body made up of private citizens who provide the President with advice and counsel on foreign intelligence matters.

BILL MCCOLLUM: Would you say it rendered a substantial service... that is, played a substantive role in advising the President, or is it just one of those boards that takes up space in the Federal Register?

SANDY BERGER: As I've said, I'm not that familiar with how the board operates, but yes, to my understanding, it's substantial.

BILL McCOLLUM: And in past administrations, Democratic, Republican, it's been made up of substantial foreign policy, intelligence experts. Is that correct?

SANDY BERGER: I'd have to see a list, but in general, yes. I think that would be the case, not only in the past but today.

BILL McCOLLUM: Well, that being the case, Mr. Berger, could you enlighten us on the foreign intelligence qualifications of two current members of the board, appointed by President Clinton...

SANDY BERGER: I'm not...

BILL McCOLLUM: ...one Stanley Shuman and one Richard Bloch?

SANDY BERGER: Mr. McCollum, I make no claim to knowing the qualifications of each and every person appointed to this or any other board, but I'd be happy to get and forward that information.

BILL McCOLLUM: I'd appreciate that, Mr. Berger, though I can save you some time. What you'll find on checking Mr. Shuman's qualifications is that he'a New York investment banker with no, absolutely no background in the foreign intelligence field, and the same is true of Mr. Bloch, whose experience lies exclusively in the field of Texas real estate investment. But the two do have one distinction in common. Would you like to know what it is?

SANDY BERGER: Well—yes, I guess—could you repeat the question?

BILL McCOLLUM: The question, Mr. Berger, is, what do these two Clinton appointees to the Foreign Intelligence Advisory Board— Stanley Shuman, a New York investor, and Richard Bloch, a Texas real estate operator—have in common that brought them to the President's attention? And the answer, Mr. Berger, is that like our friend Mr. Hotung, they both made $100,000 contributions to the Democratic National Committee. In Mr. Shuman's case, in fact, he got what you might call a two-fer. An appointment to a board for which he is totally unqualified, along with one of those overnight stays in the Lincoln Bedroom. But I guess, as in the Hotung case, you're not familiar any of that.

SANDY BERGER: No, sir, I am not.

BILL MCCOLLUM: Who contributes and what they receive in return, that's none of your concern, is it, Mr. Berger. Like everyone else in the White House, see no evil, hear no...

CHARLES SCHUMER: Mr. Chairman...

BILL MCCOLLUM: Thank you, Mr. Berger. No further questions, Mr. Chairman.

• • •

CHARLES SCHUMER: Thank you for being with us today, Mr. Berger, and let me congratulate you for the manner in which you've represented yourself and the White House...

SANDY BERGER: I appreciate that, Mr. Schumer.

CHARLES SCHUMER: —under adverse circumstances. I have only one question, and I ask it in order to cut through the partisan rhetoric, and separate fact from fiction about American foreign policy interests in a world fraught with danger. Bottom line, Mr. Berger: In all your years as an observer, an expert on American foreign policy, can you recall any period—any period—in which this country's prestige was ever higher and the prospects for lasting peace more promising than they've been in the past five years?

SANDY BERGER: No, Mr. Schumer, I can't.

CHARLES SCHUMER: Thank you, Mr. Berger. And keep up—regardless of partisan carping, keep up the good work.

CHAPTER SIXTEEN
A VOICE-ACTUATED
ELECTRONIC SYSTEM

---■---

SMOKING GUN: Along with John Dean's "cancer on the presidency," it became the metaphor-of-choice during the final phase of the Watergate hearings, and John Conyer's use of the term was enough to send Bob Barr back to the books during the committee's midday recess. Barr had originally planned to take time to review his notes prior to questioning Sandy Berger in the afternoon session. Instead he spent his lunch hour re-reading the Watergate Committee testimony of Alexander Butterfield.

More than Woodward and Bernstein, it was Butterfield, a White House military aide, who had uncovered the incriminating weapon that doomed the Nixon presidency. Answering a late-in-the-day question from young Fred Thompson, then Minority Counsel for the Watergate Committee, Butterfield told of the voice-actuated electronic system that provided the President with an aural record of every conversation that took place in the Oval Office.

To Bob Barr, already struck by the irony of Bill and Hillary Clinton's moving step-by-step down the road Nixon had travelled, the only thing surprising about the idea the Clinton White House would have a similar system was that it hadn't occurred to him before.

Within hours, the Chairman approving, a subpoena *duces tecum*, for tapes, discs and other aural devices was served on Counsel Charles Ruff at the White House. For Ruff, who had been the last independent counsel in the Watergate case a quarter-century before, it was a matter of coming full-circle.

CHAPTER SEVENTEEN
FRIENDSHIP

■

RERUN — Excerpt, Associated Press, 6/12/97

Congressman Says Evidence Shows Fund-raiser Breached Security

BY JOHN SOLOMON

A key congressman says electronic intercepts confirm that former Clinton administration official and Democratic fund-raiser John Huang "committed economic espionage" by passing government secrets to his previous Asian-based employer.

House Rules Committee Chairman Gerald Solomon, R-N.Y., said he confirmed with government officials that the intercepts substantiated that Huang passed classified information to the Lippo Group, which is based in Indonesia but has substantial dealings with China....

Huang, who has emerged as a central figure in the growing investigation into political fund-raising abuses, had access to top-secret information as a political appointee at the Commerce Department in 1994 and 1995. He left last year, with President Clinton's blessing, to raise money for the Democratic Party.

"I have received reports from government sources that say there are electronic intercepts which provide evidence confirming what I suspected all along, that John Huang committed economic espionage and breached our national security by passing classified information to his former employer, the Lippo Group," Solomon said in a statement Wednesday night....

Huang has been under investigation since disclosures that his calendars and phone records indicated he had contact with his former Lippo employer or Chinese Embassy officials in close proximity to days in which he received classified information as a deputy assistant commerce secretary....

Commerce officials have previously confirmed that Huang attended a total of 109 meetings at which classified information may have been discussed, including 37 intelligence briefings....

[Huang's] access included "classified information at the White House" and "State Department message traffic through a computer network at the Commerce Department...."

Huang has declined to produce certain documents to congressional investigators, citing his Fifth Amendment right against self-incrimination....

Before joining Commerce, Huang was the chief of U.S. operations for Lippo.

The Associated Press reported in January that Huang had made or received calls from Lippo at the Commerce Department on or around days he had received intelligence briefings....

Huang had top-secret clearance six months before he actually got his Commerce job, and his security clearance wasn't officially revoked until a year after he left the job....

RERUN — Excerpt, *The Chicago Sun-Times*, 4/21/97

Senior Security Aide Briefed Dem Donors

BY LYNN SWEET

... Papers released last week by the DNC list Nancy Soderberg, deputy assistant to the president for national security affairs, as a speaker at two Washington Issues Conferences sponsored in June and September, 1995, for the Democratic Business Council.

The latest disclosures will add to the

controversy regarding the NSC and the Democratic Party and will raise again the issue of whether U.S. foreign policy was influenced by campaign contributors....

A DNC memo included in the documents lists Soderberg, the No. 3 person at the NSC, as a guest at a June 20, 1994, DNC donor dinner where she was to be seated at a table with Huang and James Riady, an Indonesian business executive who once employed Huang. Johnson said Soderberg had the dinner on her calendar but was not sure if she actually attended the event....

RERUN — Excerpt, *The New York Times,* 3/20/97

Asian Paid $100,000 to Hubbell Days After Visits to White House

BY STEPHEN LABATON AND JEFF GERTH

In late June of 1994, the Indonesian businessman James T. Riady saw President Clinton and some of his aides in five days of White House visits ending on a Saturday. Early the next week, one of Mr. Riady's Hong Kong companies paid about $100,000 to Webster L. Hubbell, the President's close friend, who was then facing a rapidly unfolding criminal investigation, according to people in the United States and abroad familiar with the arrangement....

Mr. Riady's visits to the White House have been known for some time, and it was recently disclosed that he paid Mr. Hubbell about $100,000 through the Hong Kong company in 1994 for services that the two men have repeatedly declined to describe. But it has not been previously known how closely that payment followed Mr. Riady's White House visits....

• • •

TESTIMONY OF SAMUEL (SANDY) BERGER, (continued)

BOB BARR: I also want to thank the witness for being here today, because it gives the committee a chance to hear someone associated with this administration's foreign policy saying something other than "I refuse to testify"... how many of them have we had, to date?

THOMAS MOONEY, SR.: Eleven.

BOB BARR: Eleven—and that's not counting the gun-merchant Wang Jun, Charlie Trie, the ones overseas we can't bring in... Incredible... Mr. Berger, if I heard you right, you said earlier that you didn't know John Huang well, that as far as you were concerned he was just an apparition who passed through the West Wing from time to time...

SANDY BERGER: An apparition?

BOB BARR: My way of making a point, because, you know, we deposed one of your former NSC colleagues earlier, Nancy Soderberg. She was also a deputy assistant to the President for national security affairs in the first Clinton administration, was she not?

SANDY BERGER: Yes, sir.

BOB BARR: And she's since, I believe, been appointed to another post. But in June, 1994, Ms. Soderberg was at the White House, the NSC, and according to documents released by the Democratic National Committee, attended a fund-raising dinner where she was seated at a table with John Huang and his boss at the Lippo Group, James Riady. You're aware of that, I assume.

SANDY BERGER: Yes, sir, though I wasn't at the time.

BOB BARR: Well, obviously she wasn't either—or claims she wasn't—because when we asked Ms. Soderberg about that fund-raiser, whether she was there, seated between Huang and Riady, her answer was that she had—I'm quoting—"no reason to believe she did not attend." So you see what I mean by "apparition."

SANDY BERGER: Not quite, Congressman.

BOB BARR: She was there, but she wasn't there. On the order of "I smoked, but I didn't inhale."

BARNEY FRANK: Cheap shot.

BOB BARR: There's nothing cheap about it, Mr. Frank. We're talking about a fund-raising dinner at $1,500-a-plate, where a top presidential adviser on foreign affairs is at a table as a guest of two men charged with—alleged to be part of a multi-million-dollar scheme to influence this country's foreign policy.

SANDY BERGER: I don't understand your question, Mr. Barr. Are you asking whether I can verify whether Ms. Soderberg was at the dinner?

BOB BARR: No, sir. Ms. Soderberg's presence isn't in question. We know she was there with Riady and Huang, at a time when the Clinton White House was in a full-court press to get Hubbell on the Lippo payroll.

SANDY BERGER: Mr. Barr, you're speaking of something about which I have no knowledge.

BOB BARR: No knowledge of the fact that Riady put Hubbell on his payroll, a $100,000 retainer, with more to come, for, as *The New York Times* put it, "services the two men have repeatedly declined to describe"?

SANDY BERGER: No, sir.

BOB BARR: What about your knowledge, then—what do you know, Mr. Berger, about meetings, at least three, in the Oval Office, between Mr. Riady and the President during the same period?

SANDY BERGER: My knowledge? Unless a meeting related to my area, national security, there was no reason for me to have any specific knowledge of who the President was meeting on any particular day.

BOB BARR: Even if the meeting involved a discussion of China policy? Extending most-favored-nation trade privileges to Beijing? I'd think that would be a matter, as you put it, related to your area.

SANDY BERGER: It would be, but I had, and have, no reason to believe that was—let me understand what we're talking about here: Are you saying that China's MFN status was the subject of the President's meeting with James Riady?

BOB BARR: No, not entirely. We can assume there was some time taken to discuss Webb Hubbell's retainer. But we know, Mr. Berger—and surely by this time you know as well—that James Riady took every opportunity in his meetings with President Clinton to press his point of view, his interest in matters relating to U.S. policy toward China. And we also know...

SANDY BERGER: May I respond to that, Congressman?

BOB BARR: Yes, I'd like to hear your response.

SANDY BERGER: Let me assure you, Mr. Barr, along with other members of this committee and Congress as a whole, let me assure you that the decision to extend China's MFN status had nothing to do with campaign contributions but was made on the merits of the case.

BOB BARR: That's good to know, Mr. Berger, but let me respond by pointing out we're talking about something else—not the merits of China's trade status, but the perception, sowed and encouraged by the Clinton White House, that American foreign policy was, as they say in high finance, in play. Perception, Mr. Berger. Wouldn't you say that the way our country is perceived in foreign capitals is crucial to America's role as a world leader?

SANDY BERGER: That depends on your definition—it's important, yes.

BOB BARR: If, for example, the word around foreign capitals is that American foreign policy is for sale—don't worry about what they claim they stand for, their leaders can be bought—if we're perceived in that light, isn't it true that would compromise our interests and security?

SANDY BERGER: If that were the case, Mr. Barr, it certainly would. But the picture you paint—the situation you describe isn't accurate. With all due respect, Congressman, it's a distortion.

HENRY HYDE: The gentleman from Georgia's time...

BOB BARR: Only a few more questions.

BILL JENKINS (R-TN): Mr. Chairman, I yield time to my good neighbor from Georgia.

BOB BARR: I thank the gentleman from Tennessee... You were saying, Mr. Berger, that there's no perception overseas that the White House can be bought.

SANDY BERGER: That's right, Congressman.

BOB BARR: Isn't it true, however, that all your colleagues at the NSC don't—didn't share your opinion? You colleague Sheila Heslin, for example. She saw the possibility, the risk that the Oval Office itself could be viewed as a place foreign operators could buy their way into. Isn't that right?

SANDY BERGER: My former colleague.

BOB BARR: Yes, former colleague. Ms. Heslin left the White House, but not before objecting strenuously—too strenuously to suit her political higher-ups—to President Clinton's meeting with Roger Tamraz in March of 1996. As a matter of fact, at last summer's Thompson Committee hearings...

SANDY BERGER: I'm aware of all that, Mr. Barr.

BOB BARR: Aware that Tamraz contributed $200,000 to the Democratic National Committee, and was rewarded with a one-on-one talk with the President of the United States at a White House dinner? A talk involving a Turkish pipeline...

JOHN CONYERS: That's what the witness just said—he's aware of all that.

BOB BARR: Aware. Mr. Conyers, but it obviously hasn't registered with the witness the way it did with Sheila Heslin. She seems to have been the only person in Bill Clinton's White House to understand that an operator like Roger Tamraz—a man wanted in Lebanon for embezzling $150 million—had no business being in the White House, buying access to the President. Let me ask, Mr. Berger, weren't the same facts at your disposal, regarding Roger Tamraz.

SANDY BERGER: The same facts...?

BOB BARR: The same information Ms. Heslin was working from. Why didn't you join her, take a stand, draw the line on mixing foreign policy with political fund-raising?

SANDY BERGER: In retrospect, Mr. Barr, given hindsight, it's clear that someone with as many questions surrounding him as Roger Tamraz should never have been...

BOB BARR: I'm familiar with that answer, Mr. Berger, we've heard it from this White House too many times—mistakes were made, if we had it to do over again... But in this instance—let me use an old Georgia expression to say, that dog won't hunt. Sheila Heslin didn't need hindsight to see what was going on, to know it was wrong.

SANDY BERGER: Mr. Barr, it's obvious you've already made up your mind, and aren't interested in anything I have to say on the subject.

BOB BARR: No, sir. It's simply that I'd prefer direct answers. Did you or did you not have information on hand that Roger Tamraz was using his $200,000 access to the White House—five visits in four months—to persuade Turkish officials that he had President Clinton's approval for his pipeline deal?

SANDY BERGER: If you'll check the record, you'll find that we took immediate steps to correct any misconception in that regard.

BOB BARR: Is that your answer?

SANDY BERGER: Yes, sir.

BOB BARR: Then you've just made my point. The word was out in foreign capitals—in this case, Ankara—that money bought access to the Clinton White House, and it affected the way we were perceived in foreign capitals. Tell us, was there a price list? One hundred thousand buys a one-on-one with Sandy Berger, $200,000 with Bill Clinton...?

RERUN — Excerpt, *The Washington Post*, 4/29/97

Democratic Fund-raiser Pursues Agenda on Sudan

BY DAVID B. OTTAWAY

Mansoor Ijaz, a 35-year-old businessman, was precisely the kind of political activist the White House was seeking last year to help finance President Clinton's reelection campaign.

Wealthy and well-connected, Ijaz was more than willing to pitch in. By Election Day in November, he had raised $525,000 for the Democratic cause, including $250,000 from his personal funds and $200,000 donated by guests at a fund-raising reception for Vice President Gore at Ijaz's New York penthouse in September, according to Federal Election Commission records, White House documents and Ijaz.

Now Ijaz is truing to reap what he has sown. Having earned access to the Clinton administration through his fund-raising prowess, Ijaz has met with a succession of senior officials in the White House, State Department and Congress to further his business interests through changes in U.S. policy toward Islamic countries, particularly Sudan, a government long accused of sanctioning international terrorism.

Much of the 1996 campaign fund-raising controversy has centered on questions about big donors currying influence and gaining access to administration officials. Ijaz's case illustrates the blurring of lines between fund-raising and the pursuit of personal political financial agendas by those whose donations helped finance Clinton's reelection.

Since last summer, Ijaz has worked relentlessly to broker a reconciliation between the United States and Sudan, an emerging African oil producer the Clinton administration has sought to isolate because of Khartoum's alleged support for international terrorism.

In half-a-dozen trips to Khartoum since July, Ijaz repeatedly has met with Sudan's president, Lt. Gen. Omar Hassan Bashir, and the country's militant Islamic leader, Hassan Turabi, advising them on how to soften the Clinton administration's position, according to Sudanese officials, Ijaz and U.S. officials familiar with his activities.

During that period, Ijaz also met

with senior White House and State Department officials—including Samuel R. "Sandy" Berger, now national security adviser—to urge a policy toward Sudan of "constructive engagement," which would include enlisting Turabi's help in curbing international terrorists. A White House spokesman confirmed Berer's meeting with Ijaz last August and said the businessman had provided helpful "insight."

Ijaz, who displays photographs in his New York office of himself with Clinton and Gore, acknowledged during six hours of interviews the leverage his fund-raising provided in gaining "political prominence" in Washington for the advancement of his causes.

Ijaz also acknowledged his commercial interests in effecting a reconciliation between the United States and Sudan. As chairman of Crescent Investment Management, a New York firm that he said handles a $2.7 billion investment portfolio—much of it on behalf of Middle East governments— Ijaz said he is particularly interested in new oil field development. Sudan, with moderate reserves estimated at 3.5 billion barrels, is expected to become a petroleum exporter soon and Ijaz said he hopes to manage some of Khartoum's foreign investment of oil profits...

[Ijaz] began pressing his case for better relations with Khartoum after Congress last spring banned all financial transactions between U.S. companies and Sudan as a punitive measure...

When the regulations were published in late August, the administration effectively gutted the prohibition by allowing a broad range of financial transactions by U.S. businesses dealing with Sudan...*

• • •

"Friendship."

—HAROLD ARTHUR, CHAIRMAN OF THE BOARD, LIPPO BANK, LOS ANGELES, on being asked why James Riady would contribute $800,000 to Clinton-Gore and other Democratic campaigns, quoted in The Washington Times, 8/10/97

---

* The Ottaway article, in its entirety, was made part of the Committee record at Mr. Barr's request, and included as evidence in support of Articles III and IV of the House Bill of Impeachment.

CHAPTER EIGHTEEN
MRS. CLINTON'S WATERGATE EXPERIENCE

■

AFTER HEARING NINE WITNESSES and taking as many depositions, the committee rounded out the fund-raising phase of its inquiry by calling two Arkansas members of the Clinton staff: Assistant to the President Bruce Lindsey and White House aide Marsha Scott. Lindsey would defend the President's dialing-for-dollars from the White House, as well as the use of Lincoln bedroom sleep-overs and $50,000-a-guest coffees to raise an estimated $37 million in contributions between 1993 and 1996.

Henry Hyde knew that though some of the fund-raising coffees had included convicted felons on their guest lists,* the Clintons' use of White House facilities for political purposes had precedents going back to the early days of the Republic. He could already hear Clinton defenders, from Arthur Schlesinger, Jr., to James Carville, rising in populist wrath to compare the incumbent's citizen-sleep-overs with Andrew Jackson's open-house policy for inaugural visitors.

No matter, thought the chairman: Bringing Lindsey, Bill Clinton's closest friend and confidant, before the cameras had made crystal clear the fact that if, as Johnny Chung said, "the White House is a subway" requiring "coins to open the gate," the chief gatekeeper was the President himself.

---

*Two examples: Eric Wynn, a New York stock promoter convicted of criminal securities fraud, bought his way into the White House to share a Starbucks hour with the President on December 21, 1995; Jorge "Gordito" Cabrera, convicted of a series of drug-dealing crimes, as well as income-tax evasion, was another 1995 guest, his photograph taken with Mrs. Clinton and Vice President Gore after he made sizable contributions to the DNC. Asked by Hyde how these and other major felons could gain direct access to the President, Vice President and First Lady, Lindsey blamed "over-zealous DNC employees" for the "administrative slip-ups."

As for Scott, she had forwarded the idea—endorsed by the First Lady—of linking the White House database with the Democratic National Committee's computer operation in fund-raising. Though only a mid-level staffer, she, like Lindsey, was close to the Clintons, and her testimony would provide direct evidence linking the President, through his wife, to a fund-raising gambit in clear violation of the law.

TESTIMONY OF MARSHA SCOTT, 8/6/98

THOMAS MOONEY: ... We have the testimony, Ms. Scott, of Mrs. Clinton's chief of staff, Margaret Williams, regarding campaign fund-taking—not fund-raising but taking—in the White House, $50,000 from Johnny Chung, which she claims she took on behalf of the DNC. We also know that DNC employees were illegally placed in White House jobs. So the question I'm asking—was your memorandum recommending DNC use of the White House database...

MARSHA SCOTT: I'll say it again, sir—I did not recommend it, I simply pointed out they might be made compatible.

THOMAS MOONEY: All right, whatever you choose to call it—the thrust of your memorandum to Mrs. Clinton was the commingling of information—names, addresses, data—from the White House database with that of the DNC, was it not?

MARSHA SCOTT: Commingling?

THOMAS MOONEY: A legal term, Ms. Scott, generally meaning the mixing of two or more things that shouldn't, under the law, be combined, like operating an official government office while soliciting or taking outside money. What Ms. Williams did was in vio-

---

(Top) Memo to Clinton's secretary from the DNC spelling out how the White House could help fundraising by hosting gatherings with the President.
(Bottom) On the right, Clinton's enthusiastic response to the memo. Clinton even adds that he wants "to start overnights [for top contributors] right away." On the left, Clinton's secretary has translated his handwriting.

DEMOCRATIC NATIONAL COMMITTEE DNC
David Wilhelm, Chairman

Do you want me to pursue #1 w/ Betsy #2 w/ the colleen #3 HANDLED Run it all by KW

January 5, 1993

MEMORANDUM TO   NANCY HERNREICH
FROM: TERRY McAULIFFE
                 NATIONAL FINANCE CHAIRMAN

During my recent meeting with the President, we discussed the following projects:

1. I would like three dates over the next month, about one week apart, for breakfast, lunch or coffee with the President and about twenty of our major supporters. The purpose of these meetings would be to offer these people an opportunity to discuss issues and exchange ideas with the President. This will be an excellent way to energize our key people for the upcoming year. We would need one hour of the President's time for each of these meetings. These individuals will come in to Washington from across the country.

2. The following individuals are our ten top supporters: — *OVERNIGHTS*

        John Connelly
        Carl Lindner
        Skip Hayward
        Miguel Lausell
        Arthur Coia
        Finn Casperson
        Paul Montrone
        Larry Hawkins
        Stan Shuman
        Ernie Greene

3. Finally, if there are any opportunities to include some of our key supporters in some of the President's activities, such as golf games, morning jogs, etc., it would be greatly appreciated.

*Yes, pursue all 3
and promptly —
and get other names
at 100,000 or more
50,000 or more
cc: Harold L Panetta Webster
ready to start overnight
right away —
give me the top
10 list back
along w/ the 100, 50, etc.*

*yes pursue
3 and promptly —
and get other in.
at 100,000 or more
50,000 or more —
cc: Hilda, L Panetta, or Webster
ready to start overnights
right away —
give me the top 10 list
back, along w/ the 100, 50 form.*

lation of Title 18, Section 607 of the U.S. Code. What your memorandum suggested, the use of federal facilities or equipment for
political purposes, was in violation of...

MARSHA SCOTT: That's not—I did not, let me make this clear, I did
not commingle, violate...

HENRY HYDE: Nobody's saying you did, Ms. Scott. We're talking
about the people you work for, in this case the First Lady. All that
counsel's trying to say, driving at, is that while you and Margaret
Williams may not be familiar with the statutes, the meaning of
commingling, a lawyer should. Especially a lawyer with Mrs.
Clinton's Watergate experience...

• • •

Tapes? What Tapes?
—FRONT-PAGE HEADLINE, *THE NEW YORK POST*, 8/14/98

White House Denies President Taped Oval Office Visitors
—HEADLINE, *THE WASHINGTON POST*, SAME DAY

White House Confirms "Limited" Taping of Oval Office Visitors
—HEADLINE, *THE WASHINGTON POST*, 8/29/98

(Opposite page) Hillary Clinton's notation on this confidential White House memo
to Harold Ickes and Marsha Scott—"This sounds promising. Please advise"—
revealed her knowledge and support of the taxpayer-financed database that kept track
of political and financial supporters.

Document 10

THE WHITE HOUSE

WASHINGTON

CONFIDENTIAL

MEMORANDUM TO:　　　　Harold Ickes
　　　　　　　　　　　　Bruce Lindsey
　　cc　　　　　　　　　The First Lady

FROM:　　　　　　　　　Marsha Scott

DATE:　　　　　　　　　June 28, 1994

SUBJECT:　　　　　　　Recommendation for Design of New Database

As you know, over the past year I and my staff have had extensive interaction with Percy's people and their system in Arkadelphia. We spent two days in Arkadelphia working with their people to learn their operation and software capabilities. Our technicians have worked regularly with their designers. In order to obtain lists for various functions and projects, I have requested from the PeopleBase system, many different types of information with varying time frames for turnaround time. (If you need specifics, I will be glad to provide the documentation). My overall impression is that while he has made some improvements, Percy's system and staff cannot adequately meet our quality or response demands and should not be considered for future use.

Currently in the White House we are preparing, as you know, to implement a new database system starting August 1. While that system is modeled after the PeopleBase software, it has major differences. The main differences are ease of use, function flexibility and correction capabilities. By the first of the year we should have any flaws identified and corrected and the majority of the White House using the new system. We will then have a year to fully train and familiarize our folks to its' many possibilities and uses. If they like it, as they seem to now, they will use it. The PeopleBase system was not used during the campaign because it was not user friendly. For the most part, only people from the Governor's staff used it. While I feel the new system far surpasses PeopleBase as a useful tool, it will be technically compatible with PeopleBase.

My team and I are also engaged in conversations with the DNC about the new system they are proposing. We have asked that their system be modeled after whatever system we decide to use outside the White House. I need you to make very clear to them that their system must be technologically compatible, if not the same, as whatever system we decide to use for political purposes later on. These discussions are currently in progress, and a clear directive from you to the DNC will eliminate much misunderstanding in the future.

The time to act is now. Cloning or duplicating database systems is not difficult if carefully planned by a good design team. We have proven that it can also be done relatively quickly and inexpensively. Therefore, I suggest that instead of continuing with an old outdated system (PeopleBase) that does not meet our current demands, let my team work with the DNC to help them design a system that will meet our needs and technical specifications. We can show them what to do and then clone another system for our specific uses later on. Any information stored with PeopleBase could then be dumped into the new system and made available, when deemed necessary, to the DNC or other entities we choose to work with for political purposes.

The time to make these decisions is now while we have the opportunity to coordinate the various projects. Please let me know your thoughts as soon as possible. In the meantime I am proceeding as if this is the plan.

CHAPTER NINETEEN
WIRED

■

WHAT WHITE HOUSE COUNSEL Charles Ruff's original reply to Henry Hyde had said was that no "known tapes or discs" were "available" for subpoena, the sort of legal feint the Clinton White House began perfecting when Hillary Clinton's mentor Bernie Nussbaum sat in the counsel's office. Though Nussbaum was gone, his spirit, given the First Lady's presence, still pervaded the West Wing. Ruff's carefully-worded answer merely confirmed Bob Barr's hunch that the Clinton White House, like Nixon's, had a recording system...

WHITE HOUSE NEWS BRIEFING, 8/31/98

PAUL BEDARD [*THE WASHINGTON TIMES*]: Mike, just a simple yes or no. Is the Oval Office wired or isn't it?

MICHAEL MCCURRY: What do you mean by "wired"?

PAUL BEDARD: Are the President's conversations being taped? And if so, does he intend to comply with the Impeachment Committee's subpoena?

MICHAEL MCCURRY: Whoa, one at a time. First, are the President's conversations taped? Yes and no...

PAUL BEDARD: What does that mean?

MICHAEL MCCURRY: You want your question answered or don't you? I'm not gonna...

PAUL BEDARD: Yes, I'd like it answered.

MICHAEL MCCURRY: Okay—a few, some of the Oval Office conversations have been taped, those relating to national security and the like. But the vast majority, no. We're not running a Nixon-type operation, regardless...

WOLF BLITZER [CNN]: Will the President honor the subpoena?

MICHAEL MCCURRY: The lawyers are, they're studying the request, trying to find a way to cooperate.

WOLF BLITZER: Then he'll turn the tapes over?

MICHAEL MCCURRY: That depends...

CHAPTER TWENTY
GENERAL ASSET REALIZATION

———————————————■———————————————

THE WHITEWATER PAPERS: thousands of them, tens of thousands. Enough to fill a dozen, two dozen Ryder trucks. There's an argument to be made, Hyde told a meeting of the Republican members' caucus, that some cases can be over-investigated. Especially cases involving late 20th-century financial transactions that touch on politics.

Whitewater, it was agreed all around, was one of those cases. Though compared to Watergate, it had never taken hold as a news story that captured the public imagination, for a number of reasons: Liberal bias aside, the Washington press corps is better-equipped to handle stories about break-ins than stories involving terms like "liquidating collateral" and "general asset realization." But more, Whitewater was essentially a sprawling Arkansas story involving allegations of wrongdoing a decade earlier, before Bill Clinton had even emerged on the national scene.

Two Congressional committees had tried to shed light on the case—actually an interlocking series of cases—with negative results. Congressman Jim Leach, deliberate to a fault, had doggedly worked to produce fresh revelations regarding the Clintons' involvement, only to see a bored, cynical press follow the lead of Congressman Henry Waxman in asking, "So what?"

On the Senate side, hearings chaired by the volatile Alphonse D'Amato ended in partisan wrangling, adding fuel to the White House campaign to portray Whitewater as nothing more than a political vendetta carried on by Right-Wing Republicans.

The long-awaited Starr Report finally brought focus to the case in the fall and winter of 1997. After more than five years of speculation and three years of investigation, Whitewater, the whole case and nothing but the case, was where it belonged—in the courts.

• • •

TRUTH

"The 1980s were about acquiring—acquiring wealth, power, privilege."

—HILLARY CLINTON, QUOTED IN THE *WALL STREET JOURNAL*, 1/5/96

... AND CONSEQUENCES

"There have been so many accusations made against us, it's hard to keep track of them."

—HILLARY CLINTON, *CBS THIS MORNING*, 6/19/96

• • •

THE LAST THING the American people want or need, the Chairman told his fellow Republicans, is another Whitewater investigation on Capitol Hill. Let the courts deal with what took place in Arkansas in the 1980s. The committee's job was to deal with what happened in Washington, in and around the Oval Office, in the 1990s. Not the crime but the cover-up, or rather cover-ups, of which Whitewater was hardly the most important.

CHAPTER TWENTY-ONE
YOU CAN'T MAKE ME

———————————————■———————————————

Clinger Tells Hyde Panel
of "Pattern of Stonewalling"

—HEADLINE, *THE WASHINGTON TIMES,* 8/25/98

• • •

TESTIMONY OF WILLIAM CLINGER, retired Chairman of the House
Government Reform and Oversight Committee, 8/24/98

HENRY HYDE: ... You say your experience with this pattern goes back
to the first months of the Clinton administration. Tell us, if you
will, how this came about.

WILLIAM CLINGER: It was early on, Mr. Chairman, in conjunction
with the First Lady's effort to reform the health care system. As
you'll recall, a number of task forces were established with members who weren't federal employees, so under the law—the Federal
Advisory Committees Act—proceedings were supposed, were
required to be open to the public. Not only were they closed to the
public, but my committee couldn't even get the names of the people serving.

HENRY HYDE: You requested them.

WILLIAM CLINGER: Repeatedly, Mr. Chairman. We, Congress, the
public—were entitled to them legally, ethically—under the kind of

open government Mrs. Clinton so fervently espoused during her days with the Rodino Committee. We requested, demanded, but to no avail. And when we finally managed to get a response from the White House Counsel...

HENRY HYDE: Bernard Nussbaum.

WILLIAM CLINGER: Bernard Nussbaum. He told me—it's the sort of line you remember—he said, "Congressman, I don't have to give you that information, I'm not going to give you that information, and you can't make me give you that information."

HENRY HYDE: But, in the end...

WILLIAM CLINGER: In the end, yes, we got the information. But only under court order.

• • •

JAMES SENSENBRENNER, JR.: In your opening statement, you referred to "the Jane Sherburne operation." For the benefit of people watching who live outside the Beltway, would you expand on that?

WILLIAM CLINGER: It's a damage-control operation, a special legal unit then headed by Special Counsel Jane Sherburne. Nothing like it ever existed in the White House before.

JAMES SENSENBRENNER: A damage-control operation?

WILLIAM CLINGER: To filter, drag out the production of documents as long as possible—for example, in Travelgate. Ms. Sherburne ran interference in that case, and the White House counsel, Jack Quinn, carried the ball. If anything, he out-Nussbaumed Nussbaum. Sat in my office and told me—another line you don't forget—that he'd go to jail for contempt before he turned over certain quote "privileged" Travelgate documents.

JAMES SENSENBRENNER: But he finally turned them over.

WILLIAM CLINGER: He did, but not until a House floor vote was scheduled to hold him in contempt. And it developed that one of those documents—those allegedly "privileged" documents—included the White House request for Billy Dale's file seven months—seven months—after he'd been fired.

JAMES SENSENBRENNER: I see. So what you're saying is that this "Jane Sherburne operation" was for the purpose of...

WILLIAM CLINGER: Stonewalling, Congressman, stonewalling.

• • •

BILL MCCOLLUM: Mr. Clinger, obstruction, as we know, was one of the grounds for impeachment set out against President Nixon twenty-four years ago, so what we're looking at here is fairly serious business. You quoted, I believe, from your former committee's Travelgate findings, September 1996, did you not?

WILLIAM CLINGER: In my opening remarks.

BILL MCCOLLUM: Well, I'm looking at the section of that report, page 165, headed "Pattern of Obstruction," in which you refer to the Clinton administration's, quote, "determined efforts to obstruct investigations by the GAO, Justice Department," and your committee. Are you with me?

WILLIAM CLINGER: Yes.

BILL MCCOLLUM: All right—in the same section, pages 167 through 170, you outline another kind of obstruction, one the courts in the mid-seventies found as bad as the withholding of White House documents. As I recall, Dwight Chapin...

WILLIAM CLINGER: You're speaking of memory failures.

BILL MCCOLLUM: Yes, memory failures. Dwight Chapin... I'm sure my Democratic colleagues remember that name, just as they do H.R. Haldeman and Chuck Colson—Dwight Chapin was a Nixon White House aide who was sent to prison, not because he lied to Congress but because he suffered memory failure a few too many

From the 1996 Clinger Committee Report on Travelgate

As Admitted Into the Record of the House Judiciary Committee hearings on H. Res. 104:

WHITE HOUSE OFFICIALS ENGAGED IN A PATTERN OF DELAY, DECEIT AND OBSTRUCTION OVER THE COURSE OF 3 YEARS OF INVESTIGATIONS INTO THE TRAVEL OFFICE AND MATTERS RELATED TO VINCENT FOSTER'S DEATH

The GAO's investigation was delayed for months by document production delays. Ultimately GAO did not receive all documents relevant to its inquiry including....

White House stonewalling forced the Public Integrity Section at the Justice Department to acknowledge it had no confidence that the White House had faithfully produced all documents "relating to the Thomason allegations."

Bernard Nussbaum obstructed the FBI investigation into the discovery of the Foster note as well as numerous other investigations, including congressional investigations, by failing to timely inform anyone in law enforcement, the White House, or Congress about the Vince Foster Travel Office notebook that he had secreted in Nussbaum's office by July 22, 1993....

The President's invocation of executive privilege over discussions about the Watkins memo ... is an extraordinary misuse of the privilege in light of the ongoing criminal investigation of these matters....

PRESIDENT CLINTON HAS ENGAGED IN AN UNPRECEDENTED MISUSE OF THE EXECUTIVE POWER, ABUSE OF EXECUTIVE PRIVILEGE AND OBSTRUCTION OF NUMEROUS INVESTIGATIONS INTO THE TRAVEL OFFICE....

The pattern of behavior of the White House Counsel's office, including unprecedented misuse of executive privilege, was designed deliberately to obstruct all investigations....

Covering up the true story behind the Travel Office matter led to the White House's obstruction of numerous investigations. This obstruction was conducted, overseen and encouraged by those at the "highest levels" of the White House....

times under questioning. The courts found that when a witness repeatedly answers, "I don't remember," it takes the form of a pattern of obstruction as surely as outright lying. Would that be your interpretation?

WILLIAM CLINGER: As I've read the decisions, yes, it is.

BILL McCOLLUM: With that in mind, beginning on page 169 of your Travelgate report, allow me—for the edification of those who say there's no parallel between what the Rodino Committee found in 1974 and what this committee is finding in 1998—allow me to read off some names and, if you'll help here, Mr. Clinger...

WILLIAM CLINGER: Yes, certainly.

BILL McCOLLUM: ...I'd like you to read off the number of times these Dwight Chapins of the Clinton White House suffered memory lapses when asked by your committee what they knew about the Travel Office firings—beginning with the White House chief of staff at the time, Mack McLarty.

WILLIAM CLINGER: Two hundred thirty-three times.

BILL McCOLLUM: Two hundred thirty-three times that he couldn't recall key events, like conversations with Mrs. Clinton, about the Travel Office... What about William Kennedy?

WILLIAM CLINGER: Three hundred forty-nine times.

BILL McCOLLUM: Harold Ickes, and George Stephanopoulos?

WILLIAM CLINGER: Ickes... 148 times, Stephanopoulos, 244 times.

BILL McCOLLUM: One more—I believe the record-holder, Mrs. Clinton's friend Patsy Thomasson, who serves as director of White House administration.

WILLIAM CLINGER: Under deposition, Ms. Thomasson couldn't recall or "recollect" 420 times.

BILL McCOLLUM: Thank you, Mr. Clinger. I think we've proved our point...

• • •

BOB BARR: I'm interested, Mr. Clinger, in your reference to the White House calling up Billy Dale's file, seven months after he left the Travel Office. You're familiar, I'm sure, with the details of the Jean Lewis file, the RTC investigator in Kansas City?

WILLIAM CLINGER: Familiar with it, though it didn't come before my committee.

BOB BARR: No, it came before Banking and Financial Services, looking into the connection between Madison Guaranty and Whitewater Development. It was one of my first committee assignments.

WILLIAM CLINGER: Then you had *(inaudible)*

BOB BARR: ...yes, quite an initiation into the ways of Washington and this White House. I bring it up because we deposed Jean Lewis last week and she recounted her experience—incredible it was given so little play by the media, the networks—how she and two associates investigating Madison-Whitewater found evidence of check-kiting and bank fraud. But when they referred it to the U.S. District Attorney in Little Rock—a Clinton friend and political appointee—the next thing they knew, they were locked out of their office and told they were on administrative leave—that an investigation was underway into allegations of mismanagement on their part. That sounds familiar, doesn't it?

WILLIAM CLINGER: If you mean, is it similar to what happened to Billy Dale, yes, very familiar.

BOB BARR: Exactly. The same pattern used by the Clinton White House in the Travel Office case. Except, with Jean Lewis their object wasn't simply to get jobs for their friends. It was to impede an investigation...

From the 1996 Clinger Committee Report on Travelgate

As Admitted Into the Record of the House Judiciary Committee hearings on H. Res. 104:

In March 1992, RTC criminal investigators based in Kansas City commenced an investigation into the failed Madison Guaranty Savings & Loan [owned by longtime Clinton supporter and business partner James McDougal]. The RTC subsequently produced ten criminal referrals related to Madison, one in 1992 and nine in 1993. The lead criminal investigator on the case was Jean Lewis. Ms. Lewis and her two supervisors, Richard Iorio and Lee Ausen, signed all ten referrals.

The Special Committee concludes that the Kansas City RTC investigators were obstructed in their investigation and were forced to contend with an environment hostile to their inquiry. Ms. Lewis testified that she "believe[d] there was a concerted effort to obstruct, hamper and manipulate the results of our investigation of Madison." The evidence suggests that Ms. Lewis' belief was well founded.

The submission of the nine 1993 referrals to the Justice Department was delayed when attorneys in the RTC Professional Liability Section ("PLS") demanded time to perform a "legal review of them." During the week long delay that ensued, the White House learned about the referrals and some of the confidential information they contained. Shortly after this event, Ms. Lewis was removed as the lead criminal investigator on the Madison Guaranty case at the urging of PLS. On August 15, 1994, the three Madison investigators were placed on "administrative leave" by RTC upper management. The three wereprovided with no warning or explanation whatsoever for this action....

The 1993 referrals alleged the commission of crimes involving, among other things, bank fraud, conspiracy, false statements, false documents, wire fraud, aiding and abetting, and misuse of position. The nine referrals identified multiple suspects of criminal wrongdoing—including Mr. and Mrs. McDougal, several former Madison Guaranty officers and borrowers, Mr. Tucker, and the Bill Clinton Political Committee Fund....

The referral further suggested that Mr. McDougal may have received benefits from then-Governor Clinton in exchange for $6,000 in campaign contributions. The referral observed that during the month the $3,000 checks were written, Mrs. Clinton, then a partner in the Rose Law Firm, had sent a letter to the Arkansas Securities Department seeking approval of Madison Guaranty's plan to issue a class of preferred stock. The referral noted that the plan was approved the next month by the Arkansas Securities Commissioner, Beverly Bassett Schaffer, who had been appointed to her post by then-Governor Clinton....

The removal of Ms. Lewis from the Madison Guaranty investigation was only part of a larger pattern of interference by senior officials in the RTC's investigation. April Breslaw, a PLS attorney, was at the center of this effort. Throughout 1994, Ms. Breslaw sought to discourage RTC employees from investigating Madison Guaranty and informed RTC investigators that senior RTC officials preferred that any such investigation reach a certain outcome....

Both Ms. Lewis and Mr. Iorio testified that obstacles were placed in the way of the RTC's investigation into Madison Guaranty and Whitewater. Ms. Lewis "believe[d] there was a concerted effort to obstruct, hamper and manipulate the results of our investigation of Madison."

CHAPTER TWENTY-TWO
EXPLETIVE DELETED

———————————————■———————————————

THE SUBJECT WAS TAPES: the White House recording system installed for the ostensible purpose of aiding future historians, but now dismantled because of the Hyde Committee subpoena.

"I assume," said the President, trying to make light of the matter, "that we're now just talking to each other, not to posterity."

Nervous laughter around the Oval Office—the laughter presidents always get when they crack a joke, however feeble. Only twenty-four hours before, the Signal Corps, under the guardian eye of the First Lady, had de-wired the system. There would be no more clandestine, potentially incriminating taping in the Oval Office or anywhere else in the White House complex.

"History" was the cover, but actually, like the Nixon tapes, the Clinton tapes were for the President's personal benefit and protection. Chief executives before Nixon—Kennedy and Lyndon Johnson—had also wired the Oval Office. But as in all things relating to presidential power and perquisites, the Clintons carried the practice to excess: beyond the Oval Office to the Cabinet Room, the chief-of-staff's office, the vice president's office—even certain areas of the residence (not, however, the fabled Lincoln Bedroom, though at one time that too had been considered).

Nixon's mistake had been to think of the tapes as his personally, forgetting that anything paid for from tax funds could be claimed as public property. That might have given another President and First Lady pause, but the Clintons were like no other couple that had ever moved into the White House. Years of living on the political edge—and surviving—had led them to believe they were in a special category, beyond the rules. The possibility that their tapes might one day be called up was too remote to think, much less worry, about.

Until, that is, the impeachment movement began to pick up momentum. On the day Hillary Clinton read the headline, NEW REVELATIONS STIR TALK OF IMPEACHMENT, she began pressing her husband not only to dismantle the system, but destroy all existing tapes. No need, said the President: booming economy, no war, more Americans concerned over whether the Bulls can win another NBA title than whether Congress acts on campaign finance reform—impeachment's going nowhere.

Not until the Hyde Committee convened did Bill Clinton finally focus on what his wife by that time was referring to as "those *(expletive deleted)* tapes." Even then the President procrastinated. The tapes were valuable, he argued. Destroy them, and if you have second thoughts (as Bill Clinton often did when making political decisions), there was no way back...

WHITE HOUSE TRANSCRIPTION, XB-422, conversation in Residence between the President and the First Lady, 6/27/98

THE PRESIDENT: If we burn 'em, they're gone, irretrievable. I don't see how we can lose anything by waiting.

THE FIRST LADY: What we can lose is, some dumb *(expletive deleted)* blurts it out, like...

THE PRESIDENT: Butterworth?

THE FIRST LADY: Butterfield—and once they're subpoenaed, what's gone, irretrievable, is any chance to destroy them.

THE PRESIDENT: How do you figure? We can always burn 'em—do what they say Nixon should have done—any time.

THE FIRST LADY: You really—no wonder they had you teaching admiralty, not criminal law. Once they're subpoenaed, they're evidence. If Nixon had burned the tapes after the committee found out about them, the *(expletive deleted)* would have hit the *(inaudible)*

THE PRESIDENT: Oh... Yeah... ummm... I see what you mean. Obstruction of justice. I always wondered why the *(expletive deleted)* didn't...

THE FIRST LADY: Never mind what Nixon didn't do. What are we going to do?

THE PRESIDENT: *(inaudible)*

THE FIRST LADY: Well?

THE PRESIDENT: Let me sleep on it.

THE FIRST LADY: *(expletive deleted)*

• • •

NOW, TWO MONTHS LATER, though there had been no Butterfield to blurt it out, Bob Barr had had his hunch about White House tapes and, as the First Lady had predicted, the *(expletive deleted)* had hit the fan. Alone among those assembled in the newly de-wired Oval Office, she sat unsmiling as her husband dropped his feeble one-liners. There would be no more tapes made. But that, she knew, was simply a case of cutting losses, shutting the barn door a day too late.

"What," the President was asking, "are our options?"

The question went round the Oval Office, as if the matter were really so complex it took a roomful of advisers to answer. Their options, as Hillary Clinton foresaw, came down to (a) a total stonewall, claiming the tapes were classified, and that releasing them would jeopardize national security, etc.; or (b) a partial stonewall, releasing some tapes, but only after their being altered, redacted in the interest of national security, etc.

"What's the problem," someone asked, "with just turning the tapes over?"

A charged silence, then: "We could do that," said the President. "We could always do that. But first, Blumenthal would have to write me a better *(expletive deleted)* resignation speech than Nixon had."

Nervous laughter all around. But, of course, he wasn't joking.

CHAPTER TWENTY-THREE

THE VICE PRESIDENT FULLY EXPLAINED

■

TESTIMONY OF WILLIAM CLINGER (continued)

BARNEY FRANK: Mr. Clinger, as a member of Congress, I generally view confrontations between the Executive branch and Congress from a legislative perspective. But isn't it true these matters aren't always black and white? Both sides have their constitutional prerogatives, isn't that so?

WILLIAM CLINGER: Yes, of course.

BARNEY FRANK: You'll concede then that just because the White House didn't turn documents over to you on demand didn't necessarily mean they were stonewalling.

WILLIAM CLINGER: I'll concede no such thing. The pattern I spoke of—withholding information Congress and the public were entitled to know—went beyond any lawful assertion of...

BARNEY FRANK: Well then, concede this much. According to your own testimony, you did, in every case, get the documents you requested. Yes or no?

WILLIAM CLINGER: Did we get the documents we requested?

BARNEY FRANK: Yes or no.

WILLIAM CLINGER: Only, Mr. Frank, after court orders, the threat of contempt, delays of weeks, sometimes months.

BARNEY FRANK: But you did, at the end of the day, get them.

Regardless of why or how, the White House did turn over the documents you requested. Again I ask, yes or no?

WILLIAM CLINGER: Yes.

BARNEY FRANK: No further questions.

• • •

TESTIMONY OF WILLIAM CLINGER (continued)

ASA HUTCHINSON: Mr. Clinger, I would like to follow on two points the gentleman from Massachusetts raised: Not only did the White House ultimately produce the documents you requested, but its manner of disputing or delaying your access to those documents was legal in form, was it not? I mean, since the Sherburne operation did not flatly refuse subpoenas, but rather raised a series of arguable technical and legal obstacles to producing those documents, isn't it perfectly legal and proper?

WILLIAM CLINGER: With respect, it is neither. In cases like this, the law tells us to consider the *mens rea*, the state of mind, of those who are being asked to provide information, but are resisting. Attempts to delay such an investigation can be considered obstruction, even if the forms of delay are not illegal per se, for instance an otherwise legal challenge to a subpoena, if the intent is to block the investigation. Intent is critical.

ASA HUTCHINSON: "State of mind?" Could you elaborate on that point? How can we possibly determine "state of mind?"

WILLIAM CLINGER: Well, it has generally been held that a pattern of resistance to a series of inquiries can suggest an intent to obstruct. If there is reason to believe that the persons in question, or their superiors, have a motive to impede the investigation—for instance because it might expose their own wrongdoing—that has generally been considered to strengthen the evidence of obstruction. There is a long history of case law...

[Handwritten notes, partially legible:]

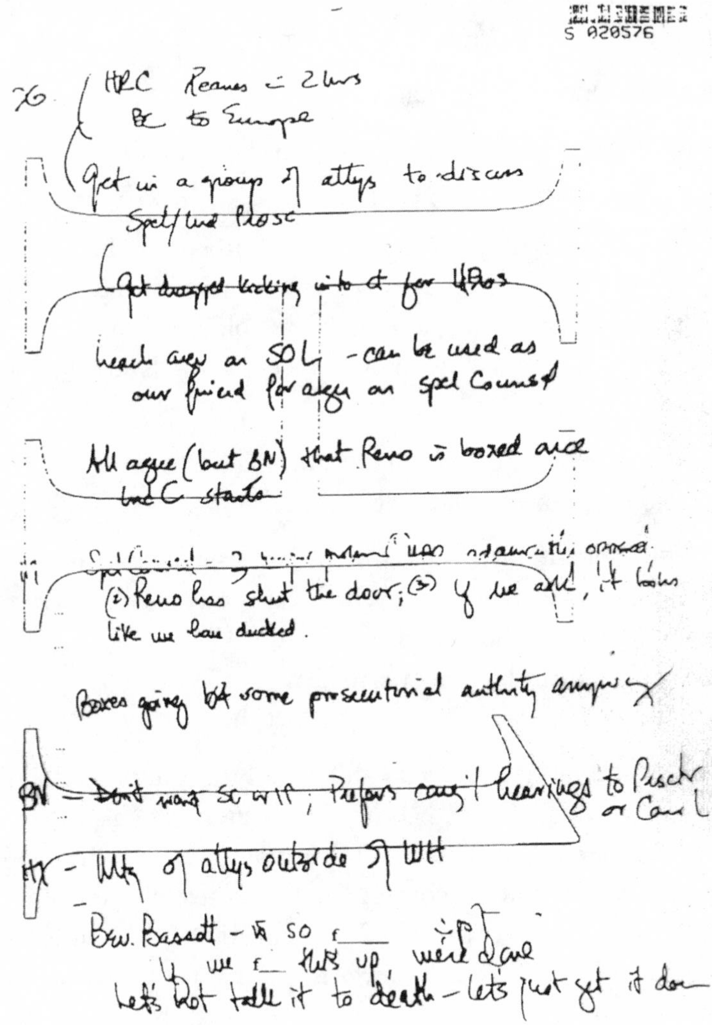

% HRC Reames = 2 hrs
    BE to Europe

    Get in a group of attys to discuss
    Spel/we Close

    Get dropped kicking into it for HBos

    reach avey an SOL — can be used as
    our friend for alegn an spel Counsel

    All agree (but BN) that Reno is boxed and
    tnc C starts

    S.[...] — ? [...] [...] ² [...] [...] ³ [...] opened
    (2) Reno has shut the door; (3) if we ask, it looks
    like we have ducked.

    Boxes going b/t some prosecutorial authority anyway

BN — Don't want so writ; Prefers cong'l hearings to Pisch
                                                  or Cam'l

EY — Mtg of attys outside of WH

    Bev. Bassett — ₹ so r___ w/ P   [...]
        if we f___ this up, we're done
    Let's not talk it to death — let's just get it done

Mark Gearan's January 7, 1994, notes quoting Harold Ickes talking about how important Beverly Bassett Schaffer's testimony was to the Clintons' account of events relating to Whitewater. Schaffer was the former Arkansas Securities Commissioner appointed by Clinton who oversaw the regulation of Madison Guaranty in the mid-1980s, and had approved Mrs. Clinton's stock plan to recapitalize the insolvent Madison S&L.

ASA HUTCHINSON: So it is not necessary to, say, lie to a police officer, or flat out refuse a subpoena to be guilty of obstruction?

WILLIAM CLINGER: Oh certainly not, in fact the Rodino Committee...

HENRY HYDE: The clock is running Mr. Hutchinson.

ASA HUTCHINSON: Thank you Mr. Chairman. Mr. Clinger, others may raise some of the Rodino issues, but I would like now to turn to one of the specific documents your committee did eventually get from the White House, after considerable resistance. I refer to the notes made at a White House meeting on January 4, 1994—a meeting in Mack McLarty's office.

WILLIAM CLINGER: Mark Gearan's notes. They were delivered only a few hours before our hearing.

ASA HUTCHINSON: It was a White House strategy meeting, wasn't it? A summit—Mrs. Clinton, even Vice President Gore were there to plan strategy on how to deal with the Whitewater investigation. Mark Gearan at the time was in charge of White House communications, is that correct? The spin doctor.

WILLIAM CLINGER: Yes, but in this case I'd say more than spin was involved. Members of the Counsel's office were also there, along with McLarty, Harold Ickes and, as you said, Vice President Gore and Mrs. Clinton. According to the notes, she entered, saying something like, "This looks like a meeting I'd be interested in." There were, as we know, more than a few White House meetings of this nature.

ASA HUTCHINSON: Yes, there were, but first, let me ask about Gearan's notes at that particular meeting. He didn't deny their accuracy, did he?

WILLIAM CLINGER: Deny? No, he didn't.

ASA HUTCHINSON: That may seem like an odd question, but along with memory failure, it appears to me that part of the pattern you referred to—the pattern of obstruction—is the habit members of

Document 1

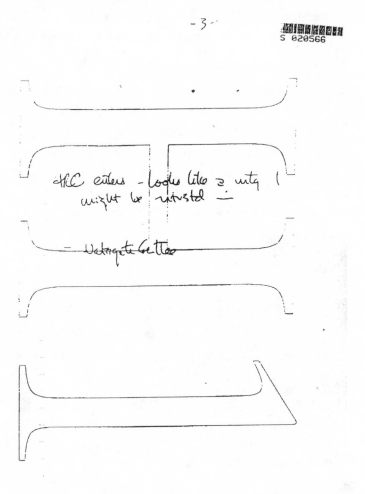

-3-

S 020566

HRC enters - looks like a mtg
might be uninvited —

— Watergate Letter

Mark Gearan's notes that reveal Hillary Clinton attended a Whitewater damage control meeting on January 4, 1994, after commenting that the meeting looked like
something she was interested in. Gearan later told the Senate Whitewater
Committee that the First Lady sat in on the meeting and expressed her disapproval
of the appointment of a special counsel.

this administration have, of repudiating words they've put on paper. There was even a case, you'll recall, of a Treasury aide who said, in effect, that he'd lied to his diary. (Audience laughter.)

WILLIAM CLINGER: I believe his name was Joshua Steiner.

ASA HUTCHINSON: And when they're not repudiating what's on paper, they're providing novel interpretations of what their words mean. In Gearan's notes, for example, we find reference to the Vice President, while talking about Whitewater papers, saying quote, "We need"—I'm going to say this slowly, so there's no misunderstanding: "We need to dump all documents." Close quote. How do you interpret those words, Mr. Clinger?

WILLIAM CLINGER: Get rid of them.

ASA HUTCHINSON: Webster's definition is, correct, "to get rid of something quickly or unceremoniously." So what the Vice President was apparently recommending, according to Gearan's notes, was that the Clintons solve their Whitewater problem by—

JOHN CONYERS: If you'll check the record, Mr. Hutchinson, you'll find that the Vice President fully explained.

ASA HUTCHINSON: I know he did, Mr. Conyers. The Vice President's interpretation—and he said it with a straight face—was that by "dump all documents," he meant, turn them over to the committees that were asking for them.

WILLIAM CLINGER: That may be so, Congressman, but if the Clintons followed his advice, my committee never got wind of it. In some cases, like the Rose law firm files...

ASA HUTCHINSON: I'm getting to that, Mr. Clinger... I believe the meeting about the Rose firm files took place at a White House meeting two months earlier, November 5, 1993, and the notes in that instance were taken by Deputy Counsel William Kennedy. And when the question of Whitewater files held by the Rose law firm came up, Kennedy's notes contained the following reference: Quote, "Vacuum Rose law files." Now, Mr. Clinger, how would

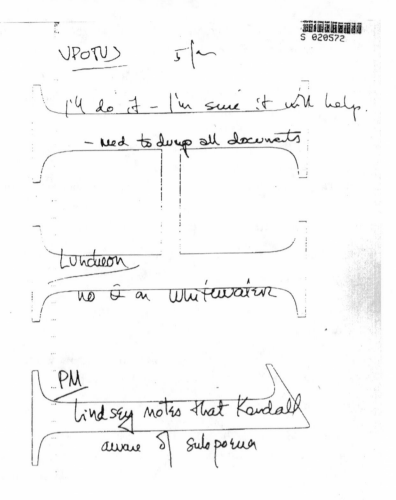

Mark Gearan's January 5, 1994, note indicating that even Vice President Al Gore was drawn into the Whitewater damage control meetings. Under VPOTUS [vice president of the United States]: "I'll do it—I'm sure it will help. —need to dump all documents."

you interpret those particular words? What do you suppose Kennedy wanted to do with those files?

WILLIAM CLINGER: I'd say he meant, clean them out, but that wasn't Mr. Kennedy's interpretation. He testified—I don't have his exact words, but...

ASA HUTCHINSON: I do, so let me report them to you. According to William Kennedy, what he meant when he said "vacuum" wasn't getting rid of the files, but rather, I quote him directly, "the information vacuum that confronted anyone trying to answer questions about the Whitewater investment."

SONNY BONO (LAUGHING): That's pretty funny. Who writes his material?

(Audience laughter)

HENRY HYDE (GAVELING): The committee will be *(laughing)* in order... Mr. Hutchinson.

ASA HUTCHINSON: Thank you, Mr. Chairman... Mr. Clinger, the President was not present at this meeting, correct?

WILLIAM CLINGER: So far as we know, he was not.

ASA HUTCHINSON: And we have no direct testimony that he authored any of these novel responses, or that he personally directed Sherburne or Quinn or Nussbaum to resist any of your specific inquiries?

WILLIAM CLINGER: No we do not.

ASA HUTCHINSON: So no smoking gun, right? Nothing that would hold up in a court of law?

WILLIAM CLINGER: Well, actually those are two very different questions. "Smoking gun" became a popular term back in Watergate days, but many an executive has gone to jail for a pattern of abuses by his subordinates even when no direct order was shown, for instance, if the abuse was known to the executive, if he even tactily approved of it, and if he had a substantial personal stake in the misconduct of his subordinates.

Document 18

William Kennedy's notes from a November 5, 1993, Whitewater control meeting referencing "Vacuum Rose Law Files WWDC Docs-subpoena." Sen. Alfonse D' Amato accused the White House of trying to suppress damaging documents. Responding, Kennedy said that what he had actually been referring to was "the information vacuum that confronted anyone trying to answer questions about the investment"—not destroying files.

ASA HUTCHINSON: And in this case?

WILLIAM CLINGER: Well, certainly the President knew that his own lawyers were resisting our investigation...

SONNY BONO: Only if he got to page A27 in the *Post*.

ASA HUTCHINSON: One last question Mr. Clinger. What was the Watergate standard? Was this issue of personal responsibility clearly addressed?

WILLIAM CLINGER: Yes, it was. In fact the chief counsel to the Rodino Committee, Mr. Jerome Zeifman, a lifelong liberal Democrat, has recently reminded us exactly what the standard was. In his new book from Regnery...

BARNEY FRANK: Oh please! Right-wing trash for Right-Wing cash!

WILLIAM CLINGER: Mr. Zeifman points out that, at the time, this committee's view was that the President could be impeached for acts of his subordinates, if those acts "were in furtherance of his policy" and he took no action to prevent them. And as Mr. Zeifman also reminds us, Leon Jaworski, the Republican Special Prosecutor, in citing Nixon as a criminal co-conspirator, noted that "one who learns of an ongoing criminal conspiracy and casts his lot with the conspirators, becomes a member of the conspiracy," especially if the alleged co-conspirator has "a stake in the success of the venture."

CHAPTER TWENTY-FOUR
STATE MORALITY

———————————— ■ ————————————

SPECIAL NEWS REPORT, NBC, 12:42 PM, 8/25/98

BRIAN WILLIAMS: It's now been confirmed by NBC Correspondent Lisa Myers that the House Judiciary Committee a short while ago approved, by a 20-to-15 vote, a seven-article Bill of Impeachment directed against President Clinton. The bill will now go to the House floor, where it's expected... We now go to the Capitol where, I'm told, Chairman Henry Hyde is about to hold a news conference...

HENRY HYDE: I have a brief written statement, after which I'll entertain questions. After long, and I might add, prayerful consideration, a majority of the members of the Judiciary Committee has voted to take the first difficult but necessary step toward impeachment by reporting out a seven-count bill, including separate articles charging President Clinton with abuse of power, solicitation and receipt of illegal campaign contributions, obstruction of justice, and by his actions dishonoring the institution of the Presidency.

I said at the outset of this procedure—this painful process—my intention has been to hold fair, open hearings aimed at arriving at the truth, un-spun and unvarnished, to bring the American people to a better understanding of the constitutional crisis now threatening our country and its free institutions.

I believe we've succeeded in this, though others on the committee and in the House as a whole may disagree. Nevertheless, I am confident that in the days ahead, the House will support the findings of our committee and will send H.R. 104 to the Senate for final action... Questions?

MARY ANN AKERS: When will copies of the Bill be available and what do you see as the timetable for bringing it to the floor?

HENRY HYDE: It's at the printer now, and my understanding is—I think within the next hour. Check with the staff. As for timetable, my hope is that we'll see it debated and up for a vote before the Labor Day break.

HELEN DEWAR: Is that just your hope, or is it a realistic schedule? John Conyers is talking about a flawed bill that needs full floor debate of up to two weeks.

HENRY HYDE: Well, that doesn't surprise me, since that's what he was talking about at our closed session. But I think I've given you a realistic schedule. We'll have full floor debate, but after eight weeks of hearings—hearings and debate—I don't think there's much to add on the House side. Any House member who doesn't understand the issues by now isn't going to understand them with another two or even four weeks of debate... David?

DAVID BRODER: You're confident then that it's going to the Senate. Would you care to predict the vote?

HENRY HYDE: I'm confident, yes, but I'm not in the prediction business. You'll have to ask John McLaughlin...

• • •

IMPEACHMENT OF WILLIAM JEFFERSON CLINTON
PRESIDENT OF THE UNITED STATES OF AMERICA
H. RES. 104

August 28, 1998
Referred to the House Calendar and ordered to be printed.

MR. HYDE, from the Committee on the Judiciary, submitted the following RESOLUTION Impeaching William Jefferson Clinton, President of the United States, for high crimes and misdemeanors. RESOLVED, That William Jefferson Clinton, President of the United States, is impeached for high crimes and misdemeanors, and that the following articles of impeachment be exhibited to the Senate:

Articles of impeachment exhibited by the House of Representatives of the United States of America in the name of itself and of all the people of the United States of America, against William Jefferson Clinton, President of the United States of America, in maintenance and support of its impeachment against him for high crimes and misdemeanors.

ARTICLE I

Using the powers and office of President of the United States, William Jefferson Clinton, contrary to his oath to preserve, protect, and defend the Constitution of the United States, has personally and through his subordinates and agents abused said powers by violating the constitutional and statutory rights of citizens, and impairing the due and proper administration of justice.

This conduct has included one or more of the following:
(1) approving, condoning, and acquiescing in, the misuse of the Federal Bureau of Investigation, in violation and disregard of the clearly established statutory and constitutional rights of citizens, by ordering, inducing, and permitting that agency to disclose to the White House raw investigative material from Federal Bureau of Investigation security clearance files, for purposes not authorized by law;

(2) approving, condoning, and acquiescing in the misuse of the Internal Revenue Service by endeavoring to cause, in violation of the clearly established statutory and constitutional rights of citizens, tax audits or other tax investigations to be initiated or conducted in a discriminatory manner;

(3) misusing other federal agencies, in violation or disregard of the clearly established statutory and constitutional rights of citizens, by directing those agencies to conduct investigations unrelated to the enforcement of laws, or any other lawful function.

Wherefore William Jefferson Clinton, by such wrongful conduct, warrants impeachment, trial, and removal from office.

ARTICLE II

In his conduct of the office of President of the United States, William Jefferson Clinton, contrary to his oath to preserve, protect, and defend the Constitution of the United States, and in violation of his constitutional duty to take care that the laws be faithfully executed, has failed without lawful cause to produce in a timely manner certain papers and things as directed by duly authorized subpoenas issued by grand juries and Congressional committees charged with investigating the White House Travel Office firings, alleged violations of the Privacy Act, alleged violations of campaign finance laws, and alleged violations of the law in what shall hereinafter be referred to as "the Whitewater matter." Acting personally and through his subordinates and agents, he has asserted improper and undue claims of privilege in a continuing effort to impede, impair, and obstruct the lawful inquiries of the aforesaid grand juries and Congressional committees.

In all of this, William Jefferson Clinton has acted in a manner contrary to his oath as President and subversive of constitutional government, to the great prejudice of the cause of law and justice, and to the manifest injury of the people of the United States.

Wherefore William Jefferson Clinton, by such wrongful conduct, warrants impeachment, trial, and removal from office.

ARTICLE III

Using the powers and office of President of the United States, William Jefferson Clinton, personally and through his subordinates and agents, in violation of his oath to preserve, protect, and defend the Constitution of the United States, has engaged in a course of conduct violating the federal election laws by:

(1) approving, condoning, and acquiescing in the solicitation and acceptance of campaign contributions from foreign nationals and the conduct of unlawful campaign financing activities on federal property including the White House, in contravention of the law;

(2) approving, condoning, and acquiescing in the use of the White House and other federal properties and facilities for the purpose of raising unlawful campaign contributions;

(3) directing and engaging in a systematic effort to mislead and deceive Congress and the people of the United States regarding the existence, nature, and extent of these illicit campaign contributions.

(4) approving, condoning, and participating in said solicitation and acquisition of political campaign funds in such reckless and improvident manner as to subvert, defame, and discredit the Office of the Presidency and the departments, agencies, and offices under his authority as Chief Executive.

Wherefore William Jefferson Clinton, by such wrongful conduct, warrants impeachment, trial, and removal from office.

ARTICLE IV

Using the powers and offices of the President of the United States, William Jefferson Clinton, personally, and through his subordinates and agents, has engaged in a course of conduct to subvert the appropriations power of the United States Congress by:

(1) causing, approving, condoning, and acquiescing in the use of salaried members of the Democratic National Committee as employees of his White House staff;

(2) causing, approving, condoning, and acquiescing in the establishment and use of a computer database, acquired with federally appropriated funds and maintained in the White House, for partisan political purposes.

Wherefore William Jefferson Clinton, by such wrongful conduct, warrants impeachment, trial, and removal from office.

ARTICLE V

Using the powers and office of President of the United States, William Jefferson Clinton, personally and through his subordinates and agents, engaged in an unlawful conspiracy to impede and obstruct the investigation of a fraudulent real estate transaction involving Madison Guaranty Savings and Loan, a federally-insured lending institution of Little Rock, Arkansas, and the Whitewater Development Corporation, by:

(1) delaying, impeding, and obstructing the investigation of those real estate transactions and related issues (collectively referred to as "the Whitewater matter"); to cover up, conceal, and protect those responsible; and to conceal the existence and scope of other unlawful acts generated by investigation into said Whitewater matter.

(2) destroying, withholding, and by other means refusing to produce relevant and material evidence or information from lawfully authorized investigative officers of the United States;

(3) approving, condoning, acquiescing in, and counseling witnesses with respect to the giving of false or misleading statements to lawfully authorized investigative officers and employees of the United States and false or misleading testimony in duly instituted judicial and congressional proceedings;

(4) interfering or endeavoring to obstruct the conduct of investigations by the Department of Justice of the United States;

(5) disseminating sensitive and confidential criminal investigative information received from officers of the United States Department of the Treasury to subjects of investigations conducted by lawfully authorized investigative officers and employees of the United States, for the purpose of aiding and assisting such subjects in their attempts to avoid criminal liability;

(6) misusing the Resolution Trust Corporation, a component of the Treasury Department, by causing the removal from their positions of three Resolution Trust Corporation criminal investigators, without cause and for reasons unrelated to any lawful function of his office, but rather in a calculated effort to impede and obstruct lawful investigations arising from the aforesaid Whitewater matter.

Wherefore William Jefferson Clinton, by such wrongful conduct, warrants impeachment, trial, and removal from office.

ARTICLE VI

Using the powers and office of President of the United States, William Jefferson Clinton, personally, and through his subordinates and agents, has recklessly and improvidently put at risk the national security interests of the United States by:

(1) causing, approving, condoning, and acquiescing in the wrongful acquisition and misuse of national security information by political appointees;

(2) causing, approving, condoning, and acquiescing in the compromise of national security interests for political considerations, by placing on the National Security Advisory Board campaign donors lacking requisite qualifications for appointment.

Wherefore William Jefferson Clinton, by such wrongful conduct, warrants impeachment, trial, and removal from office.

ARTICLE VII

Beginning on or about January 20, 1993 and continuing to the present, William Jefferson Clinton, in violation of his oath faithfully to execute the office of President of the United States and to the best of his ability preserve, protect, and defend the Constitution of the United States, has through his office managed an enterprise whose purpose it has been to engage in a pattern of illegal activity designed to conduct criminal conspiracy, bribery, obstruction of justice and violation of the laws governing national security.

WHEREFORE, BE IT RESOLVED by the House of Representatives, acting under the authority granted and responsibility imposed by the Constitution of the United States, does impeach William Jefferson Clinton, President of the United States, for said high crimes and misdemeanors and submits these Articles of Impeachment to the Senate for the purpose of trying and removing the aforesaid William Jefferson Clinton from office.

• • •

THE REAL BOMBSHELL among the Articles was Article VII, the RICO charge. Congressman Frank whispered to his colleague Congressman Schumer, "My God, that's what they got John Gotti on. They're saying that this presidency operates like a criminal enterprise," and he reread the passage from the Article "an enterprise whose purpose it has been to engage in a pattern of illegal activity." Across the aisle Congressman Barr was satisfied, musing that the RICO charge would draw immediate attention in the Senate from Senator Fred Thompson. Thompson had once had first-hand involvement in a successful RICO prosecution aimed at the office of the Governor of Tennessee. Nowadays "organized crime" was not limited to loan sharking, narcotics, and gangland executions. Now Chairman Hyde was summing up the majority view...

REMARKS OF CHAIRMAN HENRY HYDE, Judiciary Committee
hearings on H. Res. 104, 8/25/98

The question before us is not whether the President has committed a crime for which we ought to summon the Capitol Police. Just the opposite. We are neither necessary, nor qualified, nor constitutionally competent for the business of ordinary law enforcement. We are here precisely because the President is not charged with a work-a-day crime.

We are here as statesmen, to judge a statesman, for alleged crimes of state; or, in the words of the great Irish statesman Edmund Burke, for grave violations of "fundamental principles of state morality."

Our state morality is set forth in the Constitution, and in the Declaration of Independence, which records in vivid detail those state crimes which the Constitution is meant to prevent. These documents constitute, if you will, the penal code of American statesmanship, the Decalogue by which American statesmen are judged, which the President is sworn to uphold, and to preserve and protect and defend. Every count against the President—from using the police power to harass his political enemies; to obstructing justice; to compromising our relations with foreign powers constitutes a mortal violation of his oath....

And yet even conceding that these crimes are precisely the sort for which the Founders intended impeachment, I know that for many in this House one crucial question remains: Was the President himself personally responsible for these crimes?...

As to Article II, it is on this charge, obstruction of justice, that his personal responsibility has always has been most clear; for, if at any time in the years of investigations into this administration's abuse of power the President had simply told his lawyers to give their full cooperation to the investigation, certainly it would have been done....

What of the bribes, the illegal contributions from foreign powers, and especially the abuse of the police power? Whose staff was weaving this fabric of illegality, thick with offenses tediously repeated? Who benefitted from all this—*cui bono?* Even in the criminal law, which is not our guide, our investigation has developed sufficient evidence to warrant the inference that this entire campaign of obstruction was being orchestrated from the Oval Office by the President...

In the end, however, the standards of the criminal law are no more than a rough guide, by way of analogy, to our obligations. The standard by which Presidents are judged, by which we in this room will be judged, should it ever come to that, are higher than those of the criminal law, not lower. That is the essence of republican government...

Did the President, by deliberate and personal act, or by connivance, tacit consent, or negligence, betray his oath by undermining or by allowing those around him to undermine the fundamental law he is charged to defend? If so then by the standards by which statesmen are judged, he is as guilty as if he had scooped up John Huang's bribes with his own hands or personally ordered the FBI to make a criminal of Billy Dale...

CHAPTER TWENTY-FIVE
CALLING
WILLIAM JEFFERSON CLINTON

CLINTON IS IMPEACHED!

—FRONT-PAGE HEADLINE, *THE NEW YORK POST*, 8/28,98

House Votes to Impeach the President, 242-193; Clinton "Confident" as Bill Goes to the Senate

—BANNER HEADLINE, *THE NEW YORK TIMES*, 8/28/98

"Down But Not Out"
Clinton Vows to Take Fight Against "Right-Wing Coup" to the Country

—FRONT-PAGE HEADLINE, OVER EXCLUSIVE DAVID MARANISS
INTERVIEW WITH THE PRESIDENT, *THE WASHINGTON POST*, 8/29/98

• • •

BILL LIVINGOOD was the man-of-the-hour. One of his predecessors, William "Fishbait" Miller, became in his time not only a fixture but a celebrity in Washington, made famous by the booming way he had of calling out, "Mr. Speaker, the President of the United States!" whenever the President came to the Capitol to make his State of the Union Address.

Now Livingood, though hardly a match for his predecessor in flair or flourish, would in one brief hour attract more cameras and reporters than "Fishbait" had in a lifetime. For it fell upon the sergeant-at-arms, by law, to deliver the Articles of Impeachment to the President of the United States, calling William Jefferson Clinton to account and ordering him, at a time certain, to appear before the Senate, to answer charges made by the House.

At 4:25 PM, August 28, 1998, a typical hot, humid, late August day in the nation's capital, the sergeant-at-arms, a small army of reporters, photographers and TV cameramen in his wake, arrived at the White House, was passed through the southwest gate and ushered into the President's reception room, outside the Oval Office. There he waited... ten... fifteen... thirty-five minutes in all. He'd been expected, but this was Clinton Time.

Finally, at 5:07 PM, the President arrived, apologized for his tardiness ("Sorry. They told me you'd be here five-thirty."), accepted the document only one President before him had ever been handed, and asked his visitor whether—it being "a scorcher of a day"— he'd like a cold drink. Iced tea, lemonade, Coke? No sir, said the Sergeant-At-Arms, he really had to leave. He was required, under law, to report back to the speaker, to tell him the Articles had been served. Oh well, said the President. Maybe another time. Then he opened a desk drawer, pulled out a small box and handed it to Bill Livingood. A souvenir, he said. You can't leave the White House without a souvenir. On the way out, Livingood opened the box, and found a pair of presidential cuff-links. Not the cheap kind, but the A-list variety, reserved for VIPs and fat-cat contributors.

You warned me, and you were right, the sergeant-at-arms told the Speaker after he'd returned to the Capitol. Bill Clinton really is a very charming fellow...

THE
SENATE TRIAL

Chief Justice Will Preside
Over Senate in Clinton Trial
First "Grand Inquest" in 130 Years

—FRONT-PAGE HEADLINES, *THE WASHINGTON POST*, OVER PICTURE OF CLINTON DEBARKING AIR FORCE ONE CARRYING COPY OF JFK'S PROFILES IN COURAGE, 9/8/98

President Clinton Assails
"Radical Right" as Senate
Prepares for Historic Debate
He Warns Labor Rally of "the Enemy Within"

—FRONT-PAGE HEADLINES, *THE NEW YORK TIMES*, OVER PICTURE OF CLINTON ADDRESSING LABOR DAY GATHERING, SAME DATE

CHAPTER TWENTY-SIX
REHNQUIST'S DILEMMA

■

SINCE THE ROBERT BORK confirmation hearings in the mid-eighties, the cautionary rule for anyone aspiring to the U.S. Supreme Court had been "Publish and Perish." Leaving a trail of articles and books—evidence of politically-incorrect opinions—had brought Bork down and only added to Clarence Thomas's confirmation problems.

The lesson seemed to be that it was better to have written nothing, like the bland New Englander David Souter, than risk being waylaid at some future time by hostile critics.

In ordinary times no sitting judge, especially not the Chief Justice, would be affected by the rule. But writing in 1992 about the impeachment of President Andrew Johnson, Chief Justice William Rehnquist could hardly have foreseen a day when his extra-judicial writing would become live ammunition in the most heated political battle of the century...

THE WASHINGTON POST OP-ED article by Professor Laurence Tribe, Harvard Law School, 9/1/98.

"As Rehnquist rightly observes in his book *Grand Inquests*, the radical Republicans behind the move to oust Johnson were less interested in constitutional principles than, in Rehnquist's words, 'looking into what charges might be made against a political opponent.'... Had they succeeded, the Chief Justice concludes, 'the future independence of the President would have been jeopardized.'

"The parallel between the 1868 impeachment of President Johnson and the 1998 impeachment of President Clinton is striking—frighteningly so. But fortunately, Rehnquist, whatever his other faults, has been a model of consistency in acting out his role as the supreme jurist of the land; a blessing indeed that a judge with his perspective should be in charge of the President's Senate trial at a time when the radical Republicans of the 105th Congress are bound and determined to jeopardize not merely the independence of the presidency but the very fabric of the Constitution itself..."

• • •

REMINDERS OF REHNQUIST'S jaundiced view of the Johnson impeachment would also come from a half-dozen anti-impeachment pundits: Garry Wills, Richard Cohen, Lars-Eric Nelson, Anthony Lewis, Michael Gartner, and Ken Bode. And in her last appearance as a panel member on the McLaughlin show, Eleanor Clift, who was joining Sidney Blumenthal as a member of Bill Clinton's communications staff, would predict that as presiding officer at the Senate trial, "Chief Justice Rehnquist will disappoint his Republican friends by keeping Right-Wing zealots like Jesse Helms and and Rick Santorum on a short leash."

Should the Chief Justice Recuse Himself?

—EDITORIAL HEADLINE, *THE WASHINGTON TIMES*, 9/4/98

The editorial came down on the side of Rehnquist's staying on, rejecting arguments that the chief justice step aside and let one of his colleagues preside at the trial.

But who? The Constitution is specific: the chief justice shall preside. Beyond that, there being no precedent other than the Johnson impeachment, the obvious choice would have been the senior member of the Court, the liberal John Paul Stevens—a prospect that led pro-impeachment forces to dismiss as irrelevant what columnist George Will called Rehnquist's "idle historical musings."

• • •

"I haven't the slightest doubt in the world that Bill Clinton is going to come out of this (bleep) smelling like roses. If you threw him into a pile of (bleep), he'd come up with a pony. The man is the luckiest (bleep) in the world."

—JIM MCDOUGAL, IN AN INTERVIEW WITH GERALDO RIVERA, 9/8/98

CHAPTER TWENTY-SEVEN
THE HEAD COUNT

———————————————■———————————————

IN THE SENATE TRIAL of President Andrew Johnson the House leadership, under the whip hand of the irascible Thaddeus Stevens, took charge of the prosecution. That only made sense, given the strict-constructionist logic of the time: If members of the House wanted a President removed from office, let them come across the Capitol to make their case. The same impeccable logic dictated that the President hire his own lawyers to defend him—in Johnson's case, a former associate justice of the Supreme Court, a former Attorney General, and a prominent lawyer from his home state of Tennessee.

But those were the days when U.S. Senators, though conscious of their station, didn't view themselves as members of an exclusive club. One hundred thirty-two years later, the idea that any non-Senator—especially a mere member of the House—should be allowed floor privileges in the self-described "world's greatest deliberative body" was considered outlandish. The House leadership and Bill Clinton's lawyers would have to watch the proceedings like other common folk—from the sidelines. The players, as on any other resolution sent over from the "lower chamber," would be members of the Senate alone, operating under their own club rules.

As for the "trial," even in Johnson's day that was something of a fiction. In all probability no witnesses would be called, no new evidence presented. The factual record would be the House Report recommending approval of the articles of impeachment: essentially the testimony from the Hyde committee plus the report and testimony of the Clinger, Leach, Thompson, Burton, and D'Amato hearings adopted by Hyde as part of the record.

The trial would consist almost entirely of the Senate debate of the established facts.

CBS EVENING NEWS, 9/3/98

DAN RATHER: Floor managers were named today for next week's historic Senate trial of President Bill Clinton, accused by the House of seven quote "high crimes and misdemeanors." Leading the prosecution team will be Republican Senators Orrin Hatch of Utah and Arlen Specter of Pennsylvania, with Democratic Senators Edward Kennedy of Massachusetts and Patrick Leahy of Vermont in charge of the defense. The trial, expected to last two to three weeks, will be televised live, gavel-to-gavel, over the CBS Television network. An exclusive White House interview with the President by this reporter may be seen tonight at 10 PM, eastern standard time. Consult your local listings... Elsewhere, in Paris, it was announced that President Clinton and British Prime Minister Tony Blair will travel to France in early November for a ceremony marking the 80th anniversary of the end of World War One. Under secretary of State Strobe Talbott, in the French capital for a NATO conference, accepted the invitation on the President's behalf...

• • •

HAVING COME FROM House Judiciary, H. Res. 104, like any other bill, would be floor-managed by Senate Judiciary. On the Republican side, Hatch was Chairman, Specter second-ranking; on the Democratic, Joe Biden of Delaware ranked first, with Kennedy and Leahy right behind him...

WHITE HOUSE TRANSCRIPTION XB-723, telephone conversation, the President and Senator Tom Daschle, 9/1/98

THE PRESIDENT: Come again? He says...

TOM DASCHLE: He says he's troubled. That's his word, troubled. It wouldn't be fair to you, he says, if he took the lead and couldn't give it one-hundred percent.

THE PRESIDENT: *(expletive deleted)*

TOM DASCHLE: Yeah, that's the way I feel, but...

THE PRESIDENT: I never have, you know, it shouldn't surprise me because I've never really trusted the *(expletive deleted)*. Talks out of both sides—*(inaudible)*—hair transplant, *(expletive deleted)*, what he needs, what he really needs is a spine transplant.

TOM DASCHLE: Well... I wish I could say there was some way to un-trouble him, like—there's a friend, a Wilmington lawyer he'd like on some commission. But I don't think that would do it. He has his own agenda.

THE PRESIDENT: Like what?

TOM DASCHLE: Two thousand, running for...

THE PRESIDENT: Unbelievable. How does he figure...?

TOM DASCHLE: Don't ask me. I gave up trying to figure Joe Biden years ago.

THE PRESIDENT: You know... you know, to tell the truth, I think Kennedy will do a better job, but you get a drop-out, your lead horse, it just looks like *(expletive deleted)*.

• • •

IN THE WHITE HOUSE WAR ROOM...actually an office suite once occupied by Henry Kissinger, on the third floor of the old Executive Office Building—Paul Begala, one of the President's head-counters, wrote Biden down as questionable, a senator who could go either way when the vote was taken on the Bill of Impeachment.

But even if Biden, for whatever reason, supported the bill, Begala and other members of Clinton's war council felt comfortable about holding proponents of H. Res. 104 below the two-thirds mark needed to remove a President from office. Republicans would need thirteen Democratic cross-overs to reach that number; assuming, of course, they could hold their own troops in line.

The council's list of possible Republican cross-overs was short. It consisted in fact of only one name, Jim Jeffords of Vermont. Not a probable, Begala told the President, but a name to remember if it began to look as if the vote might be close.

As of Labor Day recess, however, the council, though not happy about the fourteen Democratic cross-overs in the House impeachment vote, saw no cause for panic on the Senate side. Despite the sharp decline in the President's poll numbers since the summer of '97—a result of the Starr indictments, the Hyde Committee hearings, the cooling of the economy—it could still be argued by Clinton apologists like *Time*'s Margaret Carlson that the country was "better off today that at any time in history."

Still, the President, for all the sanguine reports brought in by his head-counters, had private misgivings. Bill Clinton kept his own count when it came to numbers that threatened him personally. Nixon-like, he kept it on a long yellow legal pad, scrawling in his awkward left-handed style the names of senators he regarded as "soft" or questionable. As the Senate trial got underway, he listed a half-dozen in all: Biden; Joe Lieberman of Connecticut; Bob Kerrey of Nebraska; Fritz Hollings of South Carolina; Russ Feingold of Wisconsin; and Paul Wellstone of Minnesota.

That left the opposition seven votes short, still cause for White House optimism. But optimism, if Clinton's roller-coaster political career had taught him anything, was an emotional luxury he could never afford.

• • •

DAN RATHER INTERVIEW with the President, 9/3/98

DAN RATHER: Mr. President, there are those who say that since you've done what you set out to do—grown the economy, balanced the budget, got the peace process moving—they say since you've done all that, aren't you pretty much like the Texan who's struck a gusher, can cap his well and go out a winner?

THE PRESIDENT: I'm afraid I don't follow you, Dan.

DAN RATHER: Well, for example, this morning's *New York Times*...

THE PRESIDENT: Oh, that.

DAN RATHER: ...in a lead editorial on your impeachment, they say you could save the country and yourself a lot of anguish by gracefully stepping down...

THE PRESIDENT: Quit, you mean—like Nixon.

DAN RATHER: They go on—I only repeat it, sir, because it echoes what's being said behind closed doors by some members of your own party—the *Times* goes on to say that even if you win in the Senate, you end up losing. Your presidency wounded, you're a one-legged duck...

THE PRESIDENT: Well, the *Times*—even if I'd read their editorial, which I haven't—the *Times* has a right to its opinion, but the bottom line is, they want me to quit, like Nixon, and this President—I think the American people know, even if the *Times* doesn't—this President's no quitter. And as much as I ought to resent being invited on your show to talk—at least that was my understanding—talk about my administration's accomplishments, then get this instead, much as I have a right to resent it, I don't...

DAN RATHER: Just doing my job, sir.

THE PRESIDENT: ...and I appreciate that, believe me, I do. But you've actually done me a favor, Dan, a big favor, letting me get the word out that no matter what our critics, the special interests and Right-

Wing extremists say—no matter what, I intend to stay on the job, because neither I nor anyone connected with me has done anything outside the law or even come close to what the Founders called high crimes and misdemeanors.

DAN RATHER: Mr. President...

THE PRESIDENT: Please, Dan—you asked a question and I'm just trying to answer it. I've done nothing wrong, and on the contrary, it's what my administration has done right the past five years that's brought us to this. And if I were to do what they ask...

DAN RATHER: They, meaning the *Times*?

THE PRESIDENT: The *Times*, all our Right-Wing critics—if I were to do what they ask—cut-and-run from my responsibility to the American people, the poor, the less-fortunate, our kids, our working families, then—if I were to quit, it would play directly into the hands of the extremists, the special interests that just can't deal with the fact that for the first time in fifty years we have a liberal Democrat in the White House who's been elected to not one but two terms...

• • •

THE "L" WORD: Dick Morris came out of his chair cheering when he heard his favorite client utter it. Watching the President from his suite at the Jefferson, the diminutive spin doctor could only marvel at how well Bill Clinton performed under pressure. Postpone the Rather interview, the war council had advised. There's more to lose than there is to gain.

Only Morris thought otherwise; that Rather, if Clinton went at him, would rattle and fold, just as he had with George Bush ten years earlier. And only Morris, whom the President considered his lucky if sometimes oafish charm, could have convinced Bill Clinton of the need, in his hour of trial, to forget the polls, forego the focus groups, abandon the broad appeal of centrist politics that had brought him to the presidency.

Popular opinion—mass approval—was no longer, at least for this fight, the ultimate weapon. The battlefield had narrowed, the target was limited, the game now one of defense. The object now wasn't to get votes, but to hold on to those you had. If the votes of thirteen Democrats were needed to remove a Democratic President, where were they most likely to come from? Where did his position most need shoring up? Which faction of Bill Clinton's party felt most aggrieved, for real or imagined reasons, by his policies and appointments? Which wing least happy with a President they saw as, in the jaundiced view of Ralph Nader, "a deal-making Republocrat"? Which most likely to defect?

Move left, Dick Morris advised his client. De-triangulate. No more Mr. New Democrat. No walking the middle line. Make it a choice of Left or Right, Liberal or Conservative. And you're the Liberal.

In short, as Morris told the war council, Let Clinton be Clinton.

• • •

I sense high drama here, on the order of the grand inquisition that befell my royal namesake three hundred years ago. Of course, there are profound differences, the foremost being that while His Majesty Charles lost his head, His Excellency Mr. Clinton will, if judged guilty, lose only his seat. That, at least, is the general presumption.

—PRINCE CHARLES, WRITING AS SPECIAL CORRESPONDENT COVERING THE SENATE TRIAL OF PRESIDENT CLINTON (THE NEW YORKER, 9/13/98).

CHAPTER TWENTY-EIGHT
THE PROFESSOR

■

DANIEL PATRICK MOYNIHAN, up early after a restless night, antici-
pated the workday ahead with mixed feelings of dread and curiosity. The 71-year-old New York senator wasn't merely troubled, like
his colleague Joe Biden, but torn by the prospect of sitting in judgment of a president.

In a few hours the United States Senate would convene for the
trial of William Jefferson Clinton, the leader of Moynihan's own
party, a man duly elected, then re-elected by the people. That
accounted for Moynihan's feeling of dread. The curiosity rose from
his being at heart an academician with a dual sense of being not
only a participant in the history that was being made, but an
observer as well...

DAY OF RECKONING:
Clinton in the Dock

On his way to the Capitol, Moynihan checked the front-page
headline of *The Washington Times* and the story that followed by
Paul Bedard, reporting on Bill Clinton's strategy of—in the phrase
of an unnamed White House spin doctor—"reverting to his basic
Kennedy instincts" in defending his presidency.

Kennedy instincts: Pat Moynihan recoiled at the reference. If
invoking the memory of the president Moynihan most admired was

aimed at bringing old liberals like him closer to the party hearth—
if that was the White House "strategy"—it was misguided. Bill
Clinton was many things to many people, but in Pat Moynihan's
eyes, he was no Jack Kennedy.

• • •

ALEC BALDWIN:

*"It had the unmistakable odor
of a Munich beer hall."*

BARBRA STREISAND:

*"It was scary... I felt I was watching the
American version of the Reichstag fire."*

—LEADERS OF THE HOLLYWOOD CONTINGENT OF FRIENDS OF THE PRESIDENT,
on being asked their reaction to the first day of the
Senate trial (*Entertainment Tonight*, 9/9/98).

• • •

THOUGH THE PRESIDENT'S war council would have preferred that
they watch the trial from Malibu, the Hollywood contingent—
Alec, Barbra, Kim, Sharon, Harry, Linda, and a half-dozen supporting players—flew in the night before, held a news conference,
and were seated front-and-center in the spectators' gallery when, at
precisely 9:30 a.m., Chief Justice Rehnquist entered the chamber,
took the seat usually reserved for the vice president, and gavelled
the Senate to order.*

As in the trial of Andrew Johnson, the articles would be taken up
one-by-one, though it was widely understood that the first vote
would be decisive. It was critical, the prosecution felt, that they lead

---

* One minor fashion note on the first day of the trial: Justice Rehnquist came attired as he
would if hearing a case before the Supreme Court, an appropriate reminder that this was no
ordinary day in the life of the Senate (though, on seeing Rehnquist enter, *Time* correspondent
Margaret Carlson is said to have remarked to a colleague that the robe was "a bit much.")

with the article that made the strongest case for conviction, had the broadest appeal to senators on the fence.

To Arlen Specter, the onetime Philadelphia prosecutor, that could only mean leading with Article II, the count that directly charged the President with "a continuing effort to impede, impair and obstruct the lawful inquiries of Congressional committees and other investigative bodies"—the accusation members of the Rodino Committee (assisted, ironically, by staff lawyers Bernard Nussbaum and Hillary Rodham) leveled against President Richard Nixon in the summer of 1974.

• • •

"What Richard Nixon has done is attempt to stain the reputation of the agencies of our government by using them to obstruct justice, harass political enemies, illegally spy upon citizens, and cover up crimes. What Richard Nixon has done is show contempt for the Congress by refusing to provide information necessary for the Constitutionally legitimate conduct of an inquiry... What Richard Nixon has done is threaten the Constitution by declaring himself and the Office of the Presidency beyond the reach of law, the Congress, and the courts."

—CONGRESSMAN CHARLES B. RANGEL, MEMBER, JUDICIARY (RODINO) COMMITTEE, AUGUST 1974

CHAPTER TWENTY-NINE
FIREWALL

—■—

AFTER MONTHS OF televised House hearings—of witnesses examined and cross-examined and the introduction of hundreds of documents and exhibits—the proceedings in the Senate would play out as less an inquest than the closing arguments in a case already tried. Only one witness remained to be heard from—the defendant. But before that high drama could unfold, there was still unfinished business left over from the House hearings...

OPENING DAY DEBATE, Senate trial of the President, 9/9/98

PATRICK LEAHY: If Your Honor please, and the gentleman from Utah will yield...

ORRIN HATCH: Is this about the tapes?

PATRICK LEAHY: Yes, the tapes subpoenaed during the House hearings. In conversations with White House Counsel over the past several days, I've learned it's their feeling...

THE CHIEF JUSTICE: Feeling, Mr. Leahy, or position? Let's be explicit.

PATRICK LEAHY: Position. It's their position that the termination of proceedings in the House raises a constitutional question as to the validity of the Committee subpoena.

ORRIN HATCH: I can't see that there's a question. The subpoena was issued and served.

PATRICK LEAHY: But the issuing authority...

THE CHIEF JUSTICE: Let's cut through this, Mr. Leahy. Is it the contention of the defense that because the House has adjourned, the subpoena is no longer valid?

ORRIN HATCH: If it please the Court, let me point out that had the material subpoenaed been turned over as directed...

THE CHIEF JUSTICE: True, Mr. Hatch, but let's address the question anyway, to clear up any misunderstanding regarding the nature of these proceedings: The process set out in the Constitution, Mr. Leahy—impeachment by the House, trial by the Senate—is indivisible. I would think that was obvious, but in any case, the subpoena remains valid and you may so inform the White House. Mr. Hatch, are you ready to proceed with opening arguments?

ORRIN HATCH: We are, Your Honor. Under terms agreed to by the prosecution and the defense...

• • •

FIFTEEN HUNDRED MILES removed and 35,000 feet above the skirmish in the Senate, Al Gore sipped Evian and watched the proceedings from the privacy of his front-cabin compartment aboard Air Force II. The Denver event had gone well: a good crowd, the speech well-received—all he could have hoped for, except...

New Memo Links Gore To Tobacco Lobbyist

—FRONT-PAGE HEADLINE, *THE DENVER POST*, 9/9/98

It wasn't exactly the headline the vice president expected after a six-day speaking tour rallying the Democratic troops behind their beleaguered President. The memo in question, Gore knew, could only have come from a White House leak. What was especially galling was the fact that the "tobacco lobbyist" was really a friend of the Clintons, passed on for Gore to stroke only because the President wanted to avoid him...

TELEPHONE CALL, White House to Air Force II, 0735 hrs. EDT, 9/9/98

THE PRESIDENT: I have no idea where the leak came from, Al, absolutely none, but take my word for it, I'm gonna get to the source, track it down...

THE VICE PRESIDENT: Well, one way—do we have any idea who broke the story, where the AP picked it up?

THE PRESIDENT: I'll get Mike on that right away—but listen, old buddy, the important thing is, we can't afford to lose our grip, get divided. That's the headline they're looking for, you know? "Clinton-Gore split." And whoever's behind this *(expletive deleted)*—you know, I wouldn't be a bit surprised to find the Republicans slipped a mole into...

• • •

THE CALL HAD LEFT AL GORE at first queasy, then irritated. A Republican mole? Halfway through the conversation, he was tempted to say, Bill, this is Al, remember? Whose chain do you think you're pulling?

Get to the source? If Clinton were serious, he wouldn't have to look very far. Across the breakfast table would about do it. Amazing, Gore thought, that with as many legal problems as Hillary Clinton had, she could still make time to play White House power games.

The vice president knew most, if not all, there was to know about the first lady's behind-the-scenes work with Begala's war council. Her frequent stop-bys in the War Room had been noted and reported by his staff in the EOB. There had also been rumors—though Gore discounted them at first—that a low-road campaign code-named "Firewall" was underway to save Clinton's presidency by discrediting his back-up. A source at *The Washington Post* had overheard the hyper-loquacious James Carville spell out the campaign, in detail, over a boisterous dinner with some Louisiana cronies at the Palm restaurant.

As Carville told it, the genesis of "Firewall" was Hillary Clinton's reaction to a poll that showed the public didn't see any difference between Gore and Clinton on substantive issues.

NBC-*WALL STREET JOURNAL* SURVEY, week of August 24-28, 1998

If the Hyde Committee impeaches President Clinton and he is forced out of office, do you think Vice President Al Gore is qualified to run the nation's affairs?

Yes, Gore is qualified	65%
No, he is not qualified	23%
Don't know	12%

What difference do you think a Gore administration would make in the conduct of American foreign policy?

A great deal of difference	17%
No difference	68%
Don't know	15%

Do you think the nation's economy would benefit, be hurt, or remain the same in the event Gore replaced Clinton?

Benefit	9%
Be hurt	13%
Remain the same	71%
Don't know	7%

THE FIRST LADY read these numbers as a dual threat to her husband's presidency: first, they told her that Bill Clinton, far from getting credit for the success of his own administration, was considered as disposable as a plastic razor; second, they gave credibility to the line put out by Marty Peretz's *New Republic*, that Al Gore in the White House could give Democratic candidates running in November everything they could get from Bill Clinton—without the soiled baggage.

Thus "Firewall," the equalizer—giving Marty Peretz's friend Al some soiled baggage of his own. Al Gore wondered, reflecting on his morning phone call, how many like it he'd get from his old buddy in the weeks ahead.

• • •

COMPARATIVE HEADLINES, 9/11/98

Tape Dispute Ties up Senate Trial
Rehnquist Awaits White House Brief Before Ruling
—FRONT PAGE, *THE WASHINGTON POST*, 9/11/98

Hatch Charges Clinton With "Compounding Crime"
Rehnquist Orders Defense to "Show Cause" for Tape Hold-out
—FRONT PAGE, *THE WASHINGTON TIMES*, SAME DAY

• • •

IN FACT, THE FIRST DAY of the Senate trial had covered more than the question of whether the White House, for averred reasons of "national security," could refuse to honor the Hyde Committee's subpoena. The trial format called for opening arguments and general debate—following Senate rather than court procedure—then closing arguments, with September 25 set for the final vote. For the prosecution Hatch would open, Specter would close; for the defense, Leahy would open, with Kennedy having the last word.

By the time Orrin Hatch would be called on to deliver the most important speech of his life, the art of rhetoric in the Senate, as in American politics generally, had long since gone the way of speeches written in longhand by the very people who would make them. There were still some lawmakers around—Pat Moynihan was one—who could write and deliver a well-framed address. But by and large, the art had died on Capitol Hill in the 1960s, with the advent of television talk shows.

Given Rehnquist's presence in the chamber—a no-nonsense presiding officer uneasy with his assignment and anxious to move things along—it was just as well that Orrin Hatch was more the legal technician than a prairie spellbinder. His opening argument, all of twenty-five minutes, went to the basic question of whether the President had committed "high crimes and misdemeanors," as defined by the framers of the Constitution.

A week before, speaking to the American Bar Association, the case was advanced by the attorney general—a new-born strict-contructionist—that there were no legal grounds for removing President Clinton from office because "the charges levelled by the Hyde Committee are political in nature, not criminal... "

OPENING ARGUMENT of Senator Orrin Hatch,
Senate trial of President Clinton, 9/9/98

ORRIN HATCH: ... I could cite numerous legal authorities to refute the Attorney General's argument, but I think one will suffice... Nearly a quarter-century ago, in February, 1974, a group of lawyers here in Washington was given the task of writing a report setting out the constitutional grounds for presidential impeachment. Two notable members of that group were a New York attorney, Bernard Nussbaum, and a recent Yale Law School graduate, Hillary Rodham...

What the Nussbaum-Rodham report said in reviewing the history of the process was that since the 14th century, impeachment has been, I quote, "one of the tools used by the English" people to make their government "more responsive and responsible...." Responsive, responsible—and something else as well. On page seven of the Nussbaum-Rodham study...

THE CHIEF JUSTICE: Mr. Hatch, are you speaking here of a staff report—actually, memorandum—to the House Judiciary Committee?

ORRIN HATCH: Yes, sir.

THE CHIEF JUSTICE: Then for the record—you may refer to it as you wish—Nussbaum, Rodham, whatever—but I think the record should indicate your source with some specificity.

ORRIN HATCH: Yes, sir—the House Judiciary Committee 1974 Staff Report on Impeachment. The Rodino Committee...

THE CHIEF JUSTICE: Specific enough. You may proceed.

ORRIN HATCH: Thank you, Your Honor... The report memorandum goes on, page thirteen, to cite the Federalist, Number 65, in which no less an authority than Alexander Hamilton defines grounds for impeachment as, I quote, "misconduct of public men, or... the abuse or violation of some public trust"—that is, and these are Hamilton's own words, not those of Orrin Hatch, or the Hyde Committee—"abuse or violation of some public trust of a political nature"—I repeat—"political nature."

ARLEN SPECTER: Will the gentleman yield for a question?

ORRIN HATCH: Yes...

ARLEN SPECTER: Is the point you're making—am I correct, that the point you're making is that the theory of impeachment that Mr.

Nussbaum and Ms. Rodham applied in the case of President Nixon twenty-four years ago is every bit as applicable to the case of President Clinton today?

ORRIN HATCH: Yes, that, and the fact that our current attorney general might take time to do a bit of homework before making speeches to the American Bar Association.

• • •

"In retrospect, Nixon's release of the Oval Office tapes did the country incalculable harm. It not only eroded the American people's confidence in the institution of the presidency, but to a large extent is the source of the widespread cynicism we see around us—the fact that fewer Americans go to the polls and participate in the process. In the short run, it seemed necessary; but in the long run, it's been utterly destructive. Knowing what we do about Nixon, I wouldn't be surprised to learn that's why he released them."

—COLUMNIST GARRY WILLS, EXPLAINING WHY HE THINKS PRESIDENT CLINTON WAS RIGHT IN NOT RELEASING HIS WHITE HOUSE TAPES, 9/8/98.

• • •

PAT LEAHY DID not relish his assignment as Senate point man for the Clinton defense, but with Joe Biden removing himself from the ball game, there was no way out. Like most if not all his Democratic colleagues in Congress, Leahy's enthusiasm for the President was less than ardent. But for all Bill Clinton's personal flaws, he had done what only one other Democrat had done since the 1960s—get to the White House. Whatever Biden's professed "problem," for Leahy there was the matter of party loyalty to consider, not to mention the lure of White House assistance on projects close to the hearts of his Vermont constituents.

Still, there were limits he had to place on requests from a White House given to extravagant rhetoric. Leahy had no intention of delivering the Jacobin speech ("suggested remarks") sent over from Clinton's political office, with its class war theme and gratuitous assault on "media merchants of hate and fear." Sufficient unto the day, Leahy felt, without going out of your way to kick the shins of radio talk-show hosts and Right-Wing publishers. To date, Rush Limbaugh and Rupert Murdoch hardly knew Pat Leahy was alive. Leahy wanted to keep it that way.

A workmanlike speech, one that kept its audience awake, if not on the edge of their chairs, would do the job...

OPENING ARGUMENT of Senator Patrick Leahy, trial of President Clinton, 9/9/98

PATRICK LEAHY: May I remind my colleagues on the other side of the aisle that the genius of our political system—what separates it from that of most societies throughout history—is the section of our Constitution that bears on the way we choose our leaders, not the way we remove them...

Only once before in American history has this Senate been called together to sit in judgment of a President. The story of that trial— a trial that the distinguished legal scholar Laurence Tribe fairly describes as a partisan witch hunt—is told in this book written by one of our own, a United States Senator who revered this body, and himself rose to the highest office in the land...

(At this point, Senator Leahy read passages from John F. Kennedy's Profiles in Courage *regarding the Senate trial of President Andrew Johnson.)*

What is remarkable about this episode in our history is that Andrew Johnson had become President of the United States through succession, not election. Not a single vote—not one—had ever been cast to send him to the White House. After his impeachment by the House it must have seemed, given the partisan spirit of the age, that his days as President—some called him acting president—were numbered.

Yet Andrew Johnson and the system prevailed—testament to the fact that even in times of mean-spirited partisanship there are those American leaders who can rise above the passions of the moment to become "profiles in courage."

With that history in mind, consider the question now before this Senate, these 130 years after the trial of Andrew Johnson: Should we, little less than two years after the American people went to the polls and re-elected, in overwhelming numbers, the leader they chose to take our country into the twenty-first century—should we, in contravention of the people's will, remove that man from office? I think the answer is obvious...

CHAPTER THIRTY
THE STAND-OFF

■

President "Eager" to Go Before Congress; Offer is Made to Address Joint Session

—HEADLINE, *THE NEW YORK TIMES*, 9/10/98

THE IDEA—a preemptive stroke—was for the President to testify, then take questions from the floor, not simply before the Senate but both houses of Congress. And this time, it hadn't come from Dick Morris but from a half-forgotten figure from Bill Clinton's first administration, the once ubiquitous David Gergen. Though eased out of the White House as Clinton's resident Republican, Gergen had stayed in touch with the President and was quick to relay an idea he knew would play to Clintons' ego as well as his strength.

Clinton bought the proposal immediately. Without even running it past his war council, he told McCurry to release news of the offer—made in an early morning call to Trent Lott—at his afternoon press briefing. Even a grudging Dick Morris agreed that it would upstage a formal Senate request that the President appear personally on Capitol Hill "to testify and respond to questions raised by the House inquest into your conduct of office..."

Given the history of such requests, no one had seriously expected Clinton to honor it. The constitutional provision for co-equal branches had insulated presidents from Congressional subpoenas, orders and requests to "testify" on Capitol Hill for over 200 years. When presidents did go to the Hill to talk to a committee of Congress, as Lincoln once had, they came of their own volition, not under legal duress.

Nor was the President's annual message to Congress an exception to this rule. All the Constitution mandates is that presidents "shall from time to time give Information of the State of the Union" (Article II, Section 3). An appearance before Congress to deliver that Information, far from being mandatory, is a presidential option turned into a major media ritual since the arrival of television in the 1960s and 1970s.

In the 1980s, Ronald Reagan turned this ritual into a spin doctor's dream—the President on-stage before the nation, bathed in cheers and adulation.

In the 1990s, Bill Clinton, ever the quick learner, mastered Reagan's technique and judged it worth a five-to-seven-point boost in his polls. That was the format the President offered his Senate auditors. Not mere testimony but a prime-time production.

Republicans were having none of it.

• • •

KATIE COURIC INTERVIEW of Senate Majority Leader Trent Lott, NBC *Today* show, 9/14/98

TRENT LOTT: Well, first, Katie, let's put this into perspective. The Constitution provides for a Senate trial—deliberations, weighing the case made by the House for removing the President. A serious, probably the most serious matter ever to come...

KATIE COURIC: You're not answering the question, Senator.

TRENT LOTT: But I am, Katie, if you'll let me finish... The President, in other words, is on trial, on serious charges, and if he comes before the Senate to testify, it has to be in that context. He's a defendant. He doesn't have to appear, that's his prerogative. But if he does, it's not as a President coming to deliver a message concerning the State-of-the-Union, but...

KATIE COURIC: I'm sorry, Senator, but we have to break away for our local stations... Coming up when we return, Senate Majority Leader Trent Lott... And in the next half-hour, Demi Moore to tell us about her latest blockbuster, and a report on the newly approved one-hour out-patient procedure for liposuction...

We're back, with Majority Leader Trent Lott, here to defend the refusal of Senate Republicans to let President Clinton testify at his own trial. I'm not a lawyer, Senator, but it seems to me, as I'm sure it does to most of our viewers, that there's something basically unfair about accusing someone of high crimes and misdemeanors, then not letting him tell his side of the story.

TRENT LOTT: That's not exactly accurate, Katie, and if you'll allow me—what the President wants to do is stage a media event, make a political speech. But this—I repeat—this isn't a campaign, it's a trial.

KATIE COURIC: But he also said he'd answer questions. Isn't that a first? A President answering questions from Congress? How can you possibly be against that?

• • •

GOP Blasts Clinton Offer to Appear As "Sham and Diversion"

—HEADLINE, *USA TODAY,* 9/14/98

"A LOT OF SMILING FACES..."

That was the phrase Wolf Blitzer led with, in a report describing White House reaction to the news play given the Senate's rejection of what Dick Morris was now claiming as his (not David Gergen's) original idea. Once again, it appeared, the White House had turned the tables—outmaneuvered, outflanked, out-spun—its slow-footed Republican adversaries. Capping the President's success: an offer from what CNN was now promoting as "The People's Forum"— *Larry King Live*, prime-time—the night before the final Senate vote...

MEET THE PRESS, 9/13/98

TIM RUSSERT: Senator Lieberman, in your Friday speech, you said you had "serious concerns" about what you called "the President's delaying tactics" regarding the White House tapes. That caused quite a stir—but this isn't the first time you've parted company with your Democratic colleagues, is it?

JOSEPH LIEBERMAN: I wouldn't call it parting company, Tim, because I'm not alone in my concern. We're speaking of compliance—that is, complying with a duly-authorized subpoena from a committee of Congress. That's not a partisan matter.

TIM RUSSERT: I don't think the White House would argue that point, Senator. What they say is, given the amount of material subpoenaed—the fact that much of it is classified—it has to be vetted. Let me quote White House counsel on that...

JOSEPH LIEBERMAN: I'm aware of their position, but keep in mind it's been five weeks, more than a month, since the subpoena went out. That's a lot of time for vetting. We should have had something by now.

TIM RUSSERT: When you say you're not alone in that position...

JOSEPH LIEBERMAN: Definitely not. Other senators...

TIM RUSSERT: Democrats?

JOSEPH LIEBERMAN: Some Democrats, yes. They don't care for these delaying tactics any more than I do.

TIM RUSSERT: Enough to vote for removal?

JOSEPH LIEBERMAN: As I said, it's a serious concern...

• • •

WHATEVER PART OF THE WHITE HOUSE Wolf Blitzer had visited to find those "smiling faces," it wasn't the Political Affairs Office, where minds were focussed on Senate votes, not ephemeral headlines. Even as Bill Clinton's spin doctors were celebrating their latest PR coup, his political scouts on Capitol Hill were sending up flares, warning that unless something was done, and quickly, the tape hold-out would become a serrated-edge for republican arguments that the President was guilty of obstruction of justice.

So it was that through the first week of the Great Debate,* there were reports of Democratic senators variously described as "concerned," "uneasy," and in at least one case "testy" about the tape hold-out...

FRITZ HOLLINGS (TO WHITE HOUSE POLITICAL DIRECTOR CRAIG SMITH): Tell him to give up the *(expletive deleted)* tapes. You want me to put it in writing? Give up the *(expletive deleted)* tapes! *(expletive deleted)*, even Nixon gave up his *(expletive deleted)* tapes...

• • •

NBC RADIO, noon report, 9/16/98

NEWSCASTER: The Senate drama heightens as eight of his fellow Democrats call on President Clinton to release the White House tapes. Back after this...

• • •

THE PRESIDENT RE-READ the letter from the Hill, then took out his yellow legal pad, to add two new names to the six he had original-

---

* A label applied to the trial by Fox News guest-commentator William F. Buckley, Jr., who added that "while the rhetoric might not be de maximus, the issue most definitely is."

ly put down as potential crossovers on the final Senate vote, now less than two weeks off.

Eight in all: (1) Lieberman, (2) Hollings, (3) Feingold, (4) Kerrey, (5) Biden, (6) Wellstone, (7) Reid, and (8) Moynihan. He studied the names, then added a note in the margin: Check leverage—Clinton code for is there anything they want? Anything to give (or take away) that might make a difference? A judgeship for a Senator's friend? A reprieve on the shutdown of an Army base or naval installation?

Leverage. A meeting of the minds, a point of light, as that term was best understood in Washington. Nothing crass, on the order of what occurred the last time the Senate had tried a President, a time when—as John F. Kennedy wrote in *Profiles in Courage*—"attempted bribery and other forms of pressure were rampant."

Since June, when the Hyde Committee first convened to consider impeachment, Clinton-the-policy-wonk had become Clinton-the-history-wonk, devouring everything there was to read about the trial of Andrew Johnson, learning all there was to know about the bribery used and pressure exerted to swing individual votes...

TELEGRAM sent to Senator Edmund Ross of Kansas, May 15, 1868

KANSAS HAS HEARD THE EVIDENCE AND
DEMANDS THE CONVICTION OF THE PRESIDENT
(signed) D. R. ANTHONY AND 1,000 OTHERS

No change, really, between then and now, thought the President. The only difference is that D. R. Anthony, if he were alive, would be arranging letters/wires/phonecalls/e-mail from ten million "others," helped by his Right-wing talk show friends—Rush Limbaugh, Gordon Liddy, Ollie North, Michael Reagan...

Not that Bill Clinton had any intention of leaving the field to his enemies—of engaging in, as he liked to say, unilateral disarmament. Six states had been targeted for saturation advertising, with TV spots urging viewers to write/wire/call/e-mail their senators, telling them that (1) Connecticut, (2) South Carolina, (3) Wisconsin, (4) Nebraska, (5) Delaware and (6) Minnesota had heard the evidence and demanded the acquittal of the President. Now (7) Nevada, and (8) New York would be added to the list.

Still, something had to be done about those tapes...

CHAPTER THIRTY-ONE
THE OBSTRUCTION

■

"Oversight isn't a cat-and-mouse game, but this administration is making it that. You have to ask the right question, at the right time, in the right way. If you don't, you get a misleading response."

—CONGRESSMAN SPENCER BACHUS (R-AL)
on how the Clinton administration deals with Congress.

• • •

CONGRESS HAD ASKED for the White House tapes; Congress would get the White House tapes. Within reason, of course…

COMPARATIVE HEADLINES

White House Surrenders Tapes As Senate Trial Enters Final Week

—THE BOSTON GLOBE, 9/18/98

Hatch Says Tapes "Incomplete"; Charges "Criminal" Cover-up

—THE BOSTON HERALD, SAME DAY

• • •

THE TAPES HAD BEEN STORED in a vault in a sub-basement of the Old EOB. Some two thousand in all, covering everything from the President discussing chip shots with Greg Norman in the First Family residence to the First Lady's telling Vince Foster to put Craig Livingstone on the White House payroll.

Congress would get the first, but not the second. It was the same pattern, Hatch told the Senate, that Bill Clinger had outlined for the Hyde Committee…

ORRIN HATCH SENATE FLOOR SPEECH, 9/17/98

ORRIN HATCH: … To listen to the news this morning, the American people would get the impression—it was certainly the impression I received—that the Clinton White House had decided to comply with the law and deliver its tapes. At least, that's what the White House claimed. But when I arrived at my office—lo and behold, what do I discover? Yes, they've delivered tapes, but not all the tapes—only fifty-six out of a total of thousands. The remainder, we're told, will be delivered, to quote White House Counsel—"at the earliest time consistent with both national security interests and"—I continue to quote—"appropriate consideration given the authority provided the Chief Executive under the constitutional doctrine of separation of powers."

Haven't we—I ask not only my colleagues on this side, but the other side of the aisle—haven't we heard this claim of executive privilege before? An attempt to withhold White House tapes as part of a criminal conspiracy to obstruct justice? Yes, we have… nearly a quarter-century ago—and the courts struck it down.

JOHN MCCAIN (R-AZ): Will the Senator yield for a question?

ORRIN HATCH: Yes…

JOHN MCCAIN: When can we hear the tapes for ourselves, to get some idea of what's on them?

ORRIN HATCH: At the moment—to answer your question—they're being transcribed.

JOHN MCCAIN: I'm not talking transcriptions, I mean the tapes themselves. Not all fifty-six, but a sample. As I understand the procedure—*(at this point, addressing the chief justice)* As I understand, Your Honor, we're operating as a court of law, and the tapes are evidence. Is that correct?

THE CHIEF JUSTICE: If introduced, yes.

JOHN MCCAIN: Then I move they be introduced and played before the full Senate...

ORRIN HATCH: You mean here, now?

JOHN MCCAIN: Yes, here, now.

• • •

NIGHTLINE, Ted Koppel interview with John McCain, Tom Daschle, Pat Moynihan, 9/17/98

TED KOPPEL: Senator McCain, now that we've heard the tapes, it seems to many of us that the play we watched on the Senate stage today, if you'll pardon the metaphor, was much ado about nothing.

JOHN MCCAIN: I agree, Ted.

TED KOPPEL: The President going over his schedule, bidding his daughter goodbye as she goes off to college, meeting with Bill Weld—pretty bland fare. Was it what you expected? Or did you entertain a faint hope that there might be some red meat you could chew on?

JOHN MCCAIN: Not really—though I found it interesting that of all the tapes the White House sent over—only one out of every forty, you know—they managed to clear the one you mentioned, the President and Bill Weld.

TED KOPPEL: Yes, discussing the threat of—I believe Weld's exact phrase was "The Right-wing crazies." But didn't you...

TOM DASCHLE: I'd like to add something to that, if I might, Ted.

TED KOPPEL: Feel free, Senator.

TOM DASCHLE: Only that the Weld tape is more than interesting, it's highly significant. Because here you have a member of Senator McCain's own party—someone who served in the Justice Department during the Reagan years—saying essentially what the White House has been saying about this whole impeachment process. That Right-wing radicals...

TED KOPPEL: In fairness, Senator, he wasn't talking about the Senate trial, but his own problems with Senator Helms. The tape, I believe, was dated...

TOM DASCHLE: But the same elements, the very same elements, are at work here, Ted—which is why, though I at first disagreed with Senator McCain about playing the tapes, I think it performed a real service, focusing on what this debate is all about. On the one hand...

TED KOPPEL: Senator Moynihan, I see you shaking your head. You were, I believe, one of the eight dissident democratic senators who wrote the President, urging that he comply with the subpoena— that is, release the tapes. I take it you disagree with your colleague, Tom Daschle.

PAT MOYNIHAN: To the extent that he thinks what we heard today was significant, yes. What was significant, in my opinion, is what we didn't hear—the two thousand tapes the White House won't release.

TED KOPPEL: To be fair, Senator, nineteen-hundred forty. Or so we're informed. But essentially you're right, they haven't been released, and I assume—or am I right in assuming?—that you're unhappy with the extent of White House compliance.

PAT MOYNIHAN: That's one way to put it, though frustrated might be a better word.

TOM DASCHLE: About those eight Democrats, Ted...

TED KOPPEL: If you'll hold that thought a moment, Senator Daschle, we'd like to hear your colleague out on this point. You were saying, Senator Moynihan...?

PAT MOYNIHAN: Simply that, to put it into perspective, the content of the tapes is less important—whether they concern scheduling or Whitewater—than the fundamental principle involved. The idea that no person, regardless of the office he or she holds, stands above the law. Under our system, when a subpoena is served, it has to be honored, even by a President. Especially by a President.

• • •

EDITORIAL SAMPLINGS compiled by *USA Today*, week of September 13–19, 1998

ST. LOUIS **(MO)** *POST-DISPATCH*: "President Clinton will be acquitted, as he should be, and historians in future years will look back on the so-called Great Debate of 1998 as a bi-coastal book-end, the Washington answer to Los Angeles' O.J. Simpson travesty." (9/15/98)

ATLANTA **(GA)** *CONSTITUTION-JOURNAL*: "President Clinton in his radio address last Saturday, said that the people behind the impeachment drive seek to turn the clock back to the nineteenthth century. A minor quibble: the seventeenth century is more like it." (9/17/98)

MANCHESTER **(NH)** *UNION-LEADER*: "In 1868, seven Republican senators defied their leadership and voted conscience over party in the Senate trial of President Andrew Johnson. Are there thirteen Democrats to do the same in the trial of William Jefferson Clinton? A cynical White House thinks not, but the Union-Leader believes that now, as 130 years ago, political courage is the monopoly of no single party." (9/18/98)

• • •

White House Releases 500 More Tapes As GOP Warns of Court Order for Contempt

—FRONT-PAGE HEADLINE, *THE WASHINGTON POST*, 9/19/98

White House Memo Says Gore Met With "Polluter"

—PAGE-TWO HEADLINE, *THE WASHINGTON POST*, SAME DAY

AL GORE SAT IN THE FIRST-FLOOR SOLARIUM of the Vice President's residence, scanning the morning papers and waiting for the phone to ring. After five years of riding tandem with Bill Clinton, Gore knew the pattern, could almost call the shots.

On the tape front, the "stonewall" phase was obviously over. Now the White House would fire, fall back, and play for time. With the Senate vote only a week away, release of the five hundred tapes, though not total compliance, could cut some slack, possibly keep the dissidents in line.

The dissidents: First there were six, then eight, now possibly nine. Jeff Bingaman had called a few hours earlier and told of a new poll in the *Albuquerque Journal* that had mixed results on the question of impeachment but reported 82 percent of the respondents "strongly" in favor of the President's turning over the tapes. Why release only five hundred? Bingaman wanted to know. Why not release them all? It would make things so simple.

Indeed it would, but not in the way the Senator from New Mexico imagined. Al Gore had heard the tapes—not all of them, but enough: Bill and Riady (on the hiring of Webb Hubbell); Hillary and Nussbaum (on the Travelgate firings); the President and First Lady (on the Rose law firm billings).

They were devastating. Enough so that Bill Clinton had no real choice in the matter: he could hold on to the tapes and risk conviction, or release the tapes and assure it.

The phone rang. Gore picked it up. He knew what was coming, chapter-and-verse. There would be the feel-your-pain apology, followed by the promise to track down and fire whatever *(expletive deleted)* had leaked the memo; then, the caution to stay cool, because what "they" really wanted was a Clinton-Gore rift; and finally, the random presidential thought that some sinister force was behind the leak.

The first time, Clinton thought there might be a mole in the White House working for the Republicans. This time, he thought the mole might be moonlighting for Dick Gephardt.

● ● ●

THE GREAT DEBATE went into its second week, with sharp exchanges only when someone, intentionally or otherwise, went wide of Article II. Though reminded that the sole issue before the Senate was the Clinton administration's alleged obstruction of justice, New Jersey's Robert Toricelli persisted in arguing the extent of Ronald Reagan's knowledge of Iran-Contra, until called to order by the chief justice.

Republicans, on the other hand, were successful in their argument that the tape hold-out, though not specifically cited in the Article, went to the heart of whether, in Arlen Specter's words, "this President, as a matter of habit, routinely flouts subpoenas and impedes the course of justice."

For their part, the Democratic defense in the first week of the trial hewed to the White House line that the tapes were coming, it was just a matter of time. But by the second week...

"I cannot and will not defend the indefensible."

—SENATOR ROBERT BYRD, IN FLOOR SPEECH,
on learning that the 500 tapes released by the White House had
been edited "in the interest of national security." (9/20/98)

• • •

WHEN THE VICE PRESIDENT received word of Bob Byrd's defection, his first impulse was to laugh. But, given the fact that the person delivering the news had been sent by Bill Clinton, Gore contained himself. He could not, however, pass up the chance to say, I told you so.

Months before, while the Hyde Committee was still working its way through Travelgate testimony, the vice president had warned the White House that a line-item veto of one of Bob Byrd's West Virginia pork projects would come back to haunt them. Assured by the President that all was well ("I can handle Bob Byrd."), Gore walked away knowing that a payback lay somewhere down the line. Byrd would bide his time, waiting for the right moment to get even; which meant the worst possible moment for Bill Clinton.

Now Craig Smith, Clinton's political director, had been sent to get the vice president's advice on how to buy Byrd back. What would it take? An apology from the President? The promise of bigger, juicier pork projects in the offing?

The vice president shook his head. You still don't get it, he said. You can't buy Byrd back, at least not quickly. He may come around, but in his own sweet time.

A short while later, Gore got a call—again a call he was expecting. This time there were no apologies for memos leaked, but rather a request: Could old buddy Al see his way clear to stroke Bob Byrd? It was a vote they couldn't afford to lose.

There comes a moment in the career of every ambitious Vice President with an eye to the future when he goes his own way. Al Gore had no intention of serving as Bill Clinton's agent in Clinton's effort to placate Bob Byrd. First, the effort was futile; second, looking ahead to the year 2000, there was nothing to be gained from Gore's being linked to an incident that angered the most powerful Democrat in West Virginia; third, an hour before Craig Smith's arrival, Gore had learned that a White House source had tried to sell Richard Cohen on an "exclusive" column disclosing the real reason the President was holding onto the tapes: It wasn't to protect himself, but his good friend Al who (according to the source) was "up to his ears in laundered Asian money and tobacco pay-offs."

Fortunately Cohen didn't buy the story. But to Al Gore, who for five years had been Bill Clinton's loyal trouper, it was clear that the moment had come to look out for himself; though he didn't quite put it that way in refusing the President's request.

Understood, said Bill Clinton. I just thought I'd ask. No hard feelings. Those were his words, but Al Gore knew better.

• • •

MIKE MCCURRY WAS A TEENAGER at the time, but he still remembered an incident during the final months of the Nixon presidency, when the President blew up in public and shoved his press secretary, Ron Ziegler. The scene, Nixon at his worst, was shown and repeated on television as evidence of a President losing his grip.

Bill Clinton, who also remembered the Nixon crack-up, took pains never to be caught on camera showing anything but the upbeat confidence of a winner; a Gulliver temporarily tied down by little men, but with no long-term problems. Bad news, like the defections of Bingaman and Byrd, merely broadened his smile. A President in total control, he would never think of shoving his press secretary in public.

Privately, however, Clinton's press secretary was suffering his share of indignities. Not physical, but aural—Bill Clinton at his worst, an angry man given to tongue-lashing his subordinates when things went wrong.

Things were going wrong, and neither of the Clintons, Bill or Hillary, was one to suffer bad news gladly. Unfortunately for McCurry, he happened to enter the Oval Office just as the President hung up the phone after Al Gore's turn-down. McCurry had come seeking guidance on how to answer the question—sure to be asked by the press—on how Clinton had reacted to Byrd's floor speech...

• • •

MIKE MCCURRY TRANSCRIPTION of MEMCON with the
President, 9:15 A.M., 9/19/98

THE PRESIDENT: That's a stupid question.

MIKE MCCURRY: I know it's stupid but...

THE PRESIDENT: Then why take up my time with it? All the (deleted)
flying—the (deleted) in Congress, my (deleted) lawyers, the (deleted) Jones appeal...

MIKE MCCURRY: Do you want me to say...

THE PRESIDENT: I don't give a (deleted) what you say, just don't (deleted) it up like you generally do.

• • •

TELEPHONE CONVERSATION between White House Press
Secretary Michael McCurry and Fox News Bureau-Chief
Brit Hume, 9/20/98

BRIT HUME: No reaction? That's hard to believe.

MIKE MCCURRY: Not really. He's a man, you know, who's found inner
peace. I've never seen him more upbeat, confident...

CHAPTER THIRTY-TWO
BACKFIRE

■

IT WAS A SMALL PACKAGE, the kind working journalists often receive from someone pushing a cause, but distinguished by its having come by priority mail, with no return address; not to mention what it contained: three standard Memorex cassettes and a note, typed on white stock paper:

> **TO PAUL BEDARD**
> **THE WASHINGTON TIMES**
> · **Enc: FYI - White House Tapes**

Bedard, with a reputation as a political reporter who had done the White House no favors over the years, often received documents and other material from anonymous sources. Some were left at the front desk, some arrived by mail; most were legitimate, but a few came from crackpots. He would later confess that on opening this package, his initial impulse was to put its anonymous sender into the latter category—a crackpot simply trying to cause a stir. But then he played the tape. The voices were unmistakable.

When he replayed it for Wes Pruden, however, the *Times* editor-in-chief had his doubts...

WES PRUDEN: It could be an impersonator. There's one on the radio every morning, selling used cars.

PAUL BEDARD: Does he impersonate her, too?

WES PRUDEN: You've got a point. But I'll call in a voice expert anyway...

• • •

HILLARY CLINTON'S reaction to the *Times*'s tape story was, according to a Secret Service agent present at the time, sulfuric. Orders were issued, first to place a uniformed guard in the sub-basement room in the EOB where the tapes were kept, then to move them to a top-security vault in the Pentagon.

Only when it was pointed out that Paul Bedard had said the tapes he received were copies, not the originals, did the First Lady shift her attention to the Who, not the What of Bedard's story. Who was Anonymous—Bedard's admittedly unoriginal name for his White House source?* Whoever it was had to know where the tapes were, and what was in them. The First Lady ran through a list of possibilities and finally settled on one...

WHITE HOUSE TRANSCRIPTION XA-741, telephone conversation, the President and Vice President, 9/23/98

THE PRESIDENT: Al, you know, these tapes—Hillary and I were just talking, wondering how...

THE VICE PRESIDENT: How they got out? Yeah, I've been wondering the same thing.

THE PRESIDENT: You mean, you don't know.

THE VICE PRESIDENT: No, but I have an idea. Something you told me...

THE PRESIDENT: Something I told you?

THE VICE PRESIDENT: ...about a White House mole, the one you said...

THE PRESIDENT: White House mole?

THE VICE PRESIDENT: ...was working for the Republicans. Remember?

---

*"I would have called him—or her—'Deep Throat'," the *Times* reporter told a National Press Club luncheon not long after, "but that was already taken."

COMPARATIVE HEADLINES

TIMES EXCLUSIVE:

Tapes Reveal Clintons Arranged Hubbell Job as Part of Cover-up

—FRONT PAGE, *THE WASHINGTON TIMES*, 9/23/98

Tapes Purport to Tell About Clinton Concern for Hubbell

—PAGE FOUR, *THE WASHINGTON POST*, SAME DAY

WHITE HOUSE TRANSCRIPTION, conversation in residence, President and First Lady, 3/15/94, as reprinted in *The Washington Times*, 9/23/98*

THE PRESIDENT: I can't see the problem.

THE FIRST LADY: You never can. That's why we're up to our ears in *(expletive deleted)*, because you don't see a problem until it's too late.

THE PRESIDENT: I told you, Mack's talked to the man. It's a done deal.

THE FIRST LADY: Huang or Riady?

THE PRESIDENT: Riady. Webb goes on at, I don't know, three hundred, five hundred...

THE FIRST LADY: That's not what he told me.

THE PRESIDENT: Mack?

THE FIRST LADY: No, Webb. He ways Mack was supposed to call him but didn't.

THE PRESIDENT: Okay, so he hasn't gotten around to calling him. It's

---

*Unlike the other documents dated prior to September 1, 1997, there is as yet no confirmation of the existence of these tapes.

not like, you know, we don't have things going on around the White House besides getting Webb Hubbell a...

THE FIRST LADY: Things that can get us ind...

THE PRESIDENT: Okay, so what is it? What do you want? We've been over this...

THE FIRST LADY: What I've said all along—you talk to him. We've got to keep Webb happy.

THE PRESIDENT: Me talk to Riady?

THE FIRST LADY: He'll *(expletive deleted)* Mack, but not you. I told you that a month ago, when it looked like Webb was going to...

THE PRESIDENT: Yeah, but I hate it, you know. Mack does it, I don't have to know anything about it. I do it—get a guy who's about to be indicted...

THE FIRST LADY: Who says Webb's about to be indicted? I haven't heard a word.

THE PRESIDENT: Haven't heard a word?

THE FIRST LADY: Not one. We're just trying to get an old friend back on his feet, help him...

THE PRESIDENT: I see what you mean. An act of compassion...

• • •

ON THURSDAY THE 24TH, the *Times* would publish a second transcript; on Friday the 25th, a third. The second directly involved the President in Nussbaum's "stonewall" strategy of withholding documents from the Clinger and Leach committees; the third, which appeared the morning of the Senate vote, covered a meeting between the First Lady and five Clinton aides—McLarty, Nussbaum, Ickes, Kennedy, and Carville—discussing "pressure points" (The First Lady's term) in dealing with Jean Lewis and the RTC Whitewater investigation.

Interestingly enough, publication of the transcripts wasn't viewed as the "smoking gun" Clinton's critics might have hoped for. There were, after all, only three tapes, argued his defenders; and they came, as Tom Daschle told his colleagues on the eve of the Senate vote, "from a tainted Right-wing rag."

It would take the President himself, never at a loss when pushed into a corner, to come up with something better.

CHAPTER THIRTY-THREE
GLAD TO BE HERE, LARRY

■

THE PRESIDENT'S APPEARANCE on *Larry King Live*, CNN, 9/24/98

LARRY KING: With us tonight, on the eve of the most important vote of his career, the President of the United States, Bill Clinton. Glad you could be with us, Mr. President.

THE PRESIDENT: And I'm glad to be here, Larry—but I want to correct one part of that introduction: It's not just my career the Senate's voting on tomorrow—there's more to it than that.

LARRY KING: You mean, the future, where we're headed.

THE PRESIDENT: Exactly—where we're headed—not just Bill Clinton but the country and the Constitution. Our system, our values. And when those one hundred senators stand up and cast their votes tomorrow, that's what's on the line.

LARRY KING: And on the line we'll be, in just a few minutes, Mr. President. But first, I have to ask—any second thoughts?

THE PRESIDENT: Second thoughts about what, Larry?

LARRY KING: The decision to hang in, take the heat. Your hometown paper, *The Arkansas Democrat*...

THE PRESIDENT: That's only one editor's opinion, Larry.

LARRY KING: ...said in an editorial last week that you could save the country and yourself a lot of pain if you'd just resign. Step down... And just this morning, *The New York Post*...

THE PRESIDENT: They're not the folks who elected me, Larry, and I don't intend to start, at this late date, making decisions that affect the future of America—future generations of Americans—based on what individual editors or the public opinion polls say.

LARRY KING: Commendable.

THE PRESIDENT: The folks who elected me—voted for Bill Clinton not once but twice—don't, I think, want a President who'll cut-and-run from a fight.

LARRY KING: Well said—and with that we'll go to some of those very people—San Antonio, you're on the air with President Clinton.

CALLER: Thank you, Larry, and thank you, President Clinton for everything you've done for the country and people like myself since you became President...

LARRY KING: Friendly caller, Mr. President.

THE PRESIDENT: I appreciate those kind words, friend.

LARRY KING: What's your question?

CALLER: It's about the tapes...

THE PRESIDENT: Well, before you go any further, I think you and everybody watching—it's incredible, you know, President Kennedy, I recall he once said something to the effect that a lie can march twice around the world while the truth is still strapping on its boots. Are you familiar with that?

CALLER: No, sir, but from what I've read...

THE PRESIDENT: Let me give you an example. Not long ago—ten or twelve years—*Time* magazine published, was taken in and published, what they said were Hitler's diaries...

LARRY KING: Actually, it was *Newsweek*.

THE PRESIDENT: *Time* or *Newsweek*, the point is—the diaries turned out to be fake, a hoax, and I think it's important as we come down to the final days of a partisan political fight—and make no mistake, that's what this is all about—as we come down to these final days, out of the clear blue, we find a publication that from Day One has opposed everything I and my administration have been trying to do for people like yourself—at the last minute, they come up with something like this. Does that answer your question?

LARRY KING: Then you're saying the tapes are phony. Is that it?

THE PRESIDENT: Absolutely. Spliced, faked, however they do it.

LARRY KING: Interesting. Fort Wayne, Indiana, you're on the air with President Clinton.

CALLER: Good evening, Larry, Mr. President—I just heard your answer to the previous caller, about the tapes, but isn't it true that the real issue...

LARRY KING: Could you speak up, please?

CALLER: Sorry. Isn't the real issue not the tapes we've been reading about the past few days, but the ones you, the White House, won't release? If these tapes are fake, as you claim, it seems to me the best way to strap the boots on truth would be...

THE PRESIDENT: I'm having a hard time hearing...

CALLER: Louder? I said, *if these tapes are fake, why don't you just clear the air by releasing the ones...*

LARRY KING: Can you hear him now? If not...

THE PRESIDENT: What he's saying, yes, but I think the caller should know that we're talking about two different things. Two entirely different things. The tape he's referring to...

CALLER: *The White House tapes.*

THE PRESIDENT: The so-called White House tapes, yes. The first thing you have to understand is that until they were subpoenaed— until I heard about it from Charley Ruff, the White House Counsel, and read about it in the papers, I didn't even know there was a taping system in the Oval Office...

LARRY KING: You didn't know?

THE PRESIDENT: Not an inkling, Larry, and when I found out, the first thing I did—you can check the records on this—the first thing I did was have it removed. Ripped out, wire by wire. Because the idea of taping people when they're unaware—well, go back to the Nixon years—it violates every principle this country stands for, what I believe in, have always believed in, with every fiber of my...

• • •

DICK MORRIS TOUCHED the button on his remote and watched his favorite client's image shrivel and disappear as the TV screen went dark. Morris had seen enough to know that this would not be one of Bill Clinton's better nights.

Morris knew his man—the public Clinton—better than anyone (except possibly Hillary Clinton). For over a dozen years he had watched the quicksilver charmer as he smiled and seduced his way out of countless crises, corners, and tight spots. But this night something was missing. The words were right, but the music was off. Morris wondered whether, after all these years, "Slick Willie" was finally losing his Teflon touch.

Negative thoughts. The spin doctor would put them out of his mind and call Clinton after the show, to tell him how well he did. Then, just for insurance, he would call his old friend Al Gore.

CHAPTER THIRTY-FOUR
THE FINAL DAY

———————————————■———————————————

President Clinton Said to be 'Confident' as Senate Votes Today on Obstruction Charge

—HEADLINE, *THE NEW YORK TIMES*, 9/25/98

UNLUCKY THIRTEEN?
Clinton Fate in Balance

—HEADLINE, *THE NEW YORK POST*, SAME DAY.

• • •

PAT MOYNIHAN had spent the pre-dawn hours of Friday, September 25, re-reading the chapter of John F. Kennedy's *Profiles in Courage* devoted to the ordeal of Senator Edmund Ross in the Senate trial of President Andrew Johnson...

The New York Tribune reported that Edmund Ross in particular was "mercilessly dragged this way and that by both sides... His background and life were investigated from top to bottom, and his constituents and colleagues pursued him throughout Washington to gain some inkling of his opinion..."

MOYNIHAN'S ORDEAL in recent days, though not the crucible Ross had endured, was no less hectic. Since the "Nightline" appearance that marked him as a Democratic dissident on the tape issue, New York's senior senator had been "dragged this way and that" and "pursued... through Washington" by a frenetic press corps that viewed the President's impeachment as a game rather than a process, involving personalities rather than issues.

Then there had been the calls from constituents and colleagues, not to mention the White House itself, explaining, imploring, and on more than one occasion directing Moynihan's attention to polls that showed New York second only to Massachusetts in its support for the President and opposition to his impeachment; calls that continued right up to the moment he set aside his reading, drained one last cup of coffee, and left for the Capitol.

• • •

"Mr. Chief Justice, fellow members of the Senate..."

IT WAS TED KENNEDY, rising to make what Mary McGrory would call "the speech of his life, one that would have done credit to his brother Jack"—the closing argument on behalf of the President.
Orrin Hatch had opened for the prosecution, followed by Pat Leahy for the defense. Both delivered workmanlike, if passionless, speeches, leaving it to their colleagues—Kennedy and Specter—to produce the thunder that might make the difference for those Senators who remained uncommitted.

In his twenty-one years as a senator, Pat Moynihan seldom entered the chamber without a strong, if not a fixed, idea of how he would vote when the clerk called his name. But this day, still undecided about the most critical vote he would ever cast, Moynihan would take his seat and listen—first to Kennedy, then to Specter—

not so much to be persuaded as to resolve the debate going on within himself.

Kennedy would speak for forty-five minutes, a closing argument Moynihan thought notable not only for its eloquence but for the speaker's not once mentioning the allegations made against his client. In fact, until the final minutes of the speech, the client himself was hardly mentioned.

This was hardly an oversight. Given the charge of obstruction of justice, the President's refusal to honor the subpoena for the White House tapes was tantamount to a confession. To save Bill Clinton's presidency, Kennedy concluded, he would have to rise above both the facts and the law, to the higher reaches of what, until now, the President's allies had sought only to execrate—partisan politics, raw and undiluted.

CLOSING ARGUMENT of Senator Ted Kennedy, 9/25/98

TED KENNEDY: The prosecution speaks of "patterns" as well they might. For what the country and the world are witnessing here today is part of a pattern we have seen throughout the Twentieth Century—the pattern of Republican reactionaries hell-bent on destroying a visionary Democratic president...

The country and the world saw it in Woodrow Wilson's time, when the party of the Lodges and the Borahs killed the dream, the vision of our first great Democratic president of this century, Woodrow Wilson... We saw it again a generation later, when another great Democratic president—and his wife—were vilified, when the reactionaries and economic royalists of Franklin Delano Roosevelt's day tried to block, by every means at their disposal, Social Security, the minimum wage, every progressive bill a Democratic Congress passed to improve the lot of the average American, the working American, the disenfranchised and disadvantaged American...

And does anyone doubt—does anyone doubt for a moment— that if a Republican Congress had been in power when Franklin

Delano Roosevelt was President of the United States, he would have been impeached—and tried—before this very body...?

• • •

Kennedy's appeal was simple, direct, and so obviously aimed at a select audience—the Democratic dissidents—that he hardly turned to address the other side of the aisle. A few optimists on the White House staff had talked up the possibility that James Jeffords or some other Republican "moderate" might cross over to vote for acquittal. But Ted Kennedy knew where and how his client's case would be decided—on the Democratic side of the chamber, by members of the party of Wilson, Roosevelt, and John F. Kennedy— by loyal Democrats who kept the faith.

CLOSING ARGUMENT of Senator Ted Kennedy, (continued)

TED KENNEDY: ... Wilson, Roosevelt, and in our own time, John Fitzgerald Kennedy, another great Democratic president whose courage and vision led America to a New Frontier and beyond—an era of civil rights and equal justice for all—but who was fought every step of the way by the Right-wing zealots, the John Birchers, the white-robed Klansmen, the racists and bigots whose malign spirit still hovers over this country—and, yes, over this chamber—even today...

And does anyone doubt for a moment that if a Republican Congress had been in power in the brief, all too brief Thousand Days of John F. Kennedy's presidency, he too would have been impeached—and tried—before this very body?...

Make no mistake then—no mistake about what the country and the world are witnessing here today—a pattern, the same pattern we have seen again and again in this American century: a president, a *Democratic* president at the peak of his powers—a *Democratic* president who has led our nation through five years of peace, prosperity, and plenty—a *Democratic* president of hope and compassion, vision and vitality—a *Democratic* president who has lifted not only the American economy but the American spirit—a *Democratic* president who needs, has earned, and deserves the loyalty and support of *all* Democrats—and *all* Americans who share the values of the party of Woodrow Wilson, Franklin Delano Roosevelt, and John Fitzgerald Kennedy...

• • •

Ted Kennedy sat down to a loud, presumably spontaneous burst of applause from the gallery, brought up short by a gavelled warning from the chief justice. It had been, Moynihan grudgingly thought, quite a speech—Kennedy at his convention best, all hellfire-and-brimstone for the Republican heathen.

What Moynihan begrudged, however, was not his Irish Democratic colleague's rhetorical flair so much as his cold-eyed cynicism. Did Ted Kennedy truly believe that Bill Clinton walked in the path of Wilson, Roosevelt, and his brother? The Hollywood contingent in the galleries might think so, but Pat Moynihan knew better.

Now Arlen Specter was on his feet, reviewing his notes...

CLOSING ARGUMENT of Senator Arlen Specter, 9/25/98

ARLEN SPECTER: I little thought when I was preparing these remarks that our colleague from Massachusetts would, instead of addressing the issues before the Senate—the obstruction of justice by a President who considers himself above the law—I little thought that instead of addressing that issue. Senator Kennedy would impart his version of the political history of the Twentieth Century, beginning with Woodrow Wilson—called "The Incorruptible" when he served both as governor of New Jersey and as President—to William Jefferson Clinton, who as governor of his home state—and as President—has been called many things—but never, to my knowledge, incorruptible.

• • •

AT THE WHITE HOUSE, after receiving his morning update from Capitol Hill, the President watched Arlen Specter on C-Span. The conversation with Craig Smith had been brief and nasty, a clone of the last three conversations Smith had had with his boss.

Clinton's reputation as a man with a foul temper when getting bad news had grown in recent days and Smith, as the chief bad news bearer, had suffered the worst abuse. Before calling in that morning, the White House political director had even considered sugaring the news. But in the end he delivered it straight and unsweetened, then answered questions as best he could.

"You're sure about Durbin? I talked to him just two days ago... What happened to Cleland—the polls in Georgia?"

Smith's answer to the first question was "I'm reasonably sure," to the second, "I don't know," at which point, the conversation ended abruptly. The President simply hung up, scrawled a note on his yellow legal pad, and returned to watching Specter...

On his end, Craig Smith, though unhappy with the way things were going, took comfort in the fact that he had just delivered his final report before the Great Debate ended and the Senate clerk called the roll.

• • •

ARLEN SPECTER had been given an opening, and the dour, sharp-tongued former prosecutor from Philadelphia knew how to exploit it.

The substance of the case under Article II of the Bill of Impeachment—obstructing justice, impeding lawful investigations—had been argued, in painstaking detail, by Orrin Hatch. Closing the case, Specter had set out to make morality—public morality—his theme. Ted Kennedy, by placing Bill Clinton in the twentieth century Democratic pantheon with Wilson, Roosevelt, and John Kennedy, had, as Specter put it, "invited odious comparison between the high standards we once knew and expected in the White House, and the debased standards we have had since January of 1993..."

The President listened without comment as Specter—looking across the aisle at the very Democrats his opponent had addressed—ran off a series of questions comparing the Clinton White House not only to those of Wilson, Roosevelt and John Kennedy, but to Harry Truman's as well...

CLOSING ARGUMENT of Senator Arlen Specter (continued)

Would Harry Truman, as quid pro quo for lavish campaign contributions—or contributions of any size—have entertained foreign lobbyists, felons and gun merchants in his White House? Would he have opened the Oval Office door—given access to the President—to the likes of a John Huang, or Roger Tamraz?

• • •

AT THE MENTION OF HUANG and Tamraz, the President shook his head as if to say something, but instead turned back to his notes—the list of possible Democratic crossovers that had doubled since Labor Day from half-a-dozen to a eight, then ten—and if Craig Smith's new information was accurate, an even dozen.

How, he had asked Begala, Carville, the war council, the night before—how could this happen? The tape hold-out, yes; but that was a calculated risk, one the polls said would cause damage but not prove fatal. The market? Falling, yes, with alarm bells about a new recession; but that too fell short of explaining why, within a month, the improbable had become the possible.

The answers to Clinton's questions had been mixed, some skewed toward the optimistic to avoid Smith's mistake of giving the President bad news. Carville, who claimed to have his own sources on Capitol Hill, thought Smith's reports were exaggerated, that the situation wasn't nearly as bad as described. He predicted the President would lose no more than seven Democratic votes when the roll was called. Begala, not as upbeat, predicted a loss of eight.

Only George Stephanopoulos, who was in touch with people outside the White House compound, offered a less sanguine view. He thought a revolution (though he called it a counter-revolution) was brewing; a cultural backlash against the new morality of Bill Clinton's Baby Boomer generation. It could arrive full-force by the year 2000, but Clinton might be its first casualty. The President, his jaw perceptibly tightening, heard Stephanopoulos out, then simply turned to Smith and asked for another rundown on possible Senate defections. Smith gave his best vote scenario as nine defections; his worst as eleven.

Last night eleven, now twelve. Clinton wondered if Smith's information on Pat Moynihan—gleaned from a former Senate staffer— was accurate. Moynihan had been openly critical of the White House when the fund-raising scandals first broke and had lined up with Joe Lieberman and other dissidents on the tape issue. All the background needed to make him a crossover, except…

Clinton's political instinct—not the one that dealt in numbers, but the instinct that gave him a sixth sense in dealing with people one-on-one—told him that Smith's reading in this case was right: Moynihan would not break ranks, no matter how critical he had been of a Democratic White House. His party roots were sunk too deep. True, he had once worked for the Nixon White House; but even then, when the opportunity came to switch allegiance, the pull of his past—the liberal idealism that had drawn him to John F. Kennedy in the early 1960s—was too strong to let him go the way of a John Connally.

No, thought Bill Clinton, Pat Moynihan will not cross over. But the fact that things had gone his far—that he had miscalculated so badly that his presidency hinged on a single senator's vote—gave him pause. He had been wrong about the others. Could he be wrong about Moynihan?

• • •

CLOSING ARGUMENT of Senator Arlen Specter (continued)

Would Franklin D. Roosevelt have approved a plan to barter overnight stays in the Lincoln Bedroom, by the hundreds, for campaign money?

Can you conceive of a Kennedy White House in which John F. Kennedy had on his staff—as director of personnel security, no less—a former barroom bouncer whose specialty was collecting raw FBI files on private citizens? Or a Kennedy administration in which cabinet secretaries, almost as a matter of routine, were under investigation or indicted? Where the third-ranking member of the Justice Department—a member of the President's inner circle—was not only indicted but convicted, then emerged months later as a paid lobbyist for foreign interests seeking access to the Oval Office?

• • •

THE FOCUS OF BILL CLINTON'S ATTENTION, the senior senator from New York, had left home that morning not knowing how he would vote when the roll was called. In any case, he came prepared, a speech in each coat pocket—one for conviction, the other for acquittal—and bided time as Arlen Specter closed out his argument with yet another reminder to Democratic members that it was one of their own, President Grover Cleveland, who said, "A public office is a public trust."

Unsurprisingly, there were no outbursts from the Hollywood contingent as Specter took his seat. He had, however, scored points, if not in the gallery, on the Senate floor; whether enough to assemble sixty-seven votes for conviction remained to be seen.

• • •

RERUN —

"Well, ultimately, anything that happens in the White House is the responsibility of the President."
—PRESIDENT CLINTON, QUOTED IN *THE WASHINGTON POST,* 5/25/93

CHAPTER THIRTY-FIVE
THE ROLL CALL

———————————————— ■ ————————————————

"MR. ABRAHAM."
"GUILTY."

It had begun. At 4:47 PM, on Friday, September 25, 1998, three months to the day after Henry Hyde opened the House Impeachment hearings, Senator Spencer Abraham, the 46-year-old first-term Republican from Michigan, cast the first vote to remove an American president from office in one hundred thirty years.

"MR. AKAKA."
"NOT GUILTY."

The vote would be cast under the same protocol used during the trial of Andrew Johnson, with each senator rendering his or her individual verdict to the question, posed by the Chief Justice, "Do you find the respondent William Jefferson Clinton guilty or not guilty of a high crime, as charged in this Article of Impeachment?"...

"MR. ALLARD."
"GUILTY."

It would take all of fifty-eight minutes to call the Senate roll, with time allowed for remarks by members who wished to explain their vote; or, in some cases (Chris Dodd, Robert Toricelli) simply seize the moment to go on camera before what would be the largest worldwide television audience in history...

"MR. ASHCROFT."
"GUILTY."

The President, newly reclusive—he felt, he told his friend Bruce Lindsey, "betrayed" by those, notably Paul Begala and members of the war council, who "let this thing get out of hand"—watched the vote from the privacy of the residence, with only Lindsey, Webb Hubbell, and the First Lady on hand...

"MR. BAUCUS."
"NOT GUILTY."

"MR. BIDEN."

Finally, the first of the crossovers. There was a rustle in the press gallery as Joe Biden bled the moment. Then:

"GUILTY."

Jeff Bingaman, the second crossover, would follow; then, eight votes later, with stentorian flourish, Robert Byrd. There would be, in all, ten Democratic crossovers before the chief justice reached the "M"s....

• • •

AS PARIS IS THE CITY OF LIGHT, Washington is the City of Myth, and the myths that grew out of Pat Moynihan's vote that day were many and varied.

Howard Fineman, writing in *Newsweek*, had heard that New York's senior senator, after four terms, had told a colleague that he "felt a need to leave his mark on history."

Eleanor Clift, returned to the private sector, made her reappearance on *The McLaughlin Group* memorable by terming Moynihan "a latent misogynist," whose vote, while ostensibly directed at the President, was in fact aimed at his wife.

Frank Rich, with incomparable balance, wrote in *The New York Times* that Moynihan, while apparently sound, was approaching his seventy-second birthday, had "lost his compass," and did not in fact know what he was voting on.

George Stephanopoulos, citing "unimpeachable sources," told his ABC audience that Moynihan, as *quid pro quo* for his vote, would be appointed ambassador to the Court of St. James.

In fact, he was not. Nor did Moynihan, in the years to come, ever vary from the explanation given on the Senate floor, that he cast his vote purely, simply, and for no reason other than that he thought it was right for the country.

But Washington being Washington, no one, of course, bought that.

APPENDIX
CAST OF CHARACTERS

■

THE CLINTON WHITE HOUSE:

WILLIAM JEFFERSON CLINTON: Forty-second President of the United States, but only the second president to face a Senate impeachment trial

HILLARY RODHAM CLINTON: First Lady of the United States

PAUL BEGALA: White House aide who serves on the President's "war council" during the impeachment trial

ROBERT BENNETT: Member of President Clinton's legal team

SAMUEL "SANDY" BERGER: Deputy assistant to the President for National Security Affairs (1992–1996); assistant to the President for National Security Affairs (1996–   ); testifies before the House Judiciary Committee about alleged illegalities that occurred in fund-raising activities in and around the Clinton White House during the period 1993-96

RICHARD BLOCH: Texas real-estate operator, with no discernible background in foreign intelligence, appointed by President Clinton to the Foreign Intelligence Advisory Board; also donated $100,000 to the Democratic National Committee

JAMES CARVILLE: Top Clinton campaign strategist and adviser

ELEANOR CLIFT: Former journalist and political analyst on *The McLaughlin Group* appointed to the White House communications staff, Fall 1998

CATHERINE CORNELIUS: Widely held to be President Clinton's cousin, though a review of their genealogies in the May 1996 *American Spectator* revealed no relationship and suggested that the White House fabricated the kinship to explain to *Time* magazine Mrs. Cornelius's curious proximity to him; as a low-level staff member she wrote a memorandum in early 1993 outlining a plan to replace the Travel Office staff with Clinton appointees, sparking the so-called "Travelgate" episode

BILLY DALE: Former director of the White House Travel Office, fired in May 1993 after more than thirty years of service

LANNY DAVIS: White House special counsel

JEFF ELLER: Director of White House media affairs

VINCENT FOSTER: President Clinton's deputy counsel until his death in July 1993; former law partner of Hillary Rodham Clinton

PHILIP HEYMANN: Resigned as deputy attorney general following Vincent Foster's July 1993 death

SHEILA HESLIN: Resigned from the National Security Council in 1996

WEBSTER HUBBELL: Former associate attorney general and a former law partner of Hillary Rodham Clinton; convicted of two counts of defrauding the federal government

HAROLD ICKES, JR.: Former deputy chief of staff

DAVID KENDALL: President Clinton's private lawyer

WILLIAM KENNEDY III: Former deputy counsel to President Clinton; testifies before the House Judiciary Committee regarding his involvement in and knowledge about "Travelgate"

ANTHONY LAKE: Former assistant to the president for National Security Affairs; withdrew his nomination to be director of the CIA, March 1997

BRUCE LINDSEY: Assistant, and close friend, to the President

CRAIG LIVINGSTONE: Former head of the office of personnel security; had hundreds of FBI "raw" files in his possession at the White House; invokes Fifth Amendment rights when testifying before the House Judiciary Committee

ANTHONY MARCECA: Former aide to Craig Livingstone in the office of personnel security; had hundreds of FBI "raw" files in his possession at the White House; invokes Fifth Amendment rights when testifying before the House Judiciary Committee

MICHAEL MCCURRY: White House press secretary

THOMAS "MACK" MCLARTY: Former White House chief of staff, counselor to the President and special advisor for Latin American affairs

DICK MORRIS: Political advisor to President Clinton, forced to resign in disgrace in the summer of 1996 when his rendezvous with a prostitute was discovered; reinstated as Clinton's political adviser in the spring of 1998

DEE DEE MYERS: Former White House spokesperson

BERNARD NUSSBAUM: Former White House counsel; testifies in June 1998 before the House Judiciary Committee about his involvement in the handling of 900 raw FBI files, in "Travelgate," and in the removal of files from Vince Foster's office the night of Foster's suicide; during the 1974 Watergate scandal served as staff attorney to the House Judiciary Committee that prepared to impeach President Richard Nixon

LEON PANETTA: Director of the Office of Management and Budget (OMB), January 1993–July 1994; White House chief of staff, July 1994–January 1997

JACK QUINN: White House Counsel

ROBERT RUBIN: Secretary of the Treasury

CHARLES RUFF: Counsel to President Clinton; last independent counsel in the Watergate case

DOUG SCHOEN: White House pollster

MARSHA SCOTT: White House aide who suggested that the Democratic National Committee could use the White House database for fund-raising purposes; testifies before the House Judiciary Committee, August 6, 1998

JANE SHERBURNE: Special counsel who headed a special legal unit that acted as a damage-control operation

STANLEY SHUMAN: A New York investment banker with no discernible background in foreign intelligence, appointed by President Clinton to the Foreign Intelligence Advisory Board; also donated $100,000 to the Democratic National Committee

CRAIG SMITH: Clinton's political director

NANCY SODERBERG: Former deputy assistant to the President for National Security Affairs, serving in the first Clinton administration

DOUGLAS SOSNIK: White House political director

KENNETH STARR: Independent counsel appointed to investigate Whitewater, as well as "Filegate" and the death of Vincent Foster

JOSH STEINER: Aide in the Department of the Treasury who claimed, in effect, that he had lied to his own diary

GEORGE STEPHANOPOULOS: White House communications director during the first year of the Clinton presidency; later senior adviser to the President; departed White House before Clinton's second term to become a political analyst for ABC News

ROBERT SUETTINGER: Top White House intelligence expert on Asia; held a meeting with Hong Kong businessman and significant Democratic National Committee contributor Eric Hotung in the fall of 1995

STROBE TALBOTT: President Clinton's undersecretary of state

PATSY THOMASSON: Deputy Director of White House administration

DAVID WATKINS: Former White House administrator; intimately involved in "Travelgate;" forced to resign by the President for supposedly using a White House helicopter for private purposes

MARGARET WILLIAMS: The First Lady's chief of staff

GARY WRIGHT: Former deputy director of the White House Travel Office, fired in May 1993 after more than thirty years of service

THE HOUSE OF REPRESENTATIVES
Key players on the House Judiciary Committee:

BOB BARR (R-GA): Though only a second-term congressman, one of the driving forces behind the impeachment of William Jefferson Clinton

HOWARD BERMAN (D-CA): One of the senior members of the committee's minority, a defender of President Clinton

SONNY BONO (R-CA): Resident wit on the House Judiciary Committee

HOWARD COBLE (R-NC): A key interrogator of witnesses before the Judiciary Committee

JOHN CONYERS (D-MI): Ranking minority member of the Judiciary Committee

BARNEY FRANK (D-MA): Second-ranking member of the committee's minority, one of the White House's point men on Capitol Hill

ASA HUTCHINSON (R-AR): Votes to impeach Clinton despite representing the President's home state of Arkansas

HENRY HYDE (R-IL): Chairman of the House Judiciary Committee

BOB INGLIS (R-SC): One of the key interrogators of witnesses

BILL MCCOLLUM (R-FL): Third-ranking member of the committee's majority, a key interrogator of witnesses

CHARLES SCHUMER (D-NY): Third-ranking member of the committee's minority, one of the White House's point men on Capitol Hill

JAMES SENSENBRENNER, JR. (R-WI): Second-ranking member of the committee's majority, one of the primary interrogators of witnesses

MAXINE WATERS (D-CA): An important defender of President Clinton

Other figures:

SPENCER BACHUS (R-AL): Opposes Clinton Administration

DAVID BONIOR (D-MI): House minority whip and a member of the "Committee of Six," the group of six Democratic leaders who inform President Clinton in May 1998 that an impeachment trial is unavoidable

DAN BURTON (R-IN): Chairman of the House Government Reform and Oversight Committee who led an investigation into campaign fundraising activities in the Clinton White House

WILLIAM CLINGER (RETIRED): Former chairman of the House Government Reform and Oversight Committee who led an investigation of "Travelgate" in 1996

ROSA DELAURO (D-CT): A defender of President Clinton

RICHARD GEPHARDT (D-MO): House minority leader and a member of the "Committee of Six," the group of six Democratic leaders who inform President Clinton in May 1998 that an impeachment trial is unavoidable

JIM LEACH (R-IA): Chairman of the House Banking and Financial Services Committee, led an investigation into Whitewater

WILSON LIVINGOOD: Sergeant-at-arms of the House of Representatives, delivers the articles of impeachment to President Clinton

THOMAS E. MOONEY, SR.: Chief of staff and general counsel for the House Judiciary Committee

DONALD PAYNE (D NJ): Chairman of the Congressional Black Caucus

HENRY WAXMAN (D-CA): Member of the "Committee of Six," the group of six Democratic leaders who inform President Clinton in May 1998 that an impeachment trial is unavoidable

SENATE:

JOE BIDEN (D-DE): Ranking minority member of the Senate Judiciary Committee, steps down from his position as leader of President Clinton's defense in the Senate impeachment trial

JEFF BINGAMAN (D-NM): Potential Democratic "crossover" who urges the White House to turn over all tapes

BARBARA BOXER (D-CA): Friend and supporter of Hillary Rodham Clinton

ROBERT BYRD (D-WV): Democratic "defector"

AL D'AMATO (R-NY): Chairman of the Senate Banking, Housing, and Urban Affairs Committee; led an investigation into Whitewater

TOM DASCHLE (D-SD): Senate minority leader and a member of the "Committee of Six," the group of six Democratic leaders who inform President Clinton in May 1998 that an impeachment trial is unavoidable

RUSS FEINGOLD (D-WI): Potential Democratic "crossover"

JOHN GLENN (D-OH): Member of the "Committee of Six," the group of six Democratic leaders who inform President Clinton in May 1998 that an impeachment trial is unavoidable

ORRIN HATCH (R-UT): Chairman of the Senate Judiciary Committee, leads the prosecution in the impeachment trial of William Jefferson Clinton

JESSE HELMS (R-NC): Strong opponent of President Clinton

FRITZ HOLLINGS (D-SC): Democratic senator who urges Clinton to comply with subpoena of tapes

EDWARD KENNEDY (D-MA): Along with Patrick Leahy, second-ranking minority member of the Senate Judiciary Committee, charged with leading the defense of President Clinton when ranking member Joe Biden asks not to lead the defense

PATRICK LEAHY (D-VT): Along with Edward Kennedy, second-ranking minority member of the Senate Judiciary Committee, charged with leading the defense of President Clinton when ranking member Joe Biden asks not to lead the defense

ROBERT KERREY (D-NE): Potential Democratic "crossover"

JOE LIEBERMAN (D-CT): Democratic senator who speaks out against President Clinton

TRENT LOTT (R-MI): Senate Majority Leader

JOHN MCCAIN (R-AZ): Moves to introduce White House tapes to the full Senate

DANIEL PATRICK MOYNIHAN (D-NY): Leader of the "Committee of Six," the group of six Democratic leaders who inform President Clinton in May 1998 that an impeachment trial is unavoidable

HARRY REID (D-NV): Potential Democratic "crossover"

RICK SANTORUM (R-PA): Outspoken opponent of President Clinton

ARLEN SPECTER (R-PA): Second-ranking member of the Senate Judiciary Committee

FRED THOMPSON (R-TN): Chairman of the Senate Governmental Affairs Committee, led an investigation into campaign fundraising activities in the Clinton White House

ROBERT TORICELLI (D-NJ): Strong defender of Clinton in the impeachment trial

PAUL WELLSTONE (D-MN): Potential Democratic "crossover"

OTHER:

HOWARD APPLE: Head of the Crimes Unit of the Federal Bureau of Investigation, called in to investigate the White House Travel Office

LEE ATWATER: Former chairman of the Republican National Committee

TONY BLAIR: British Prime Minister; strong supporter of President Clinton

JAMES BOURKE: Unit chief of the Criminal Investigations Division of the Federal Bureau of Investigation; called in by the White House to investigate the Travel Office

JORGE "GORDITO" CABRERA: A convicted felon who attended a 1995 White House event after he made sizable contributions to the DNC

THOMAS CARL: Agent for the Federal Bureau of Investigation who investigated the White House Travel Office

JOHN COLLINGWOOD: Formerly the official spokesman for the Federal Bureau of Investigation; implicated in "Travelgate"

DON FOWLER: Co-chairman of the Democratic National Committee

LOUIS FREEH: Director of the Federal Bureau of Investigation

BOYDEN GRAY: Former White House counsel during the Bush administration, and outspoken critic of President Clinton

LARRY HERMAN: Auditor for Peat-Marwick contacted to audit the White House Travel Office; also a member of the staff of Vice President Al Gore's National Performance Review

ERIC HOTUNG: Hong Kong businessman and significant contributor to the Democratic National Committee; met with Clinton foreign policy officials in the fall of 1995

JOHN HUANG: Former Commerce Department and Democratic National Committee official who conducted extensive Democratic fundraising; accused of conflict of interest because of his former employment with the Indonesian-based Lippo Group

MANSOOR IJAZ: Important fund-raiser for President Clinton's reelection campaign who sought to use his influence with the administration to affect US policy regarding Sudan

PAULA JONES: Accused President Clinton of sexual harassment

JEAN LEWIS: Resolution Trust Corp (RTC) investigator into Whitewater who experienced stonewalling in Arkansas

JOHN LIBONATI: Former Secret Service agent who spoke to congressional committees about White House use of personnel files

JIM MCDOUGAL: The Clintons' partner in the Whitewater investment

DAVID MARTENS: Friend of Hillary Clinton; under Catherine Cornelius's Travel Office plan, Martens's and Harry Thomason's company would have received the White House air charter contract

WILLIAM REHNQUIST: Chief justice of the United States; presides over the Senate impeachment trial

JAMES RIADY: Son of the founder of the Indonesian-based Lippo Group

ARTHUR SCHLESINGER, JR.: Former adviser to President Kennedy who is an outspoken supporter of President Clinton

DENNIS SCULIMBRENE: Agent for the Federal Bureau of Investigation

HOWARD SHAPIRO: Former general counsel for the Federal Bureau of Investigation

ROGER TAMRAZ: A significant contributor to the Democratic National Committee who had a one-on-one meeting with President Clinton in the White House; also wanted in Lebanon for embezzlement

HARRY THOMASON: Friend of Hillary Clinton; under Catherine Cornelius's Travel Office plan, David Martens's and Thomason's company would have received the White House air charter contract

RANDY TURK: Attorney for Craig Livingstone

JEFFREY UNDERCOFFER: Former Secret Service agent who spoke to congressional committees about White House use of personnel files

ERIC WYNN: Convicted felon who attended a White House coffee in December 1995

WATERGATE IMPEACHMENT FIGURES:

ALEXANDER BUTTERFIELD: Deputy to H.R. Haldeman; revealed Nixon's White House taping system

DWIGHT CHAPIN: Appointments secretary for Nixon (1969–1973); served eight months in prison; his failed appeal demolished the "I can't remember" defense

CHARLES (CHUCK) COLSON: Special White House counsel (1970–1973); served seven months in prison

JOHN DEAN: Counsel to President Nixon; served four months in prison

SAM ERVIN (D-NC): Chairman of the Senate Watergate Committee

H.R. HALDEMAN: Nixon's chief of staff (1969–1973); served eighteen months in prison

PETER RODINO (D-NJ): Chairman of the House Judiciary Committee during the impeachment of Richard Nixon

RON ZIEGLER: Nixon's press secretary (1969–1974)